Transcultural Cognitive Behaviour Therapy for Anxiety and Depression

I0131135

Transcultural Cognitive Behaviour Therapy for Anxiety and Depression is a practical and accessible guide, drawing on current research in CBT and clinical practice. It aims to support therapists in taking a reflective and evidence based approach to genuinely improving access and outcomes for Black and Minority Ethnic service users. It highlights the skills that clinicians need to undertake Culturally Adapted and Culturally Sensitive CBT and provides practical ideas and case examples that will enable therapists to feel confident in adapting models of assessment and treatment across cultures.

The emphasis of this book is on practical clinical techniques and approaches but it is firmly grounded in the research literature on this topic. Therapists, supervisors and service leads will find useful ideas to support and enrich transcultural working and develop their confidence when applying evidence based interventions across cultures.

Transcultural Cognitive Behaviour Therapy for Anxiety and Depression will be of interest to Improving Access to Psychological Therapies (IAPT) trained cognitive behaviour therapists, clinical psychologists and cognitive behaviour therapists. The book will also appeal to those undertaking advanced or post-graduate studies in CBT.

Andrew Beck has been working as a cognitive behaviour therapist since 1997 and has published several research papers on transcultural CBT, including work on clinical outcomes and the views of service users who have benefited from CBT. He is Senior Lecturer on the North West England IAPT training programme and Honorary Senior Lecturer on the Doctorate in Clinical Psychology at Manchester University. Beck is Chair of the Equality and Culture Special Interest Group of the British Association for Behavioural and Cognitive Psychotherapists (BABCP) and has worked with colleagues in Chennai to establish the first stand-alone CBT training course in India. His Twitter handle is @andrewbeck45.

'Dr Beck's masterful book on CBT brings therapy to life with multiple case examples. The book is timely considering most societies are becoming more and more multicultural, and therefore therapists need to have a better understanding of their client's cultural backgrounds. Dr Beck has done an excellent job of emphasising the complexity of working across cultures while simplifying the process of delivering culturally responsive therapy. We know that both the populations in low and middle income countries and ethnic minority groups in high income countries have less access to psychological interventions; in my opinion Dr Beck's book will make a significant contribution towards reducing the huge treatment gap. This is an important book for all who are involved in offering therapies across cultures.'

Dr Nusrat Husain, Reader in Psychiatry, Lead Global
Mental Health Institute of Brain, Behaviour and Mental Health,
University of Manchester, Director of Research, Global Health,
Manchester Academic Health Sciences Centre (MAHSC)

'Central to the CBT model is a bringing together of relationship and structure. Without relationship, CBT works poorly. Similarly, CBT provides a model to help people work out why they feel as they do, and make changes that they wish to make. But classical CBT is Western-developed and can exclude rather than engage those from other backgrounds and cultures. That's why I am so excited by this essential book. It provides a wealth of ideas, tools and approaches to build relationships, and culturally adapt the CBT model to engage people from diverse backgrounds. It makes essential reading for clinicians, supervisors and service managers wanting to include all members of the community in health care delivery.'

Professor Chris Williams, University of Glasgow and
President of the British Association for Behavioural and Cognitive
Psychotherapies, lead author of www.livinglifetothefull.com

Transcultural Cognitive Behaviour Therapy for Anxiety and Depression

A practical guide

Andrew Beck

Routledge
Taylor & Francis Group

LONDON AND NEW YORK

First published 2016
by Routledge
2 Park Square, Milton Park, Abingdon, Oxon OX14 4RN

and by Routledge
711 Third Avenue, New York, NY 10017

Routledge is an imprint of the Taylor & Francis Group, an informa business

British Library Cataloguing in Publication Data
A catalogue record for this book is available from the British Library

Library of Congress Cataloging in Publication Data
Names: Beck, Andrew (Clinical psychologist), author.
Title: Transcultural cognitive behaviour therapy for anxiety and
    depression : a practical guide / Dr. Andrew Beck.
Description: Abingdon, Oxon ; New York : Routledge, 2016. |
    Includes bibliographical references.
Identifiers: LCCN 2015041552| ISBN 9781138890473 (hardback) |
    ISBN 9781138890480 (pbk.) | ISBN 9781315707419 (ebook)
Subjects: | MESH: Cognitive Therapy. | Anxiety Disorders—therapy. |
    Culturally Competent Care. | Depressive Disorder—therapy. |
    Ethnopsychology.
Classification: LCC RC489.C63 | NLM WM 425.5.C6 | DDC
    616.89/1425—dc23
LC record available at http://lccn.loc.gov/2015041552

ISBN: 978-1-138-89047-3 (hbk)
ISBN: 978-1-138-89048-0 (pbk)
ISBN: 978-1-315-70741-9 (ebk)

Typeset in Times New Roman
by Swales & Willis Ltd, Exeter, Devon, UK

Contents

Acknowledgements

I would like to thank Dr Ayesha Gurpinar-Morgan, whom I was lucky enough to work with on the research which forms the basis of Chapter 2. I would also like to thank the young adults who participated in this research and who were happy for their ideas to be disseminated to help therapists think about the way that they talk about ethnicity with service users. The section on community participation in Chapter 8 is based on work that Dr Anamika Mujamdar and I did in Tower Hamlets, which had a considerable impact on my understanding of community engagement and working across cultures. The work of Dr Ghazala Mir informs much of the thinking which forms the basis of Chapter 6 and I would like to thank her for her tirelessness and enthusiasm in disseminating her exemplary work. I am indebted to the following for their comments regarding particular chapters of the book: Bipasha Ahmed, Romilly Gregory, Bernadka Dubicka, Lydia Stone, Paul Wallis, Caroline Browne, Phil Milner and Stephen Gregson.

I would like to dedicate this book to my daughters, Santi and Mahni, and my wife Lakhbir, who are constantly teaching me about living life transculturally and a lot of other things besides.

Preface

In writing this book, my underlying assumption has been that Cognitive Behaviour Therapy (CBT) can be of considerable help to service users from Black and Minority Ethnic (BME) communities who have mental health problems. My experience as a clinician and researcher has taught me that in order for this approach to be effective, therapists need to understand and incorporate the values, beliefs and practices of service users into their work. Change also needs to happen in terms of how services are organised and in the way that services interact and engage with the communities they serve. Change at both the individual therapist and service level is the best way to ensure genuine equality of access and outcomes.

In busy clinics where therapists struggle with high caseloads and increased demands on their time it is easy for us to forget that working as a cognitive behaviour therapist can be a privilege as well as a challenge. Clinical work involves collaborating closely with people who are experiencing one of the most difficult periods of their lives and working with them to develop a shared understanding of the problem. Therapists hear about the private thoughts of the service user and their feelings of fear, shame or sadness. We also hear about the richness of the lives of the service users beyond the presenting problem and help them to draw on their personal strengths and resources in order to overcome their difficulties. There is no doubt that it is rewarding to share someone's life in this way. It can, however, be hard for us as therapists to maintain the sense of interest in and regard for others that was a likely factor in deciding on a career in mental health when we are managing large caseloads and considerable organisational pressures.

My experience has been that when therapists extend their practice with people from diverse backgrounds their curiosity about the lives of others is refreshed, as they encounter new communities, new ways of organising family life and new ways of seeing the world.

This book provides a framework and resource for therapists and supervisors using CBT with BME service users. In the spirit of CBT it is a collaborative process, as it provides different frameworks and approaches which therapists can consider in the light of their own practice. Therapists can then incorporate those ideas that fit with the groups of people they work with, their own approach to therapy and the way that their service works.

As the author, I am aware that my own ethnic background (White British) limits what I can usefully say to Black and Minority Ethnic therapists working across and within cultures. Where others with greater expertise in this area have discussed these issues I have referenced their work and tried to do their ideas justice. As a therapist with a particular interest in transcultural assessment and therapy I am aware of how much my practice is constantly changing, thanks to the generosity of colleagues and service users who help me to refine my thinking about this area. As a trainer, I very much appreciate the feedback of trainees and their generosity in taking the time to look at ideas on transcultural work in a critical but helpful way. As a parent of children who, when asked, identify themselves as Indian but who might be classified as of mixed Indian/British background, I am aware that ideas about culture and belonging are fluid and complex and that the personal perspectives that my family life brings might make some aspects of transcultural working easier for me. This personal experience might also bias which research I emphasise, or which communities I feel more familiar writing about, but the broad principles outlined in this book can be adapted for any setting where the population is ethnically diverse.

Applying CBT across cultures is very much a work in progress and there is still a considerable amount of work to be done in terms of research and refining our thinking as therapists. There are some very valid criticisms about the application of CBT across cultures which I have summarised in Chapter 1. Despite these criticisms, it is my experience that CBT has a great deal to offer people from diverse cultures and backgrounds. This book sets out some of the key principles which will support therapists to adapt and refine the way they practice CBT in order to give their Black and Minority Ethnic service users the best possible chance of a good outcome in terms of their mental health.

Finally, I would encourage readers to join in with this ongoing discussion about how we might need to adapt therapy and services to meet the needs of diverse communities, by engaging with the special interest groups within their professional organisations which are involved with thinking about culture and diversity. My own practice has been very much improved by the opportunities I have had to speak to other clinicians and researchers interested in this area and as a result of the constructive and stimulating feedback that these conversations have led to.

Chapter 1

Introduction

Why we need to think and work transculturally

Transcultural approaches to health care are based on the idea that the values and beliefs of different cultural groups need to be understood in order to provide services which reflect the distinct ways that these groups conceptualise health problems, act in response to these and engage with treatment. This framework enables health workers to collaborate with service users in a way that takes their culture into account whilst also identifying factors which are common across communities and making use of evidence based approaches to health care developed for majority ethnic groups (Andrews and Boyle 2008).

Cultural and ethnic diversity in Europe and North America has increased at an unprecedented rate over the past 70 years, and with this has come the challenge of providing mental health services which reflect this diversity and which respond to the values and beliefs of newer or growing communities. Cognitive Behaviour Therapy (CBT) is the most widely available psychological therapy in the UK and many other countries. It is supported by a strong evidence base for its efficacy for a wide range of problems and is likely to be the first psychological therapy offered to most people using mental health services.

Cognitive Behaviour Therapy was developed in clinical settings in North America and Europe where the majority of therapists, researchers and service users were from a White European cultural background. The core beliefs about mental health and its treatment implied by this model have their origins in Western concepts of emotional well-being and illness. The majority of the clinical observations and initial research which led to the development of the disorder specific models which underpin CBT were done with white clinical populations, and almost all of the subsequent research into the efficacy of CBT has been done with white participants. This does not mean that CBT cannot be helpful for service users from Black and Minority Ethnic communities – this book looks at some very good examples of adapted CBT which have shown excellent clinical outcomes – but it does mean that therapists need to think carefully about the way that CBT might be used across cultures and in different contexts in order for it to be effective.

As CBT skills have become widely disseminated in mental health settings and the populations served by teams become more ethnically diverse, cognitive behaviour therapists often find themselves working with service users from cultural backgrounds which are different to their own. This means that therapists may have to adapt their ways of working to take into account the culture and context of these service users. There is very good evidence to support the idea that culture, language, ethnicity and religion have a considerable impact on the way that mental health problems manifest themselves (Gone and Kirmayer 2010), and that these factors will shape symptoms, how people experience their problems, their explanations for the problem and the way that they might seek help. Understanding these processes will help to ensure that BME service users benefit from the same clinical outcomes as white service users.

In response to the challenge of working across cultures and contexts there have been a number of research projects evaluating both Culturally Adapted CBT (CA-CBT) and Culturally Sensitive CBT (CS-CBT), and research into these two ways of working across cultures suggests that outcomes can be as good as those for white service users. The difference between CA-CBT and CS-CBT is summarised at the end of this chapter and considered in more detail in Chapter 5, which contrasts ways of using these two approaches in the treatment of post-traumatic stress disorder (PTSD).

Who this book is for

This book is written for practitioners working across the lifespan in mental health services and who use or would like to use CBT with BME service users. It assumes a broad working knowledge of CBT but is written with both the novice and the expert therapist in mind. The assumption of much of the book is that it is written for a white therapist working with a BME service user. This is not meant to suggest that there are no challenges for BME therapists who are working transculturally or with service users from within their own ethnic group. When indicated there are specific references to the research literature looking at therapy issues relating to perceived sameness or closeness of culture.

The book does not set out to provide a step-by-step guide for success in working across cultures. Instead it sets out some broad principles and approaches which have come from both the research literature and clinical experience. The chapters are illustrated with case examples, though care has been taken to change the details of cases to protect the confidentiality of patients. Practitioners are encouraged to keep a reflective learning log in order to facilitate use of these ideas and techniques and to use supervision as a forum for further reflective practice.

How this book might help therapists using CBT across cultures

In mental health services in much of the English-speaking world there has been a growing recognition that the needs of BME communities are often not well met. This is largely because the way that services are organised, mental health is conceptualised and therapies are delivered reflects a Western view of mental health that might not sit well with the way that mental health is understood in other cultures. There is a growing recognition that interventions need to take into account diverse values and beliefs and that services need to engage with the communities they serve in order to understand how to adapt the way that therapies are provided. Although the availability of CBT has increased considerably over recent years, the evidence base regarding how to adapt and apply this model to BME groups has not kept pace with these service developments, and where evidence does exist it has often not been disseminated into teams.

This book starts from the assumption that CBT can be an effective treatment for BME service users, but that in order for it to be effective practitioners need to adapt the way that they work. This includes how they might engage service users, how they formulate presenting problems in ways that take into account culture and context, how disorder specific models are used and how confident therapists are about discussing and thinking about culture in therapy and in supervision.

Adapting CBT across cultures can be a considerable challenge for therapists. They might feel unprepared to do this, as it is seldom covered in any depth on training courses. Therapists might not feel confident discussing culture and difference with service users, might not be confident that good therapy outcomes can be achieved and might struggle to provide CBT through interpreters.

This book is written as a resource for therapists in order for them to be more comfortable and confident when working across cultures and as a resource for supervisors, managers and service leads in order for them to think about how they might need to adapt their service to meet the needs of the patients they serve.

Most cognitive behavioural therapists work with service users from BME communities, but many therapists report that they are reluctant to bring up issues regarding ethnicity or culture in case they do so in a way that undermines the therapeutic relationship. This book sets out to give therapists the confidence to think about ethnicity and culture with service users and incorporate this information into formulations in a way that will improve engagement and clinical outcomes. It also provides a framework for looking at patterns of service use amongst ethnic minorities and to consider the way that these populations can be involved with participation and service design in a way that leads to services that are responsive to the particular needs of local populations.

It seems reasonable to assume that as clinicians develop a greater understanding of a client's conceptualisation of ethnicity and its relationship to their mental health there will be improvements in the way that therapy is provided and better clinical outcomes for BME service users (Department of Health 2005). Research suggests that therapist awareness and sensitivity may be more important for service users who perceive a relationship between their ethnicity and their psycho-social well-being than for service users who see little relationship between their ethnicity and their use of mental health services (Pope-Davis et al. 2002), but it is only possible to know how someone understands these relationships through therapeutic discussion and exploration.

The rapid growth of CBT

It is almost 40 years since the foundations of CBT were established by Aaron T. Beck in his seminal book on the treatment of depression (Beck et al. 1979) and in that time CBT has become one of the most influential models to both describe and treat mental health problems, across the lifespan and in a wide variety of settings.

This expansion can be attributed to three factors. The first is the flexibility of the approach. CBT has been adapted for a wide range of presenting problems, contexts and situations. This flexibility has enabled it to be used across the lifespan from childhood mental health problems to difficulties in old age, in physical health care settings and with people with cognitive or neurodevelopmental difficulties. The second factor is that key concepts can be readily understood by mental health practitioners, service users and referrers. It is a model that is easy to explain to others and which has a great deal of face validity. The third factor is that there has been a clear commitment to establishing a credible evidence base for the efficacy of CBT from the start. This has meant the adoption of high standards of research methods, including randomised control trials (RCTs), which are seen as the gold standard for outcomes research in health care settings. This research has given CBT a reputation for demonstrable effectiveness that appeals to service users, therapists, referrers and commissioners of services.

Health economics are also likely to have driven the growth in CBT in recent years as this therapy is seen as a more cost effective form of treatment for depression and anxiety disorders than many other therapeutic approaches (Layard et al. 2006, Gyani et al. 2013). This means that scarce mental health resources can be used to help more people, but it is also assumed that individuals are more likely to return to being economically active as a result of successful therapy. From an economic point of view transcultural CBT is likely to use more resources than CBT which is unmodified. It may take more sessions and need more resources to engage individuals and families and to work with wider systems. Interpreter mediated CBT can often need longer sessions or more sessions to complete. Clinicians providing transcultural CBT are also likely to need additional support through appropriate training and supervision in order to successfully adapt the model across cultures and contexts, and this will also have additional resource implications.

Culturally Adapted CBT or Culturally Sensitive CBT?

This book considers two approaches to using CBT to meet the needs of BME service users: Culturally Adapted and Culturally Sensitive CBT. Both approaches have something to offer therapists, but it might be useful to distinguish between the two at this stage.

Culturally Adapted CBT

Culturally Adapted CBT (CA-CBT) can be best understood as

> a middle ground between the two extreme positions of considering an original evidence based intervention as applicable to all cultural groups without the need for adaptation, and a culture-specific approach with emphasis on unique culturally grounded content and process.

> (Chowdhary et al. 2014)

Taking this approach ensures that the basic active components of CBT are retained whilst incorporating elements of the distinct and culturally mediated aspects of the way that mental health problems are expressed and understood. This approach is based on an assumption that mental health problems are universal phenomena but that specific manifestations, in terms of thoughts, behaviour and family processes, might be specific to particular cultures (although Culturally Sensitive CBT is also based on this premise).

The steps for the cultural adaptation of therapies

A useful way of understanding the steps necessary in cultural adaptation for all psychological therapies has been developed by Bernal and Sáez-Sangriago (2006). This framework considers a number of possible domains within which adaptation can take place. These are summarised below:

1   The language in which therapy is conducted is considered a key element in adaptation, as language is often the means by which culture is expressed and transmitted. This dimension also includes the adaptation of communi-cation styles.
2   The degree to which the therapy considers the ethnic and cultural similarities and differences in the service user–therapist relationship. This might involve explicitly matching the ethnicity of therapist and service user or including reflective practice about the degree to which this impacts on therapy. It might also include a recognition that some cultural groups might prefer a more collaborative stance for this relationship whilst others might prefer a more didactic therapist.
3   Adaptation accounts for the use of metaphors and incorporates the particular idioms or sayings of a cultural or ethnic group into the therapeutic language and approach.
4   The content of the therapy and how knowledge about cultural practices, values and behaviours are incorporated into the therapy approach.
5   Therapy goals are seen as a key area, and the authors emphasise the need for therapists to work collaboratively with service users to establish goals that reflect the values and aspirations of the service user.
6   Therapy methods; this refers to the way that therapy techniques reflect or are compatible with the practices of the community for which the therapy is being adapted.

7   The incorporation of context; this refers to an appreciation of the setting within which the BME service users find themselves, including their economic and educational opportunities, experience of racism or other forms of discrimination and, in some cases, their migration history and degree of acculturation if the adaptation is occurring in a Western context.

Adaptations might not incorporate all of these elements, and may not need to do so in order to have successful therapy outcomes, but this list of components does provide therapists with a framework for evaluating particular approaches in order to see to what extent and how a particular therapy has been culturally adapted.

Culturally Sensitive CBT

In contrast, Culturally Sensitive CBT (CS-CBT) tends to look much more like CBT as provided to white majority service users, but with adaptations made on a case-by-case basis by therapists, service users and sometimes interpreters. Therapists using this approach will draw on a set of core principles which include an acknowledgement of the need to collaboratively discuss and understand the cultural background of the service user; to think about whether disorder specific models are the best fit to describe their difficulties; to appreciate that metaphors and ideas used in one culture may not translate into another; and to recognise that it is important to think about the lived experience of the service user as a member of a BME community and what particular strengths and challenges this might bring. Chapter 5 provides a summary of the culturally sensitive approach developed by d'Ardenne et al. (2005), and Chapters 2 and 3 provide a basis for therapists to begin to discuss and think about culture and ethnicity in a way that supports culturally sensitive working.

Therapists working in an area where there is one major BME community might find developing knowledge and skills regarding a particular CA-CBT useful. Where therapists work with service users from a broad range of ethnic backgrounds, a culturally sensitive approach might be a more useful position to take, as CA-CBT is usually only adapted for a specific ethnic group and for a specific disorder. On the whole, a culturally sensitive position might underpin the majority of transcultural work and provide therapists with the flexibility to work with someone from any community with any presenting problem.

Cross-cultural adaptations of therapies and interventions are typically adapted from a model developed for white Europeans to one suitable for BME populations living within Western countries or to majority populations in other countries. One possible exception to this is mindfulness based cognitive therapies, whose origins in Buddhist philosophy are well documented (Kabat-Zinn 2003) and which might be conceptualised as being an adaptation of Indian and Burmese approaches to alleviating distress which have been culturally adapted for white majority service users in Western countries by, for example, secularising the approach, taking out the moral and community based components and incorporating a language to describe distress that fits within a Western diagnostic framework. Developing an evidence base for this approach that fits with the positive approach to science which underpins Western models of health care could also be seen as a cultural adaptation.

Unmet needs for mental health services amongst BME communities

An increasing percentage of the UK population now identify themselves as Black and Minority Ethnic (BME) (Aspinall 2003). Research has demonstrated that some BME populations are less likely to access mental health services compared to the majority population (Kramer et al. 2000). For example, Messent and Murrell (2003) found that Bangladeshi families are less likely to seek treatment for mild or moderate mental health difficulties than white families. Similarly, young people from South Asian, Black Caribbean and African communities are under-represented in Child and Adolescent Mental Health Services (CAMHS) compared to the White British population (Kramer et al. 2000).

It is likely that the rates of mental health difficulties in the majority of BME communities are at least as high as those in the white majority population. Under-representation of BME communities in services seems to be more likely to be as a result of minority groups not being able to access services, rather than there being less need for such services in these communities. There are a number of reasons why this might be the case which we will look at in detail in Chapter 8, but this might involve stigma about discussing mental health problems, referrers not identifying mental health problems so readily in some communities or referrers believing that evidence based therapies will not help particular populations. It might also be a result of services not being set up in a way that suits how local BME communities might want to access them.

This pattern is replicated amongst adolescents, where young people from some BME backgrounds are at greater risk of developing mental health problems than the white majority population and are less likely to access appropriate services (Hull et al. 2008, National Institute for Mental Health in England 2003). As a result of these identified inequalities in the UK there is a national programme to better understand the relationship between ethnicity and mental health in order to ensure the provision of appropriate services to young people and adults (Joint Commissioning Panel for Mental Health 2015). The rapid expansion of the Improving Access to Psychological Therapies (IAPT) Adult and Children and Young People's programmes in the UK has meant that in many areas CBT is now the first line of treatment for a large number of presenting mental health problems. This means that therapists providing CBT will need a sophisticated understanding of the way that cultural differences might impact on the therapeutic relationship, the way that therapy can be adapted across cultures and the way that clinical outcomes can be measured in different populations. The drive towards improving access to therapies has to include thinking about improving access for diverse populations. However, IAPT training courses do not place a great deal of emphasis on the role of ethnicity in access to services, therapeutic approaches or clinical outcomes, and there are few resources to support therapists in this work.

This recognition of the need for changes in practice within mental health teams has led to targeted research amongst BME communities which aims to improve the way that services are organised and therapies delivered. This research should help to ensure that research outcomes are translated into tangible improvements in service delivery and quality of care (Loue 2006: 25–53).

Terms and phrases used in this book

There is a wide range of views as to how best to name and conceptualise issues relating to ethnic and cultural difference. It is inevitable that as we become more sophisticated at thinking about difference in services that terms change to reflect current thinking. Communities may also adapt the terms used to identify themselves over time. This can leave staff worried about getting the terminology wrong and being considered culturally insensitive or even racist by colleagues and service users. This in turn can lead to therapists and teams avoiding talking about ethnicity and culture altogether. The result of this is that a potentially important aspect of people's identity and experience is not thought about in services. This may have a considerable impact on the therapist's understanding of the difficulties being experienced by service users and may impact on engagement, the therapeutic relationship and therapy outcomes.

Rather than these worries becoming a barrier to constructive discussion and thinking, it seems to be more helpful to take into account our own intent and that of our colleagues when discussing ethnicity or cultural issues in team meetings and supervision. For example, if someone in your team uses terms or phrases that you are uncomfortable with but which are used with the intent of constructively thinking about how best to meet the needs of communities, it might be better to honour that intention by responding in a helpful and encouraging way. Use terms that you believe are better suited to describing the community or cultural practice in question when you respond, and look for an appropriate opportunity to discuss the use of terms with colleagues in a way that is less likely to make them feel criticised or act defensively. Be open to the idea that terms you might use with good intention might make others uncomfortable and be prepared to adapt and modify these if appropriate. The worse possible outcome is for staff to be avoidant about discussing issues of culture and ethnicity. Ideally, teams should foster an environment of respect for one another and willingness to discuss and think about culture and ethnicity that is collaborative and accepting of diverse opinions.

For the sake of clarity, some of the commonly used terms used in this book are defined below.

Service user

The question as to what to call the people who use mental health services is a contentious one. Traditionally in the UK the majority of mental health care has been provided by the state funded National Health Service (NHS) and the term 'patient' has been widely used to reflect this. In recent years a combination of preferences expressed by some mental health service user groups, the marketisation of health services and growth of non-NHS providers of mental health care has meant that this term is no longer used as widely. Some mental health service staff and advocacy groups prefer terms which do not imply any relationship between the service and the person using it. So for example terms such as 'our young people' might be used to refer to people using an adolescent mental health service. The marketisation of health services has also led to the terms 'customer' or 'client' being used in some settings. These terms come with specific underlying ideas about what mental health services are for and how they ought to relate to people who use them, as well as having implications about the way services might be funded and organised. I have used the term 'service user' in this book as it seems to be one of the most universally accepted, and it does not make too many assumptions about the relationship between people with mental health problems and the service they attend.

The definitions used below are based on the work of Fernando (2003). He has been one of the most thoughtful and eloquent writers on the subject of ethnicity and mental health over several decades, and his writing provides a much more comprehensive framework for thinking about ethnicity and mental health than this book, which is concerned mainly with CBT, can provide.

Race

The term 'race' is not widely used today. The idea that there are distinct biological sub-groups amongst humans has its origin in the scientific theories of Charles Darwin, which were taken up by his cousin Francis Galton and developed into a theory of innate racial differences. However, over 200 years before Darwin published his ground-breaking work on evolution there was a commonly held idea that there were broad categories of humans that could be differentiated based on skin colour and that there were natural differences between these groups in terms of intelligence, morality and other abilities and attributes, including character traits and personality. In Europe these ideas were widely understood to support the idea that the white race was superior to others and was naturally positioned to lead and rule the rest of the world. This belief ignored the fact that for two thousand years prior to this it had been China and India that had been the most technologically and socially advanced societies and that during the European 'Dark Ages' the Arab Muslim world was considerably advanced compared to Europe in many areas of mathematics, philosophy and engineering. These ideas saw race as something essential and fixed about people that could be used to predict things about how they would act or think. These days the idea that there are distinct biological racial groups, identifiable through physical characteristics like skin colour, is not supported by genetic research and there is much more emphasis on understanding the difference between people in terms of culture and ethnicity, or at the level of small and very specific differences in genetic traits linked to health outcomes.

From the mid-twentieth century onwards, biological ideas about race were refined into what Fernando calls a social idea of race. What this means is that a 'race' is understood as being a distinct population rather than a biological grouping. This can be considered an advance in terms of being less likely to consider difference to be an essential and fixed characteristic, but may not provide a subtle or flexible way of thinking about the role of culture in mental health.

Racism

Racism is usually understood to mean members of a powerful ethnic group having a set of prejudicial or negative views about a less powerful group of people based on beliefs about their biological or social characteristics, and acting on these beliefs in a way that harasses, marginalises or harms members of that group. It can also be used to describe the subtle ways an organisation disadvantages people from BME backgrounds who work in or make use of that institution. The experience of racism may well have a negative impact on someone's emotional health and may also impact on their ability to engage with institutions, such as mental health services, which they might experience as not understanding their experiences of marginalisation, or whose staff they might believe will have negative views about them based on their ethnicity.

Although ethnicity or perceived race are important factors in understanding the way that people are marginalised and excluded, it is important to bear in mind that other factors such as gender, social class and sexuality might increase or decrease the risk of marginalisation. So, for example, it is not enough to think about how being from a Black Caribbean background might have shaped someone's experience of exclusion: it is also important to think about their social class. For example someone who is African-Caribbean and from a working class family background may have both of these factors negatively impacting on their educational and vocational opportunities. If that person is also a gay man then they may have experienced increased marginalisation and prejudice in some aspects of their life and increased opportunities in others.

This definition of racism does not capture negative and pervasive beliefs about a particular religious group which may be equally prejudicial. Currently in many Western countries Muslims are the group of people most likely to be thought about in these negative terms, although at other times and in other contexts different religious groups have experienced this type of prejudice. This has a lot in common with racism (negative beliefs, generalised ideas about what a large population thinks and does) but when directed at Muslims it is sometimes called 'Islamophobia' to distinguish it from other kinds of prejudice based on perceived racial characteristics. There are a number of problems with this term.

The first is that what is called Islamophobia is often indistinguishable from racism and is better understood as such. The second is that as cognitive behaviour therapists we would see a phobia as a distinct diagnostic term with a clearly understood cause (paired association between a particular stimulus and the response of fear), with a clear treatment process (graded exposure and habituation). This seems to be an unhelpful term for experts in the treatment of phobias to use, and the use of the term 'Islamophobia' might obscure the political and economic context for this form of prejudice. It might be better to think of Islamophobia as another aspect of the racism that patients from some BME backgrounds may experience as part of their everyday lives.

Ethnicity

Ethnicity is a dynamic and subjective definition of one's self in relation to a range of factors including language, geographical origin, skin colour, political preferences, and religious and cultural practices (Loue 2006: 25–53). It is important that the ethnicity of service users is something that they define for themselves, rather than being a category assigned to them by mental health services or their therapist, because ethnicity is not a fixed thing, like race might have once been thought to be. Instead it is something that people use to define themselves in relation to the groups they belong to and the groups that they are in contact with. A person's definition of their ethnicity is likely to incorporate both culture – which can be understood as a set of attitudes, beliefs, values and behaviours – and ideas about their background which might include their country of origin and the country of origin of their family (Fernando 2010). Chapter 2 looks at the way that self-defined ethnicity can be a fluid process which can be shaped by the situation and contexts a person finds themselves in.

Black and Minority Ethnic

This book uses the term 'Black and Minority Ethnic' (BME) as a shorthand for groups who are ethnically or culturally different to the white majority group. As things stand, this is the most widely used term in clinical practice and mental health research. Another term that is becoming more widely used is 'Black, Asian and Minority Ethnic' (BAME). It is often used in the same way as BME but has been favoured by some in acknowledgement of the idea that one of the largest non-white groups in the UK is from India, Pakistan, Sri Lanka and Bangladesh. People whose country of origin is in this group of countries are often collectively known as 'Asian' in the UK. It is worth noting that in the United States the term 'Asian' is usually used to describe people whose family background is in China, Korea, Japan and what in the UK might be called South East Asia (Vietnam, Laos etc.). In the United States the term 'South Asian' is usually used to refer to people whose family origin is in India, Pakistan, Sri Lanka and Bangladesh. The reason that both BME and BAME include the term 'Minority Ethnic' is that using the term 'Ethnic' on its own implies that the white community has no ethnicity, or that it is ethnicity-free. This is clearly not the case. It is also helpful to bear in mind that service users who are identified as BME need not necessarily have anything in common with one another other than a shared experience of social and economic marginalisation (Modood et al. 1998).

White

There have been long-standing concerns in research which considers ethnicity about the degree to which being white, European, Caucasian or Western is poorly defined and understood (Bhopal and Donaldson 1998). In research, these terms often mean all those who are not included in other specific racial groups and the group with which comparisons are made. The term is still seldom defined with consistency or clarity in the majority of the mental health literature. In general, where the term is used in this book it refers to the ethnic group which is in the majority in terms of numbers in Europe, North America and Australia/ New Zealand and which has a greater access to power and resources within that country and internationally. The implication when using this term is that being white is helpful in terms of access to opportunities, social power, and influence, and that institutions such as health care, education and work are designed with the values, beliefs and behaviours of this ethnic group in mind. This white majority group will be seen as the norm in terms of how services are organised and how typically the majority of positions of power or influence within an organisation will be taken by people from this group. The ethnic group identified as white can vary a lot between countries in terms of the culture, values and beliefs of the people who make up that group. There is also considerable difference within this ethnic group in terms of the power, influence and opportunities that its members have. As with BME communities, the social class, gender and sexuality of people within this population will all have a marked impact on the degree to which people experience advantage in different domains of their lives.

The underlying assumptions of CBT and why it might need to be adapted for transcultural work

It might be helpful to spell out the main underlying assumptions that CBT makes before the criticisms of the use of this model across cultures are considered. The CBT approach assumes that mental health problems are to a large degree caused by problems in the way that someone thinks or acts and that it is the responsibility of the individual concerned to bring about changes to these processes. This view fits with dominant ideas about individual responsibility found in most Western cultures. There is very credible evidence that poverty, social exclusion, gender prejudice and racism play a considerable part in people's mental health difficulties (Reiss 2013, Rosenfield 2012). The implication of this research is that many of the solutions to mental health problems require society-wide change rather than individual therapy and that the individual may have only limited abilities to make changes within an unequal society. Reducing economic inequality and social discrimination is likely to be a slow process, and at times governments might in fact act to heighten rather than reduce these. In this environment of inequality, models of mental health which see the individual as having the majority of the responsibility for becoming well are likely to be treated more favourably by policy makers rather than those which challenge existing economic and social power structures.

It is worth thinking about these factors in the context of the mental health of BME groups who may disproportionally feel the effects of social inequality and economic exclusion. BME service users may also understand their problems and their solutions as being closely linked to their family, community and context, rather than as something that can be fixed through an individual therapy that does not take these factors into account.

Criticisms of the transcultural use of CBT

There are many reasons why therapists and academics might criticise attempts to adapt CBT for minority groups. Some have already been mentioned at the start of this chapter, but I will now consider these in detail. This book does not set out to resolve these criticisms as it is a practical guide for therapists written to support their work in adapting CBT with BME service users. It has, however, been written with these criticisms in mind, and where specific chapters address these concerns this has been noted. This book recognises that there is still considerable work to be done in order to understand how to best adapt CBT across cultures and that there are limits in terms of what can realistically be achieved.

The disorder specific models used in CBT were developed for white majority populations in the UK and USA

This criticism is a fair one. Very little work has been done outside of Europe and North America into the validity or usefulness of the disorder specific treatment models which underpin CBT. Even when research is done into the appropriateness of disorder specific models across cultures, the majority of this research is done on the basis of diagnostic interviews and measures of mental health problems developed in Western cultural contexts (Hollifield et al. 2002). The assumptions about emotional health and mental illness come from Western ideas about the individual and the way that distress is manifest and caused, and these ideas might not have much validity in other cultural contexts.

Summerfield (2008) discusses the degree to which cultures vary in the way that mental health problems and distress are understood and expressed. In many non-Western contexts distress is understood in terms of disruption to the social and moral order and might also involve supernatural or moral explanations. The idea that mental illness is situated in the mind or body alone would not fit with these ideas.

There is a substantial body of research demonstrating that the way distress is expressed and explained varies considerably between cultures, and it seems premature to think that CBT as it is currently understood and used is able to wholly explain and treat mental health problems across all cultures and in all contexts. Even what might seem like a relatively straightforward diagnostic category like depression does not necessarily translate across cultures. Summerfield (2008) highlights that in central and southern Africa a condition that roughly translates as 'thinking too much' has some overlap in terms of physiological symptoms with the Western diagnostic term 'depression', but that how it is understood in terms of cause and cure varies considerably. A cognitive behaviour therapist might think that 'thinking too much' sounds like a problem of rumination, and superficially it does, but it does not necessarily follow that CBT techniques to reduce rumination would alleviate this problem and no research has been done to establish whether or not this is the case.

The majority of research evidence for the efficacy of CBT comes from research which uses white majority service users as participants

One of the cornerstones of CBT is the commitment to evidence based practice (EBP). That means that there is a clear recognition of the importance of establishing a firm foundation of high quality research evidence to demonstrate the efficacy of interventions. It follows that CBT with BME service users should be supported by research demonstrating the efficacy of this intervention with diverse communities. This evidence base could be established by research looking at community specific Culturally Adapted CBT, through research into outcomes using Culturally Sensitive CBT, or through the participants of mainstream outcomes research including a significant proportion of people from BME backgrounds. There is a small but growing body of research into the efficacy of CA-CBT, but even a cursory look at the mainstream outcomes literature shows, on the whole, either that the ethnicity of participants in studies is not reported or that the participants were largely or wholly from the white majority community. Increasingly, systematic reviews or meta-analysis are used as a basis for establishing the efficacy of CBT and these are even less likely to take into account or even report the ethnicity of participants. Kirmayer (2012) suggests that this is a problem throughout mental health research, not just within CBT. Kirmayer also raises the very interesting point that developing interventions in non-Western communities based on diagnostic categories that not do not fit with how members of these communities experience or manifest distress means that this research is more likely to show that interventions are ineffective. In order for research into the efficacy of CBT with BME populations to be helpful it needs to start by ensuring that the presenting problem that is being treated is in fact grounded in the lived reality of the population in question.

Increasing the cultural competence of clinicians is not enough

This book is based on the idea that increasing the cultural competence of clinicians by supporting them to develop skills in adapting assessment, formulation and intervention across cultures will improve outcomes for BME service users. Kirmayer (2012) points out that this approach makes the assumption that mental health services are the right institutions to reduce mental health problems, that the interventions offered are more effective and accessible if delivered by staff who are skilled in cross-cultural working and that practitioners can acquire the necessary skills and knowledge through training or supervision. Kirmayer offers several criticisms of these points of view.

Mental health problems may predominantly be caused by social factors (such as racism, poverty and gender inequality) that are not amenable to change in the short term, so individual therapy that locates responsibility for change in the individual who has experienced these things is unlikely to be genuinely effective. Although this argument has some merit it can be argued that in the absence of society-wide change, therapists in mental health services have a duty to work to alleviate the mental health problems of service users as best as the situation and resources allow. They might work towards society-wide change but this is not their role as a therapist who is part of a mental health team.

Kirmayer also offers the possibility that effective interventions may not need to be culturally adapted and that in fact focusing on the cultural aspects of problems presented by BME service users might ignore core maintaining factors that are unrelated to culture. This is possible for some service users but assumes that mental health problems are universal conditions and that there are no difficulties in taking disorder specific models across cultures. This might be the case for some disorders and some communities, as Chapter 4 illustrates, but there is no evidence that this will always be the case. Kirmayer suggests that providing staff with training to help change their beliefs about mental health in a diverse cultural setting might not necessarily change their behaviour when it comes to assessment, formulation and intervention. This may be the case particularly when staff are not supported by supervisors who can consolidate learning and look at transcultural processes on a case-by-case basis in order to ensure new approaches are integrated into therapy. Chapter 10 sets out a framework for using supervision to support more effective work across cultures.

Another concern raised by Kirmayer is that trainers and therapists might simplify culture to key points of difference, and in doing so fail to acknowledge just how dynamic and complex questions about ethnicity and culture are. This is a valid criticism but one that can be addressed by therapists adopting a Multidimensional Approach, which is discussed in Chapter 3.

Asylum seekers and refugees need political and social justice, not psychological therapies

This argument is important when thinking about service users who have fled political persecution, war or community-wide disasters. Summerfield (1999) and others have argued that providing psychological therapies disempowers asylum seekers and fails to address the material realities of the injustice they have suffered or their understandable feelings of loss, anger and sadness following their experiences. I would argue that seeking psychological help and seeking justice or working for reparation are not mutually exclusive. For example, cognitive behaviour therapists can help service users look at what practical actions they might want to take in response to experiencing political injustice or community-wide disasters. This might involve political activism or awareness raising for victims of political injustice, or fundraising and relief work for people who have experienced community-wide disasters. These activities can be understood as part of Behavioural Activation (BA) with depressed service users (Martell et al. 2013), or the process of reclaiming one's life in PTSD as detailed in Ehlers and Clark (1999).

Looking at one form of discrimination at a time risks ignoring others

There are many aspects of people's identities that might lead to them experiencing marginalisation and exclusion. Although ethnicity is an important one, any approach to adapting CBT that only focuses on this aspect of someone's experience risks therapists and service users missing out on developing an understanding about the way that other factors such as sexuality, social class, disability and gender also contribute to the difficulties that someone might be experiencing. This is another fair criticism of the idea that transcultural approaches to adapting CBT are in themselves all that is necessary to ensure equality in terms of access and outcomes. Ethnicity is, however, an important aspect of a service user's identity, and one that is likely to have a considerable part to play in the way that they understand and respond to their mental health problems. Although this book focuses on ethnicity as an important factor, therapists are encouraged to see this as just one aspect in the life of a service user. The Multidimensional Approach detailed in subsequent chapters can be used as a framework for understanding how the many different aspects of the identity of a service user can be understood as part of the process of assessment and treatment.

Summary

There are, then, some very thoughtful and credible critiques of the idea of adapting CBT for BME populations. However, currently, CBT is the best-evidenced and best-resourced therapeutic approach available to help service users manage psychological distress. In this opening chapter the case has been made that CBT as usually taught and practised is largely neutral about ethnicity, culture and difference, but that these are likely to be important factors to consider when working with BME service users. There are a growing number of researchers and therapists working to adapt CBT across cultures and develop a high-quality evidence base regarding its effectiveness. Over the course of this book their work will be used to look at the ways in which therapists can work more effectively with BME service users. In subsequent chapters this book will look at how to bring up and discuss ethnicity and culture with service users, how to incorporate this information into formulations and treatment, what we know about the outcomes of CBT for BME service users, whether therapists should use disorder specific or generic approaches, and when Culturally Adapted CBT might be more helpful than Culturally Sensitive CBT. Subsequent chapters will also look at how to best understand patterns of service use and make services more responsive to the needs of minority groups, and how supervision can be used to support transcultural work. This book provides ideas as to how staff groups, team managers, service leads and commissioners can work together to ensure that the way services are organised is adapted so that there is genuine equality of access to evidence based psychological therapies for everyone, regardless of their background and ethnicity.

References

Andrews, M. M., and Boyle, J. S. (eds). (2008). *Transcultural concepts in nursing care.* Philadelphia, PA: Lippincott Williams & Wilkins.

Aspinall, P. J. (2003). The conceptualisation and categorisation of mixed race/ethnicity in Britain and North America: Identity options and the role of the state. *International Journal of Intercultural Relations, 27*(3), 269–296.

Beck, A. T., Rush, A. J., Shaw, B. F., and Emery, G. (1979). *Cognitive therapy of depression.* New York: Guilford.

Bernal, G., and Sáez-Santiago, E. (2006). Culturally centered psychosocial interventions. *Journal of Community Psychology, 34*(2), 121–132.

Bhopal, R., and Donaldson, L. (1998). White, European, Western, Caucasian, or what? Inappropriate labeling in research on race, ethnicity, and health. *American Journal of Public Health, 88*(9), 1303–1307.

Chowdhary, N., Jotheeswaran, A. T., Nadkarni, A., Hollon, S. D., King, M., Jordans, M. J. D., Rahman, A., Verdeli, H., Araya, R., and Patel, V. (2014). The methods and outcomes of cultural adaptations of psychological treatments for depressive disorders: A systematic review. *Psychological Medicine, 44*(06), 1131–1146.

d'Ardenne, P., Capuzzo, N., Ruaro, L., and Priebe, S. (2005). One size fits all? Cultural sensitivity in a psychological service for traumatised refugees. *Diversity in Health and Social Care, 2*(1), 29–36.

Department of Health (2005). *Delivering race equality in mental health care.* London: Department of Health.

Ehlers, A., and Clark, D. M. (1999). A cognitive model of persistent posttraumatic stress disorder. *Behaviour Research and Therapy, 38,* 319–45.

Fernando, S. (2003). *Cultural diversity, mental health and psychiatry: The struggle against racism.* Oxford: Psychology Press.

Fernando, S. (2010). *Mental health, race and culture*. London: Palgrave Macmillan.

Gone, J. P., and Kirmayer, L. J. (2010). On the wisdom of considering culture and context in psychopathology. In T. Millon, R. F. Krueger and E. Simonsen (eds), *Contemporary directions in psychopathology: Scientific foundations of the DSM-V and ICD-11*. New York: Guilford, 72–96.

Gyani, A., Shafran, R., Layard, R., and Clark, D. M. (2013). Enhancing recovery rates: Lessons from year one of IAPT. *Behaviour research and therapy*, *51*(9), 597–606.

Hollifield, M., Warner, T. D., Lian, N., Krakow, B., Jenkins, J. H., Kesler, J., Stevenson, J., and Westermeyer, J. (2002). Measuring trauma and health status in refugees: A critical review. *JAMA: The Journal of the American Medical Association*, *288*(5), 611–621.

Hull, P., Kilbourne, B., Reece, M., and Husaini, B. (2008). Community involvement and adolescent mental health: Moderating effects of race/ethnicity and neighborhood disadvantage. *Journal of Community Psychology*, *36*(4), 534–551.

Joint Commissioning Panel for Mental Health (2015). *Guidance for commissioners of mental health services for black and minority ethnic communities*. London: JCPMH. Available at: www.jcpmh.info/resource/commissioning-mental-health-services-for-bme-communities/.

Kabat-Zinn, J. (2003). Mindfulness-based interventions in context: Past, present, and future. *Clinical Psychology: Science and Practice*, *10*(2), 144–156.

Kirmayer, L. J. (2012). Cultural competence and evidence-based practice in mental health: Epistemic communities and the politics of pluralism. *Social Science & Medicine*, *75*(2), 249–256.

Kramer, T., Evans, N., and Garralda, M. E. (2000). Ethnic diversity among child and adolescent psychiatric (CAP) clinic attenders. *Child Psychology and Psychiatry Review*, *5*(4), 169–175.

Layard, S., Bell, D. M., Clark, M., Knapp, M., Meacher, M., and Priebe, S. (2006). *The depression report: A new deal for depression and anxiety disorders*, London: London School of Economics.

Loue, S. (2006). *Assessing race, ethnicity and gender in health*. New York: Springer Sciences-Business Media.

Martell, C. R., Dimidjian, S., and Herman-Dunn, R. (2013). *Behavioral activation for depression: A clinician's guide*. New York: Guilford Press.

Messent, P., and Murrell, M. (2003). Research leading to action: A study of accessibility of a CAMH service to ethnic minority families. *Child and Adolescent Mental Health*, *8*(3), 118–124.

Modood, T., Berthoud, R., Lakey, J., and Nazroo, J. (1998). *Ethnic minorities in Britain: Diversity and disadvantage*. London: Policy Studies Institute.

National Institute for Mental Health in England (2003). Inside outside: Improving mental health services for Black and Minority Ethnic communities in England. London: Department of Health.

Pope-Davis, D. B., Toporek, R. L., Ortega-Villalobos, L., Ligiéro, D. P., Brittan-Powell, C. S., Liu, W. M., Bashshur, M. R., Codrington, J. N., and Liang, C. T. (2002). Client perspectives of multicultural counseling competence: A qualitative examination. *The Counseling Psychologist*, *30*(3), 355–393.

Reiss, F. (2013). Socioeconomic inequalities and mental health problems in children and adolescents: A systematic review. *Social Science & Medicine*, *90*, 24–31.

Rosenfield, S. (2012). Triple jeopardy? Mental health at the intersection of gender, race, and class. *Social Science & Medicine, 74*(11), 1791–1801.

Summerfield, D. (1999). A critique of seven assumptions behind psychological trauma programmes in war-affected areas. *Social Science & Medicine, 48*(10), 1449–1462.

Summerfield, D. (2008). How scientifically valid is the knowledge base of global mental health? *BMJ: British Medical Journal, 336*(7651), 992.

Chapter 2

How to discuss ethnicity and culture with service users and why it can improve outcomes

Overview

For CBT to be effective the therapist and service user need to establish a good therapeutic relationship, and for therapists working with Black and Minority Ethnic service users this working relationship will be enhanced by asking about and showing interest in their cultural and ethnic background. This discussion will then enable service users and therapists to begin to think about the degree to which cultural factors impact on the presenting problems. Chapter 3 looks at approaches to exploring these issues in greater depth and Chapter 6 looks at the degree to which religious beliefs and practices might be understood and incorporated into therapy. Often service users will have been given some sort of ethnicity monitoring form to complete as part of their initial paperwork when attending clinic. This may be given by a receptionist or by the clinician as part of the administrative process but, although it is vital that this information is collected to ensure that mental health teams have a good understanding of who is and is not accessing their services, it is not something that will particularly help the therapist to develop a good understanding of the life of the person they are about to begin to work with. For some cognitive behaviour therapists a discussion of ethnicity is something that happens routinely and is seen as part of the engagement and assessment process; however, this is not the case for all practitioners. It is helpful to see this initial discussion about background and culture as being very much in the collaborative spirit of CBT and part of a process whereby the therapist begins to understand something of the world of the person they are working with.

One of the many strengths of CBT is that it is a truly collaborative treatment. Collaboration includes an agreement about what will be discussed in each therapy session when the agenda is negotiated. It might not be helpful for therapists to ask if 'a discussion about ethnicity' could be an agenda item and it is unlikely that service users would ask for this, so the way that this topic is raised needs to be negotiated in a more subtle way. This will be considered in this chapter.

Barriers to discussing ethnicity with service users

Amongst therapists there seems to be a degree of reluctance to discuss ethnicity with service users in mental health settings. Knox et al. (2003) interviewed clinical psychologists about their practice in terms of asking service users about their ethnic background as part of their assessment or ongoing work. Many practitioners were clear that they found discussing ethnicity with service users uncomfortable and avoided this topic even if it specifically came up during a session. One possible reason for this avoidance is highlighted in more recent research which found that practitioners are concerned that service users might see this type of discussion as being intrusive, racist or indicative of negative therapist views about their background (Dogra et al. 2007). Therapists in this study also reported worrying about discussing ethnicity with service users in case it made service users feel uncomfortable or judged. Practitioners also reported that getting this wrong might impact on the therapeutic relationship in a negative way and thus make therapeutic work difficult.

What BME service users say about discussing ethnicity in therapy

What we know from research asking BME service users what they want, in terms of the way that ethnicity is raised in therapy, is that they are clear that this discussion is valued and that it is likely to impact positively on the quality of the therapeutic relationship if handled well. Service users are also likely to play an active part in deciding when and how this issue is raised, though the therapist still has responsibility for asking about it if the service user does not provide an obvious opening. Given that service users often actively manage discussions of ethnicity during therapy, and that research suggests that the therapeutic relationship may be adversely affected if they feel unable to discuss ethnicity with their therapist, it seems likely that mental health practitioners who do not pick up on these cues risk compromising the effectiveness of the therapeutic relationship (Pope-Davis et al. 2002).

There is clear evidence that when therapists do join in a discussion about cultural issues and ethnicity with service users they are seen by the service user as being more culturally competent and better able to understand aspects of their life despite the difference in backgrounds between them (Knox et al. 2003, Pope-Davis et al. 2002). The service user's beliefs about the ability of their therapist to respectfully discuss and understand their cultural background is thought to subsequently enhance the therapeutic relationship (Fuertes et al. 2002) and ultimately improve the chance of a successful outcome in therapy (Flicker et al. 2008).

The concern about getting it wrong appears to be one of the main barriers that stops therapists raising questions about ethnic background as part of therapy. In order for therapists to feel confident that they can get it right enough, it would be useful to look in some detail at what service users have to say about how this discussion can most helpfully take place.

Service user perspectives on why, how and when to discuss ethnicity

This section is based on qualitative research done with BME service users in Manchester, an ethnically diverse city in the north of England, by Gurpinar-Morgan et al. (2014). This work is reported in detail as it provides an opportunity to hear the voices of young adult BME service users discussing a topic that is central to this book: the degree to which ethnicity and culture are important topics to consider during Cognitive Behaviour Therapy. This study interviewed a group of BME mental health service users aged between 16 and 18, who were mainly British born and identified themselves as being from a variety of ethnic backgrounds, including British Pakistani, Iranian, British Indian, Libyan and Ugandan. Adolescence is a time when ideas about identity and cultural background can be particularly pertinent, so this is an important age group to interview in terms of understanding how service users would like therapists to think about these issues as part of assessment and formulation. All of the participants had worked successfully with cognitive behaviour therapists from white majority backgrounds.

The interviews highlighted four interrelated themes, which are presented below with illustrative quotes from participants.

The impact of discussing ethnicity on the therapeutic relationship

The first theme described emphasised how important service users thought that a discussion of their ethnicity was in terms of their use of mental health services and engagement with their therapist. This emphasis has important implications for subsequent discussions about ethnicity during therapy. It was striking that each participant offered a highly personalised definition of their ethnic background that distanced them from a specific category or membership of a particular group, and that their conceptualisations of ethnicity were complex and multifactorial. The participants defined their ethnic background in terms of their skin colour, religion, social class, culture (which they defined as expected ways of behaving), parental origin and country of residence. Generally they did not use the term 'ethnicity' but preferred terms such as 'background' or 'culture'. This diversity and breadth of responses when young adults were asked to define their backgrounds emphasises the importance of asking BME young people to self-identify, without the constraints of forced-choice categories (Panter et al. 2009). It also highlights that it might be more helpful to begin discussion with a request like 'Could you tell me about your family background?' rather than 'Could you tell me about your ethnicity?', as the term 'background' provides a very broad set of expectations that the service user can respond to in a way that is comfortable and meaningful to their own understanding of how they fit into the world.

All of the young people discussed their ethnic background with their therapist. Some described this discussion as being primarily about their religious identity; however, for others the discussion was more broad and included thinking about the impact of their parents having been born and raised in another country and then moving to England. One common theme was that thinking about their ethnicity was related to their developing identity as a young adult. As the participants struggled with their emerging identities in their social relationships, they reported that the expectations placed on them by others who shared the same religious beliefs, by family and peers, led to a dilemma between conforming to and rejecting expectations:

> Yeah I wonder where do I fit in? Do I fit in with this group or do I fit in with that group and I feel like I'm just in the middle of it all and trying to make everyone happy.
>
> (Laila)

This dilemma was particularly relevant for the participants whose parents had different ethnic backgrounds to one another. Feeling forced to choose between groups is a common experience for adolescents with parents of different backgrounds (Campbell and Eggerling-Boeck 2006) and to a lesser extent for adults. During adolescence there can be an additional set of social roles to negotiate, as there is also the question of fitting in with ethnically similar or white British-born peers at the same time as facing the dilemma of whether to conform to the expectations of one parent or the other.

Participants described therapy as being useful for working through some of these conflicts and addressing the negative impact on mood that this tension caused. For instance, Laila described how the therapist validated her experience, by explaining that other BME adolescents also reported similar challenges. Normalising difficult experiences allowed Laila to explore the importance of developing her own identity and to resist peer-group expectations she was not comfortable with:

> . . . to know that if other people are struggling with this as well, so you if you're not the only one you don't have to like . . . conform to what everyone else is expecting . . . you can just carry on being who you are.

Many of the young people only became aware of the influence of their ethnic background on their presenting difficulties through the process of exploration and discussion in therapy:

> Having therapy helped me to understand why I didn't get along with my parents . . . because I really didn't get it at the time.
>
> (Amaya)

Amaya described conflict between herself and her parents, who expected her to behave in ways that were the norm in their country of origin. The implications of this in terms of her relationship with her parents and her long-standing low mood were formulated as part of therapy. There is an interesting question about whether providing a space for exploration and contextualising problems can be strictly considered to be CBT. It might not fit with disorder specific models of working; however, it does fit with what we are calling Culturally Sensitive CBT, and it is possible to begin to formulate these issues within a CBT framework, as seen below:

Trigger: conflict with parents about activities after school.

Cognitions: 'They don't allow me any independence, this is not fair, my life is totally unfair.'

Affect: sadness, agitation.

Behaviour: withdrawal from family life, rumination.

Impact of behaviour: parents believe that Amaya is not interested in the culture and practices of the family, and try to bring her back into family life by increasing demands to participate.

Cognitions: 'They are only happy when I am totally busy with family activity. I have no independence.'

By beginning to understand the family context it was possible to begin to develop an understanding with Amaya about the nature of the culturally informed family beliefs which underpinned this cycle of conflict, low mood and rumination. As we will see in the next chapter, work with BME service users can usefully consider the thoughts, feelings and behaviours of their family members and how these might need to be understood and modified as part of the intervention.

One young man in the study reported that ethnicity was not important in understanding his presenting difficulties but that it was important in developing interventions, as he described how:

> One of the techniques I'm using now is based on religion.
>
> (Umair)

This link was made by the young person, and understanding CBT techniques in this way appeared to have been helpful in terms of making use of them in his day-to-day life. Without a discussion about ethnic background and spirituality during the initial stages of the therapy, the therapist and service user might not have been able to discover the common ground between his religious practice and CBT techniques.

There is some research which suggests that clients do not necessarily view their ethnicity as important or relevant to their difficulties until it emerges as part of the reflective process of therapy, and that this is often initiated by the therapist (Fuertes et al. 2002, Knox et al. 2003). This raises a difficult question. Are issues to do with ethnicity or culture part of the presenting problem or is the therapist, perhaps unused to the background of their patient, thinking about ethnicity as a problem? In the spirit of collaboration at the heart of CBT, it might be assumed that formulations are developed jointly, are seen as provisional and that the service user is able to say that they disagree if the therapist makes suggestions that do not fit with their understanding of the presenting problems. However, as therapists we should be aware of the power we have in sessions and the way that this might make it difficult for service users to challenge our own unhelpful assumptions. It might be even more difficult for a service user to disagree when the therapist is white and so in a position of perceived relative authority compared to the BME service user. A good principle to help frame this dilemma is the idea that the therapist's and the service user's understanding of the presenting problems are, as Beck (1995) said, 'an ever evolving formulation of patients' problems', implying that any understanding of what maintains the distress is tentative and subject to review as part of the therapy process.

Working with BME service users where issues of cultural practice or belief are being incorporated into formulations is a process likely to benefit from the therapist taking an even more non-expert, hesitant and provisional view about the formulation than usual. In practice the most helpful formulations are usually the ones that the service user discovers for themselves through Socratic dialogue. Using this principle to develop formulations which include cultural factors is likely to reduce the risk of the therapist imposing their ideas about the relationship between culture and the presenting problems of service users.

Harper and Iwamasa (2000) surveyed adolescent users of mental health services and recommended that a discussion of the ethnic background of the client should take place regardless of whether the client raises the issue or identifies ethnicity as a precipitating or maintaining factor. The case examples of Amaya and Umair above illustrate the value of the therapist raising this issue if the service user does not. This principle holds for adult and adolescent service users as well as both parents and children who use CAMHS services.

Discussing ethnicity and identity in therapy may be particularly useful for BME adolescents with parents from two different ethnic backgrounds, who are more likely to undergo multiple shifts in their self-concept compared to BME adolescents with parents who share the same ethnic background (Rockquemore et al. 2009).

Talking about ethnic differences and establishing the therapeutic relationship

Service users were very clear that they thought it was important to have a therapist who could acknowledge ethnic or cultural differences and similarities. Therapist willingness to begin this discussion was universally seen as a positive thing. Umair described his preference for acknowledging their differences:

> So you got better understanding of how people live their lives . . . and so you are more open and aware.

Some service users might be interested in learning about the therapist's background to establish whether there is common ground on which the therapeutic relationship can be built. This could explain why therapist self-disclosure (relating to factual information regarding ethnic background or experiences of discrimination) is strongly correlated with BME service users' satisfaction with therapy in adult settings (Chang and Berk 2009). In the majority of cases, though, the service user–therapist relationship will be built on difference rather than similarity, so the task for the therapist is to communicate that the difference between them has been recognised and that the service user is respected and accepted for who they are. This might begin to address any concerns that service users have regarding negative views that therapists might have about them on the basis of their ethnicity.

When the discussion about ethnicity should take place

Given that this discussion is likely to have a marked positive impact on the therapeutic relationship, it seems likely that the timing of the discussion about culture and ethnicity is an important factor. Participants in the study had different preferences for when conversations about ethnicity should take place. For example, Umair said that this discussion could take place:

> Maybe at the beginning of your therapy. Just so you know more about each other and you can start from there.

Although some service users are likely to initiate conversations about ethnicity with their therapist, it is likely to be the case that some will not bring this as a topic for discussion in therapy. Participants recommended that the therapist prompt the client to discuss ethnicity if the client did not mention it first:

> I don't think the most people would talk about it at first. I think it needs the therapist to encourage them, to ask questions about it.
>
> (Laila)

One participant reporting discussing the differences between her own ethnicity and the therapist's, which put her at ease and strengthened their rapport:

> I wasn't like I was in a strange room talking to a complete stranger about my life . . . some of the things we talked about I wouldn't be able to say to my mum or my dad . . . whereas I'm saying it to a person I don't know. Finding out about his background and about him . . . it felt a lot more comfortable.
>
> (Laila)

It is likely then that some service users value the opportunity to discuss ethnic differences between themselves and their therapist, and that this could lead to a better rapport and a more trusting and open therapeutic alliance (Knox et al. 2003). A different participant in the study, Jahzara, commented on how the therapist acknowledged their own discomfort in raising the issue of her ethnic background, but thought that by being open about this her therapist improved the quality of the therapeutic relationship, as she stated:

> I would definitely empathise with why they didn't particularly want to speak about certain subjects . . . so it was okay that they said that.

Service users often comment that it can feel strange to talk about their own ethnicity, as it is not something they are used to doing, particularly with a stranger and in an open and purposeful way. However, it is clear from the research literature that on the whole service users prefer to talk about their ethnicity rather than for it not to be acknowledged at all. Although this might be true for the majority of service users, it is important to bear in mind that it might not be the case for everyone. For example, in the study one participant, Amaya, thought that talking about the difference in backgrounds between herself and her therapist was likely to have a long term negative impact on the therapeutic relationship, as she described how:

> The topic would just keep coming up in my brain . . . about how different we are . . . talking about how different we are made me felt uncomfortable.

It is therefore important for therapists to check and seek feedback about how, when and to what extent explicitly discussing ethnicity is helpful for the service user. This seems to be very much in the spirit of collaboration central to CBT.

The timing, sensitivity and context within which ethnicity is talked about are therefore of great importance. Discussing ethnicity could be used in developing the formulation of the client's difficulties and is generally recommended to occur towards the start of therapy. However, it might be the case that an initial discussion can take place as part of the assessment process, but that detailed and potentially more difficult discussions might need to wait until a stronger alliance has developed. This is particularly important where the discussion is linked to topics the service user might find difficult to discuss with a white therapist, such as the experience of racism or what might be seen as private family or community matters.

Research into addressing ethnic differences between client and therapist in adult psychotherapy settings (Fuertes et al. 2002, Maxie et al. 2006) suggests that therapists who believe that asking questions at the wrong time would make the client feel uncomfortable are ultimately less likely to discuss cultural background and how it might relate to the presenting problems. The participants in this study generally emphasised that the discussion about ethnicity should occur in the context of an already established rapport, rather than being the way to develop one.

Explaining the rationale for asking about culture and ethnicity

If ethnicity is raised by the therapist without a clear rationale, it is also possible that this might have a negative impact on the therapeutic alliance. Some of the participants in our study suggested that the therapist's motives in initiating such a conversation could be interpreted as a sign that the therapist was being racist or was unsure of their ability to help someone from a different ethnic background:

> to have the conversation at all would make me think that maybe he thought that it needed to be said . . . that we were different . . . so I would have thought that he had a problem with my culture and that would have worried me if it wasn't handled properly.
>
> (Amaya)

This could be experienced as a microaggression, which are defined as 'brief, everyday exchanges that send denigrating messages to people of colour because they belong to a racial minority group' (Sue et al. 2007: 72). These can have a negative effect on the therapeutic alliance (Chang and Berk 2009). One participant, Naomi, suggested that it would be very helpful if the rationale for asking about ethnic background was made explicit to the service user in terms of how this information would support the therapist to understand the service user and the way that therapy might be helpful for them:

> they would be explaining something: 'we know from our side that people from different backgrounds have different ways of thinking, so we just want to know about your background and how your family works' . . . because obviously you need to know that for you to work with them.

However, another participant, Jahzara, suggested that the conversation should be initiated in the context of 'delving deeper' into an issue already up for discussion, rather than setting it up as part of a formal agenda:

> so if we were speaking about food for instance, like in a random thing and I happened to say my favourite food and he could say 'oh perhaps you should tell me more about your culture', that's fine.
>
> (Jahzara)

It is clear that one thing that many service users value is to be able to have a say about how ethnicity is talked about in therapy, and to have the ability to either withdraw from or engage in discussions with the therapist depending on what is happening in their lives or in the therapy process at that time. This decision making about what is brought to the session and when it can be understood as being part of what Pope-Davis et al. (2002) called 'client processes' in their model of multicultural counselling competence. Expecting a service user to educate or guide the therapist in terms of cultural issues might be a considerable burden at times when service users are already experiencing high degrees of distress, but it might also be an empowering process that enhances their sense of working collaboratively with the therapist.

Case examples

To illustrate the dynamic nature of self-ascribed ethnicity, two case examples are presented below. They are both of women who might be typically classed as British South Asian but whose self-ascribed ethnicity might vary considerably depending on the context of who is asking and in what circumstances they are asked.

Case example: Harvinder

Harvinder is a 74-year-old woman born in the Indian part of the Punjab (an administrative State within India which was divided into Indian and Pakistani Punjab at the time of Indian independence from the United Kingdom in 1947). Harvinder came to the UK with her husband at the age of 20 and worked in a factory in the West Midlands until she retired. She has remained an Indian citizen but has full legal right to live in the UK and has raised a family here.

In different circumstances she might define herself as:

Indian (country of birth, geographical positioning, citizenship) – for example when asked by someone who is white in the UK.

Punjabi (linguistic/geographical/cultural grouping) – for example when asked by someone from India in the UK or in India.

From the Jalander district (a geographical district of the Punjab, with some distinct cultural implications) – for example when asked by someone in the Punjab from the Punjab.

Sikh (religious affiliation) – in a context where she might want to stress her spiritual values and affiliations; this also implies geographical and cultural affiliations, although technically Sikhs can be from any number of countries or ethnicities.

Jat (caste affiliation) – the largest caste group amongst Punjabi Sikhs; although the Sikh faith rejects the notion of caste, some Sikhs would describe themselves by caste when, for example, considering marriage arrangements.

British Indian (place of residence, ethnicity) – for example when asked in India, in order to stress the country where she lives and her cultural and community affiliations there.

(continued)

(continued)

> Non-Resident Indian (an Indian citizen but living abroad) – for example when dealing with banks, government offices etc. in India.

Harvinder would not use the terms 'BME', 'BAME', 'British South Asian', 'Asian' or 'minority' in any circumstances. She would describe herself as working class and a woman and identify both these factors as having led to discrimination at times. She would not define herself in terms of her sexuality but would say that she is heterosexual if asked, although she never has been before.

Case example: Jasmine

Jasmine is a 34-year-old woman with a senior professional job in the National Health Service. She was born in the UK. Her parents are from Dhaka in Bangladesh; they came to the UK in the 1960s (when Bangladesh was known as East Pakistan), and are university educated and worked in professional jobs before retiring. They are a Muslim family.

At various times Jasmine would describe herself as:

> Bengali (a cultural, linguistic and geographical affiliation: Bengal was a state in British-ruled India, divided during Indian independence when one half became East Pakistan. Following civil war between East and West Pakistan in 1971 it became known as Bangladesh) – she would use this term when asked about her ethnicity in the UK; this category never appears on ethnic monitoring forms.

> Bangladeshi (the nation where much of her extended family lives) – when asked her ethnicity in the UK when she has to fit this into a category box; this country did not exist when her parents came to the UK, and Jasmine has never visited Bangladesh.

> British Asian (citizenship and ethnicity) – when emphasising her common experiences with people of Indian, Pakistani and Bangladeshi origin in the UK.

> British South Asian (citizenship and ethnicity) – when she wants to be more specific than the above and where she wants to distinguish her background from that of people whose family origin is China, Japan etc.

> From a Muslim family but not a Muslim – when questions of religious faith are being considered; although 'Muslim' is not an ethnic category, many people use it in place of one to emphasise the common experiences and values of people who are members of this faith group.

An atheist – when questions of religious beliefs are being considered in more detail; identifying as an atheist may be important when matters of religious practice or belief are being considered: again this is not an ethnic category but it might be used as a way of communicating something about herself that is similar to how ethnicity might be used.

Minoritised – when emphasising her shared experience with marginalised people from other ethnicities – this term is used in some of the academic literature about ethnicity and identity in recognition of the idea that someone is not born into a minority but that minority status is conferred on people by the majority ethnic group; she would not, however, use the term 'BME'.

English but not British (national identification but not related to citizenship) – as she would associate the latter with a colonial national entity, the term 'British' being a colonial term used to describe a number of countries united under a common monarch and government but comprised of distinct nations with their own histories and characteristics.

She would not use the terms 'BME' or 'Asian' to describe herself, but might describe herself in terms of her sexuality (bisexual), her social class (middle class) and her gender. She would identify her ethnicity, gender and sexuality as causes of discrimination.

The distinctions discussed in the case examples are dynamic; that is, they change with the circumstances of when and how the questions are asked, and may also change with time depending on the social and political climate and how someone sees themselves in relation to that. They are also just one aspect of how someone would describe themselves and the way they might experience marginalisation and exclusion. It is important to consider the ways that gender, sexuality, social class and disability might also be important in understanding someone's lived experiences.

What service users say about working with ethnically similar and dissimilar therapists

Service users' views about the impact of ethnic difference between themselves and the therapist are important to consider. Generally, this difference occurs where a white majority therapist is working with a service user from a BME background. Some of the themes discussed here might also be relevant to or inform work where the service user is from a white background and the therapist is from a BME community, or where therapist and service user are from different BME communities. Quantitative studies have suggested that client outcomes for ethnically matched and non-matched client–therapist pairings are the same (for example, Erdur et al. 2000). A review of the use of health services by BME individuals also concluded that the communication style and manner of relating to the patient was more important than the ethnicity of the clinician (Scheppers et al. 2006). Dogra et al. (2007) reported that the ethnicity of the therapist was seen by service users as less important than the personality and general demeanour of the therapist. It may be that children and young people share similar views regarding the importance of therapist communication style; however, older adolescents may be more explicitly aware of the concepts of a therapeutic relationship, such as empathy and rapport, whereas BME children and younger adolescents may express the same concepts in terms of having a friendly therapist.

It is likely that most if not all service users privately reflect on differences between themselves and their therapist, although the degree to which this is important to them will vary. During the research into the views of young adult BME service users, one related theme was that during initial sessions most of the participants had questioned the ability of an ethnically dissimilar therapist to understand and help with their difficulties. For example, Amaya said that:

> I thought that maybe he wouldn't understand where I was coming from because of how I grew up and I didn't think he had grown up like that.

Regardless of the clinician's ethnic background, over the course of therapy service users are likely to be involved in an ongoing process of working out whether or not the therapist can sufficiently understand their difficulties. One participant in our study, Naomi, described listening out in early sessions for signs that the therapist understood her situation. She was explicitly looking for a degree of expressed empathy but also psychologically informed knowledge of the presenting difficulties and how her own ethnic background might be related to this. She described a process of evaluating the therapist for their level of understanding and deciding within a few sessions:

> that you know what, I think they can help me.

Believing that you are understood seems to be an essential aspect of the therapeutic relationship for both adolescents and adults (Chang and Berk 2009). If the therapist can effectively demonstrate an understanding of the service user in terms of their ethnic background and culture this will increase service user confidence that the therapist will be able to help them (Pope-Davis et al. 2002). This level of confidence in turn will facilitate engagement.

The use of key Socratic skills such as summaries, reflections and interpretations is likely to help develop a rapport and demonstrate that the therapist has heard and understood what has been said. Fuertes et al. (2002) found that therapists reported using skills such as reflecting, paraphrasing, conveying an open, non-judgemental, empathic attitude and demonstrating understanding to establish the working alliance with BME service users. These core skills are central to the successful development of all therapeutic relationships, regardless of therapist or client ethnicity (Chang and Berk 2009), and provide a basis from which the therapist can begin to seek clarifications or a deeper understanding of the context and background of the service user.

Although we will discuss religious practice and spirituality in Chapter 6, it is worth noting that an acknowledgement of and questions about difference early on in therapy might also cover this topic. One participant, Umair, described how having an ethnically dissimilar therapist who was confident enough to ask him about his religious practices early on therapy was of great benefit:

> I thought, he understands what I think and believe, so it will help him to find better ways to help me.

This is consistent with the cultural competency literature that highlights the benefit of adding techniques to the existing model within which the therapist and BME client are working (Fuertes et al. 2002). Techniques can be adapted or replaced with culturally appropriate equivalents (Sue et al. 2009), which may include approaches which are linked to religious practices.

There may also be other barriers related to difference which impact on the alliance. One participant in our study believed that the therapist would be unable to understand topics relating to her background which were as much to do with social class as ethnicity:

> I don't think he relates to me though . . . like he wouldn't relate if I had a problem that I said I needed money for instance . . . because I doubt he's ever been in the situation where he was to not have money . . . so sometimes I find our sessions are hard, I'm not as enthusiastic because [therapist's name] wouldn't be able to relate to me and my frustration, which is fair enough, it's not his fault.
> (Jahzara)

This demonstrates the complexity of thinking about difference, and the way that this might also include social class and the experience of poverty as well as gender, sexuality and disabilities.

It is also worth considering how service users conceptualise work with a therapist from an ethnically similar background. Some studies support the idea that ethnic similarity is associated with higher scores on measures of the therapeutic alliance compared to non-matched therapists (Farsimadan et al. 2007). In the present study, Laila described how ethnic similarity may facilitate the process of talking about ethnicity and its impact on the client's difficulties, thereby strengthening the rapport. Laila reported that:

> It would be a lot easier to open up to them, whereas it would probably take time if there was no understanding or there was no connection between the psychologist and the patient . . . but having a simple basic connection, it would be easier to open up and obviously to explain things to them.
> (Laila)

Although having an ethnically similar therapist is not a requirement for successful transcultural CBT to occur, it might be helpful in terms of the service user believing that the therapist would be more likely to understand their life, behaviour, views and religious beliefs. It is also likely that service users will find it easier to raise their experience of racism with ethnically similar therapists, as they might believe that white therapists would find that topic a difficult one to understand.

In the adult literature there is some research suggesting that the strength of the therapeutic alliance mediates the relationship between ethnic matching between the client and therapist and the therapeutic outcome (Farsimadan et al. 2007). Ethnic similarity is by no means a guarantee of enhancing the alliance. Service users may believe that an ethnically similar therapist would be more likely to make assumptions about them based on their expectations of how a member of their ethnic group should behave, and that the therapist may be critical if they did not conform to those standards. It does not necessarily follow that shared ethnicity automatically equates to shared experiences. As one participant said:

> She'd try and say that she understood me, but I really don't think she did, 'cause I don't think she had been through what I had been through . . . she had been through something else.
>
> (Amaya)

How to manage difficulties when difference impacts on the therapeutic alliance

The rupture-repair model of therapy processes might be a useful framework for some of the difficulties that might arise as a result of threats to the therapeutic alliance brought about by difference or sameness not being sufficiently managed. This model suggests that where there has been a threat to the therapeutic relationship it is possible for the alliance to be re-established in a way that might in fact strengthen this relationship over time (Keenan et al. 2005). In transcultural work this rupture might be precipitated by therapist assumptions or misunderstandings relating to issues of ethnicity or culture. In order to repair this alliance the therapist and service user would need to explicitly discuss this misunderstanding and the reasons for it, and the therapist would need to seek the advice of the service user in terms of how they might better consider these issues in therapy in the future. It might be helpful to say something like:

> As a white therapist I might not always get things right in terms of understanding where you are coming from. How could I do things differently in order to be more helpful?

This might place a considerable burden on the service user in terms of managing this aspect of the therapy process. It is important that the therapist has considered the degree to which the service user is able to collaborate around directing them in this area at that particular time during the therapy.

A sample dialogue where ethnicity is discussed as part of an initial assessment

It might be helpful to provide an example of a dialogue in therapy where ethnicity is discussed in order to illustrate how this process might work. This dialogue is between a white, middle-aged male therapist and Ahmed, a 22-year-old patient who was born in the UK to parents who were born in Bangladesh but migrated to the UK for work several years before he was born.

Therapist: So could you tell me a little bit more about the sort of worries you have when you are feeling anxious and depressed?
Ahmed: It is usually when I'm having an argument with my mother.
Therapist: What sort of things do you argue about?
Ahmed: She doesn't like how I spend my free time, she says I embarrass her.
Therapist: What is it that embarrasses her?
Ahmed: Well she doesn't really get what it is like these days. It is not like it was when she was growing up.
Therapist: How would it be if I asked you about your family background so I could understand things better?
Ahmed: Yes, that's fine.
Therapist: So could you tell me about where your parents were from before they moved to the UK? When did they move here?

This allows a discussion about country of family origin, migration history and where the service user was born. It might also expand into a wider discussion about intergenerational values and roles, but we will look at how that might work in Chapter 3.

This discussion starts with a question about whether it is okay to ask for this sort of information. It is usually the case that service users are happy to discuss this, but checking that it is an acceptable topic seems to be very much in the spirit of collaboration which underpins Cognitive Behaviour Therapy. Once this permission has been given, the therapist has several options in terms of what specific questions they might want to consider first, but country of family origin and migration histories can be a useful starting point.

Using behavioural experiments to change therapist cognitions about the adverse effects of asking service users about their ethnicity

We can begin to understand therapist reluctance to raise this topic using a cognitive and behavioural model. Thoughts about the likely negative, or even catastrophic, consequences of raising this topic may lead to heightened anxiety in the therapist, which they understandably manage through avoidance. It might be useful to consider how behavioural experiments can help in this situation. If we consider the target cognition to be something like 'Asking about ethnicity and culture will negatively impact on the therapeutic relationship', then the counter belief might be 'Asking about ethnicity and culture will at worse have no impact on and may enhance the therapeutic relationship'. The avoidant therapist might rate the strength of these beliefs and then undertake to ask about this with the next few BME service users they assess in order to test whether or not their predictions come true. In the spirit of a good behavioural experiment, they might want to operationalise how they would measure the impact that asking has on the therapeutic relationship. In most services there are likely to be therapy rating scales that service users can complete in order to provide feedback regarding the session and the therapeutic relationship. These would provide robust measures and might be better than relying on the 'felt sense' of the therapist as to whether this was a successful approach, particularly if they are anxious about trying this. Therapists can use supervision to review these results and reflect on what they have learnt as a result of this behavioural experiment, and complete the learning cycle by planning what they would do differently next time.

Summary and clinical implications

Cognitive behaviour therapists working in diverse communities must be able to be confident in asking about the backgrounds of BME service users and demonstrate both empathy for the service user's presenting problems and an appreciation of how their background might impact on their presenting difficulties. This seems particularly important where the presenting difficulties include relational difficulties, or when the maintaining factors are linked to cultural practices or beliefs. There are likely to be additional factors to consider when the client identifies themselves as being multi-ethnic and where managing multiple identities and roles is a challenge. The therapist should have the confidence to provide a therapeutic setting in which service users are invited to talk about their background, as this will strengthen the therapeutic alliance and may be useful in developing a shared formulation which includes culturally specific factors likely to have implications for the interventions used. For many service users talking about religion as part of this discussion will be welcomed and may offer opportunities to integrate their faith and spiritual practices into therapeutic approaches.

Ethnically similar therapists may be seen by service users as having similar experiences and values to themselves, and this may provide opportunities for discussing experiences such as racism, culturally driven family difficulties or spiritual practices that might be harder to discuss with a white therapist. However, service users might also believe that ethnically similar therapists may make more assumptions about them. It is possible that clients could feel judged for not conforming to expectations in their family, peer or other social relationships, and this dynamic could then be reinforced by interactions with the therapist. Ethnically similar therapists should therefore also discuss the similarities and differences between them and the service user as part of engagement.

Therapists should take the lead from the client in talking about ethnicity and follow up on the client's comments about their background with further questions. The therapist should, however, be prepared to initiate such a conversation during assessment if the client does not talk about it spontaneously. Preliminary research has suggested that client ratings of the therapeutic alliance are the same regardless of whether it is they or the therapist who initiates the discussion. The important point seems to be that at some point fairly early on in the assessment and treatment process the issue is raised and responded to in a facilitative and respectful way.

Where the service user does not initiate this discussion, the timing, context and rationale for talking about ethnicity should be carefully considered by the therapist and decisions about when and how to introduce the topic of ethnicity should be made on a case-by-case basis.

Asking about ethnicity in this way is a good start; however, as we will discuss in the next chapter, a more subtle and detailed approach to considering ethnicity might be helpful for some service users.

References

Beck, J. S. (1995). *Cognitive therapy*. New York: John Wiley & Sons, Inc.

Campbell, M. E., and Eggerling-Boeck, J. (2006). 'WHAT ABOUT THE CHILDREN?' The psychological and social well-being of multiracial adolescents. *The Sociological Quarterly, 47*(1), 147–173.

Chang, D. F., and Berk, A. (2009). Making cross-racial therapy work: A phenomenological study of clients' experiences of cross-racial therapy. *Journal of Counselling Psychology, 56*(4), 521–536.

Dogra, N., Vostanis, P., Abuateya, H., and Jewson, N. (2007). Children's mental health services and ethnic diversity: Gujarati families' perspectives of service provision for mental health problems. *Transcultural Psychiatry, 44*(2), 275–291.

Erdur, O., Rude, S., Barón, A., Draper, M., and Shankar, L. (2000). Working alliance and treatment outcome in ethnically similar and dissimilar client–therapist pairings. *Research Reports of the Research Consortium of Counseling & Psychological Services in Higher Education, 1*(1).

Farsimadan, F., Draghi-Lorenz, R., and Ellis, J. (2007). Process and outcome of therapy in ethnically similar and dissimilar therapeutic dyads. *Psychotherapy Research, 17*(5), 567–575.

Flicker, S. M., Turner, C. W., Waldron, H. B., Brody, J. L., and Ozechowski, T. J. (2008). Ethnic background, therapeutic alliance, and treatment retention in functional family therapy with adolescents who abuse substances. *Journal of Family Psychology, 22*(1), 167–170.

Fuertes, J. N., Mueller, L. N., Chauhan, R. V., Walker, J. A., and Ladany, N. (2002). An investigation of European American therapists' approach to counseling African American clients. *The Counselling Psychologist, 30*(5), 763–788.

Gurpinar-Morgan, A., Murray, C., and Beck, A. (2014). Ethnicity and the therapeutic relationship: Views of young people accessing cognitive behavioural therapy. *Mental Health, Religion & Culture, 17*(7), 714–725.

Harper, G. W., and Iwamasa, G. Y. (2001). Cognitive-behavioral therapy with ethnic minority adolescents: Therapist perspectives. *Cognitive and Behavioral Practice*, 7(1), 37–53.

Keenan, E. K., Tsang, A. K. T., Bogo, M., and George, U. (2005). Micro ruptures and repairs in the beginning phase of cross-cultural psychotherapy. *Clinical Social Work Journal*, 33(3), 271–289.

Knox, S., Burkard, A. W., Johnson, A. J., Suzuki, L. A., and Ponterotto, J. G. (2003). African American and European American therapists' experiences of addressing race in crossracial psychotherapy dyads. *Journal of Counseling Psychology*, 50, 466–481.

Maxie, A. C., Arnold, D. H., and Stephenson, M. (2006). Do therapists address ethnic and racial differences in cross-cultural psychotherapy? *Psychotherapy: Theory, Research, Practice, Training*, 43(1), 85–98.

Panter, A. T., Daye, C. E., Allen, W. R., Wightman, L. F., and Deo, M. E. (2009). It matters how and when you ask: Self-reported race/ethnicity of incoming law students. *Cultural Diversity and Ethnic Minority Psychology*, 15(1), 51–66.

Pope-Davis, D. B., Toporek, R. L., Ortega-Villalobos, L., Ligiéro, D. P., Brittan-Powell, C. S., Liu, W. M., Bashshur, M. R., Codrington, J. N., and Liang, C. T. (2002). Client perspectives of multicultural counselling competence: A qualitative examination. *The Counselling Psychologist*, 30(3), 355–393.

Rockquemore, K. A., Brunsma, D. L., and Delgado, D. J. (2009). Racing to theory or retheorizing race? Understanding the struggle to build a multiracial identity theory. *Journal of Social Issues*, 65(1), 13–34.

Scheppers, E., Van Dongen, E., Dekker, J., Geertzen, J., and Dekker, J. (2006). Potential barriers to the use of health services among ethnic minorities: A review. *Family Practice*, 23(3), 325–348.

Sue, D. W., Capodilupo, C. M., Torino, G. C., Bucceri, J. M., Holder, A., Nadal, K. L., and Esquilin, M. (2007). Racial microaggressions in everyday life: Implications for clinical practice. *American Psychologist*, 62(4), 271–286.

Chapter 3

Using family systems, migration histories and acculturation in assessment and formulation

Overview

As the previous chapter has shown, asking about ethnicity is likely to be a key part of establishing good therapeutic relationships with BME service users, and provides therapists with a better understanding of how the person they are working with sees themselves and their place in the world. What this information does not do is help the service user and therapist begin to formulate the way that ethnicity and cultural practices might be part of the presenting problem and the solutions to that problem. Where therapy time is limited, for example within some IAPT services or where the presenting problem is straightforward, it might be enough just to ask about ethnic background and there may be no need for further exploration of this aspect of the service user's life and identity. There are, however, likely to be cases where it is necessary to think in greater depth about family context and cultural issues.

This chapter draws on two papers that together provide a useful framework for cognitive behaviour therapists working with BME service users. The first is Dummett's (2006) paper on systemic CBT with children, young people and families. Although written from the point of view of a CAMHS clinician this paper has a lot to offer clinicians working with adults, as it provides a framework for formulating the way that the thoughts, feelings and behaviours of family members can impact on presenting problems. The second paper is by Falicov (1995). This paper was written for Systemic Family Therapists, who have historically had a much more sophisticated way of thinking about diversity than cognitive behaviour therapists. This paper looks in detail at the ways in which ethnic diversity can be understood, and provides a framework that has a lot to offer cognitive behaviour therapists looking to enrich the way that they think and talk about diversity. This chapter will also look at the way that drawing up a genogram with service users can provide a more detailed way of thinking about ethnicity and culture and how this works in their family.

Thinking about systemic issues in a CBT framework

Dummett (2006) begins by reminding therapists that formulation is central to the work that cognitive behaviour therapists do, in that it provides a way for service users and therapists to understand the processes that are maintaining the presenting problem. The need for collaboratively derived formulations is as important when working with children and families as it is when working with adults. Although amongst CAMHS based cognitive behaviour therapists there has been a growing recognition that the thoughts, feelings and behaviours of family members can play an important part in maintaining problems, there is less recognition of this amongst therapists working with adults. Part of this is likely to be because the majority of evidence based interventions developed for anxiety and depression have focused on the individual and have not included family or partner based work. These models have been very successful in treating the majority of people with depression and anxiety disorders presenting to mental health services; however, as we have seen in Chapter 1, they were developed primarily with white majority service users in mind. This is not so much of a problem in services where almost all referrals are of white ethnic backgrounds, but where service users are from diverse cultural backgrounds it might be necessary to incorporate thinking about the wider family context into how the problem is understood.

Within some BME communities life is organised around the family much more than it is around the individual. In some BME communities what is considered to be the family unit may also be different to how this might be understood within white majority cultures. Aunts, uncles and grandparents may have a more prominent role in decision making within the family than the core dyad of the married parental couple recognised in most Western contexts. Adults within the family unit may place more emphasis on ensuring good family relationships and family functioning, and the needs and wishes of individuals may be seen as subordinate to this. That is not to say that this will be true for everyone from a particular minority group or that this is not true for some white majority service users. It is, however, a factor that would benefit from some sort of consideration when applying CBT transculturally. In order to begin to understand the family context of service users it is helpful to draw up a genogram as part of the initial assessment process.

Mapping the family system with a genogram

A genogram, or family tree as it is sometimes called, is a relatively quick way to learn a lot about the context of the person you are working with. Most mental health staff will be familiar with these but, unless they work in CAMHS, may not have drawn one with a service user for many years. Given this, it is worth looking at the key principles again. A genogram has three main purposes: it maps out the structure of the family, including who currently lives at home with the service user; it can be used to outline key relationships between family members; and it can be used to record important information about family members, such as physical and mental health problems, whether they are in work and their age. Typically, a genogram will start with immediate family members but may expand to include the wider family and family friends. The ways of describing relationships using genograms have become increasingly sophisticated to account for more subtle and complex ways that families might be organised, and clinicians interested in looking at these should refer to current Systemic Therapy journals for updates.

The task of drawing a genogram can be introduced by saying something like:

> It would really help me to get to know you better if I could get an idea of who is in your family and who is important to you. Could we draw it out together?

Each person in the genogram is represented by either a circle (for female) or a square (for male), and typically the name and age of the person is recorded in or beside the symbol. It is helpful to start with the service user, drawing their symbol close to the bottom of the page but leaving room below this for their children or grandchildren, depending on their age. From there you might typically start by mapping on their parents and siblings. The relationship between married or co-habiting couples is shown by a horizontal line connecting them. If they are divorced or separated then a double vertical line is made in the centre of the line connecting them, usually with a year to indicate when this happened. The children from that relationship can be added to the line connecting the parents, by adding a downward vertical line with a horizontal line at the bottom to which each sibling can be added. Some clinicians also record still births and abortions on this axis, though this seems to be a lot of detail to get on an initial assessment and may not be necessary information to know in terms of the presenting problem. When someone has multiple marriages/relationships of significance these can be represented by additional lines, as shown in the illustration of Iftar (see Figure 3.1).

Iftar is a 23-year-old man of Pakistani origin who is the eldest of five siblings. He is a post-graduate student. His parents separated when he was a child and his father now has a new wife and family with three children, but lives close by and visits Iftar and his siblings every one or two days. His mother has not remarried. By convention, children are included on the genogram in age order, with the eldest child represented by a circle or a square on the left hand side of the relevant line. In this genogram Iftar, as the eldest, is the first square on the left of the line of siblings.

Adopted or fostered siblings are connected to the horizontal sibling line by a vertical broken line. Sometimes couples who are together but not married are connected by a dashed line rather than a continuous one, but this convention is becoming less common as it seems to imply that a long term steady relationship that has not been legally or religiously sanctioned is in some way less important. A more detailed account of these conventions can be found in McGoldrick et al. (1999).

If the initial discussion about ethnic origin has not yet taken place when the genogram is drawn, this can be a good time to ask about where family members were born and are currently living, and when they came to the country where the assessment is taking place. This can also be a good time to ask about the emotional and physical health of family members. It might be important, where the service user is in a relationship, to include the genogram of their partner as well. Therapists should be aware that their assumptions as to what constitutes a family

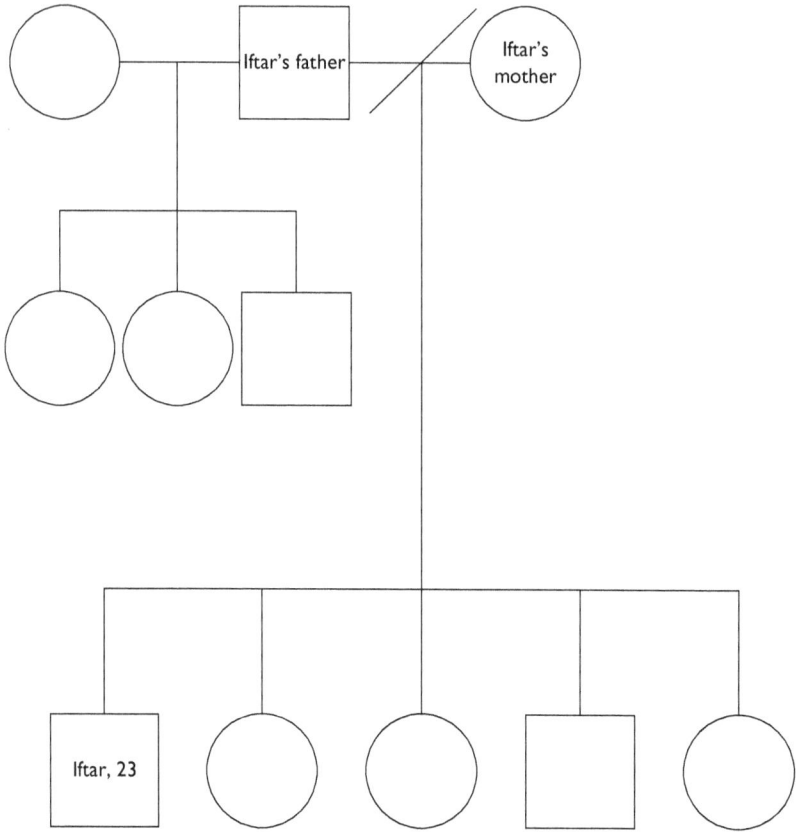

Figure 3.1 Iftar's genogram

may not be shared by different communities, and the discussion about who to include can be helped with questions like:

> What other people are important in your family? Who has a role in decision making about finances or how people behave? Out of this group of people, which relationships are the most important in making decisions?

It can be helpful to use gender neutral terms when asking initial questions to enable lesbian, gay, bisexual and transgender (LGBT) service users to feel more able to discuss their relationships and gender identities. Lesbian, gay and bisexual service users from BME backgrounds may expect therapists to assume that they are heterosexual and may find it harder to raise their sexuality than a white service user. Equally, transgender BME service users may be concerned about therapists making assumptions about their gender identification. Using gender neutral terms may make these discussions easier. For example, rather than asking a male service user, 'Do you have a girlfriend or wife?' it might be better to ask, 'Are you in a significant relationship with anyone right now?'

Some therapists may take a whole session to develop a genogram, particularly where the family situation is complex because of multiple migration histories, complex patterns of relationships, larger families, or multiple instances of physical or mental health problems. In practice though, this can be a relatively quick exercise, taking just 5–10 minutes of the initial assessment but providing a wealth of detail about the life of the service user. Where the service user has attended alone, it also provides an opportunity for the therapist to ask:

> Is there anyone else in the family it would be helpful to get along to a future session? Perhaps who has a good understanding of how difficult things are for you right now?

As well as being a source of potentially important information about culture and migration histories, developing a genogram also provides the opportunity for the therapist and service user to begin to think about the role of systemic factors in the maintenance of presenting problems.

Therapists who have not used genograms in therapy before or who have not done so for some time could practise this technique by developing a genogram for their own family. Once they are familiar with how this works they could enhance this practice by developing a genogram for a friend or colleague in order to become comfortable with the idea of asking very specific questions about the way that a family is organised.

Including significant family members in the formulation

The widely used 'five areas' approach in CBT formulation (Williams 2001) incorporates environmental and relationship factors when developing formulations with service users. This model, developed initially in the treatment of depression, lends itself to thinking about the impact of family processes in maintaining the thoughts and behaviours which underpin depression. It can be argued that in the process of incorporating family processes into idiosyncratic formulations, cultural practices are also captured. The assumption of this approach is that each family is a unique culture in itself, and this has a lot in common with the Particularist approach summarised later in this chapter. This approach could be used to define culture as the core beliefs, assumptions and subsequent behaviours of an individual which provide a framework for their daily lives and long term decision making. These beliefs, assumptions and behaviours can be understood as having arisen as a result of membership of a particular ethnic group which largely shares the same beliefs, assumptions and behaviours.

The disorder specific models for anxiety disorders such as Obsessive Compulsive Disorder, Social Anxiety Disorder, Panic Disorder and Generalised

Anxiety Disorder do not specifically consider environmental or relational aspects of presenting problems, and may need to be adapted to fully incorporate these factors into the shared formulation. These adaptations will be familiar to staff working in CAMHS, who treat these disorders in children and young people but who typically pay much more attention than might therapists working elsewhere to the way that family members act to maintain presenting problems. Typically, the disorder specific formulations are augmented by the thought-feeling-behaviour cycles of family members. The triggers for these cycles are typically the behaviours or expressed emotions of the service user.

One way to begin to do this is to include family processes in the formulation is to begin to describe the way that the service user's maintenance cycle interacts with the specific thoughts, feelings and behaviour cycles of people they are close to in their family. Take, for example, Iftar, whose genogram we have begun to develop above. Iftar has a problem with Obsessive Compulsive Disorder (OCD) and the maintenance cycle includes intrusive thoughts about harm coming to family members which elicit strong feelings of anxiety. He appraises these obsessive thoughts as supporting the belief that he needs to order objects in the home in a specific way to keep family members safe. Iftar attends with his mother, Samina, who is a first generation British Pakistani. The therapist and Iftar draw up the initial formulation and then the therapist works with Samina to understand any role she might have in the presenting problem.

Therapist: So I wondered if I could ask about what happens when you first notice things are difficult for Iftar?

Samina: Yes, that's fine. It is awful seeing him like that. He looks so upset.

Therapist: So you can tell how distressed he is by looking at him. How does it make you feel?

Samina: Really upset and scared as well if I am honest. I worry that Iftar might be going crazy.

Therapist: So the thoughts you have are that he might be going crazy. How do you think that might happen?

Samina: All that anxiety might have a permanent effect on his mind.

Therapist: So what do you do to help him feel better?

Samina: I tell him everything is going to be okay and help him get the room ordered so he feels better.

Therapist: Okay, so can we sketch this out so I can make sure I've understood what is going on? When you see your son's anxiety is getting high this leads to lots of worrying thoughts about him which trigger strong feelings of anxiety in you as well. In order to help to keep him safe you reassure him and help with his compulsions. Did I get that right?

The therapist would then add this cycle to the formulation already developed. The trigger for Samina's cycle is her son's distress and her appraisal of the possible impact of this. The therapist will probably be curious about what impact helping out has on Samina's emotional state and might ask:

Therapist: It sounds as though you feel very anxious when you see him like that. What happens to your level of anxiety once you have helped out and Iftar seems to be better?

The therapist might then begin to ask questions that will lead to the introduction of some sort of change method, such as:

Therapist: So I am wondering what message your son gets from you helping out? What does it tell him about how real the danger is?

It might also be helpful at this point to formulate the role of reassurance-giving in reducing Samina's anxiety level and to explore this as a part of the maintenance cycle.

Even at this early stage in therapy adding this additional cycle to the formulation helps the service user and their family members begin to see how they might all need to do things differently in order to bring about change. It begins to move the responsibility for solving the problem from the individual to the wider system, and although this does not mean that without family processes changing no change at all is possible, it does begin to draw on the resources of the family in ways that are often helpful. However, it is important to also keep in mind that the service user might not want family members involved in their recovery process, so consent for this should be established as part of the routine collaborative process.

At the stage of initial formulation it can be difficult to think about which family members need to be incorporated into the formulation. The therapist might ask, 'Is there anyone else in the family who you think might be playing a part in keeping this cycle going?', or might leave the discussion for later as new information emerges through home practice and homework assignments. It is helpful to hold to the idea that the formulation is a continually evolving process, and that as new information comes to light the roles of different family members can be incorporated. It is also important to maintain the therapeutic stance that being collaborative and Socratic enables service users and family members to develop their own insights into the role of the wider system in maintaining problems.

It is often the case in adult services that family members do not attend with the service user, either for reasons of practicality or availability or because the service user wishes to have a degree of confidentiality around their mental health. It is still possible to use a systemic perspective when a service user attends alone. A Socratic approach can be used to ask the service user to map out how members of their family system respond to particular situations. The service user can be encouraged to speculate about the thoughts and emotions elicited in family members as a result of specific triggers, which would typically be the behaviours or expressed emotions of the service user. They can then be encouraged to think about how the responses of their family members might perpetuate unhelpful patterns to do with the presenting problems. Once a provisional formulation has been developed, the service user can begin to plan how they might discuss this with members of their family in order to involve them in bringing about change.

When to develop a more detailed perspective on ethnicity, culture and families

It may often be the case that asking a service user to tell you about their ethnicity and developing a genogram which maps out the migration history of the family is enough to enhance the therapeutic relationship and gain some understanding of the background of the person you are working with. For some service users it might also be necessary to add some systemic thinking in terms of incorporating family members and their beliefs, emotions and behaviours into the formulation.

There are, however, likely to be service users whose presenting problems create a need for a more detailed understanding of issues relating to ethnicity and culture and how these impact on the presenting problem. For example, it might be necessary to consider culture in greater depth when the issues raised by the service user are linked to complex patterns of migration and acculturation within the family and where the negotiation of these challenges is part of the presenting problem. It might also be useful to develop a richer understanding of the service user's background when the presenting problem is maintained by beliefs or behaviours that are embedded in specific cultural practices. There might also be a need to consider ethnicity and culture in greater depth where the service user is ambivalent about engaging in CBT because the explanation the therapist has provided about their distress does not fit with their own model of mental illness.

This section draws on the work by Falicov (1995) but is adapted to fit with the way that a cognitive behaviour therapist might typically work. Falicov refers to this framework as a Multidimensional one, as it takes into account the idea that someone's culture is fluid and dynamic and that individuals do not just belong to one culture but are typically connected to many different cultures in a variety of ways. Family members will each belong to a number of cultural sub-groups depending on their own histories, interests and educational or vocational activities. It might also be helpful to think about these different cultural affiliations as having overlapping characteristics, or being antagonistic to one another. For example, someone might belong to an Evangelical Christian congregation which places great emphasis on hard work and diligent study, but also be part of a social circle through a sports team where people do not value these qualities. People negotiate these tensions all the time in their everyday lives, but where difficulty reconciling value systems contributes to a presenting problem it becomes of interest to the therapist and service user.

Individuals are thought of as occupying what Falicov calls an 'ecological niche' (1995: 376); that is, the way that they uniquely fit in with these various and overlapping cultures and contexts. The Multidimensional approach sees the value of asking about membership of and relationships with specific groups, and in doing so information about factors such as ethnicity, religious affiliations, social class and acculturation can be incorporated into the shared understanding of the problem. Once this basic information has been obtained, the therapist is encouraged to become curious about just how these affiliations interact in the day-to-day life of the service user. In terms of how this approach might be used by a cognitive therapist, a good general principle might be to limit the exploration of these topics to the degree to which these factors impact on the maintenance of the presenting problem. As CBT tends to focus on symptom reduction and working towards the goals of the service user, it follows that this is where the focus of this extended consideration of culture and context should be. Before looking at how to apply this model to mapping and understanding family functioning, it will be helpful to summarise the four ways that Falicov suggests that therapists typically understand the role of culture in presenting problems and the adaptation of therapy approaches,

Models of how ethnicity can be understood in the context of therapy

The focus of this book is on the role of culture and ethnicity in therapeutic work, but that is not to say that other aspects of diversity are not important. The gender, social class and sexuality of a service user are also likely to play an important part in how they understand their problems and how they might work with the therapist. The physical health and physical or neurological disabilities of the service user might also be important and these factors deserve careful consideration, particularly in the way that these aspects of difference interact, but detailed consideration of this in relation to CBT is beyond the scope of this book. It is helpful at this stage to consider the different ways that ethnic diversity might be thought about in terms of how therapy is adapted and which of these models might be the most helpful. The framework outlined in a landmark paper on working therapeutically with BME service users by Falicov (1995) will be used as a basis for this. Although this paper was written with Systemic Therapists in mind, it provides a useful way of thinking about adaptation that can be applied to any therapy modality. Falicov discusses four possible ways of approaching diversity within therapy, which are outlined below.

Universalist

This approach starts from the assumption that people and their family systems are more alike than different. This position is often based on the idea that humans constitute one species and that the way we think, feel and act is more or less the same across all contexts and cultures. This position would also see family

composition and organisation as being more or less consistent, with any variations being minor and of minimal importance. Therapists who take this approach
are likely to have little interest in contextual variables such as ethnicity, social
class or sexuality and the way that these might shape the experiences and relate
to the problems of service users.

In the context of CBT, a Universalist might take the view that basic emotions
such as fear and sadness are common across humanity, and that everyone has the
same cognitive frameworks and architecture to do with processes such as threat
identification and monitoring and the same basic repertoire of behaviours to manage these threats. It follows from this that disorder specific models developed
through work with white majority populations, and on the whole researched in
trials composed primarily of white majority service users, can be applied without
modification to BME service users. As we will see when looking at the research
evidence for interventions across cultures, there may be some support for this idea
in some populations.

It is, though, clearly going beyond the available evidence base to think that all
of the specific models of formulation and treatment that have been developed in
the West can be applied to people from any culture group without modification or
adaptation apart from directly translating concepts and materials. But looking at
the majority of core CBT texts, therapy manuals and textbooks, it would be easy
to imagine that this is the majority opinion of the therapists and researchers who
developed CBT. There is typically little or no discussion of context or culture
and no mention of how and when particular models might be adapted for BME
groups. Typically the ethnicity of participants in key studies is not recorded, or
if it is they are of white majority background. Although this Universalist view is
implied in the lack of consideration of cultural and contextual factors in most CBT
literature, it is unlikely that the majority of the authors of these texts take the view
that this issue is unimportant. It is likely to be the case that in developing and disseminating these ideas the first priority was to describe the presenting problems
through a credible disorder specific formulation and provide an evidence base for
the specific approach that followed from this model. Research participants would
be recruited pragmatically from available clinics, and so would be more likely to
be of white majority background. Non-English speakers would be excluded from
trials for the sake of simplicity. It seems likely to be the case that cultural and ethnic factors are not included in core texts as a result of the pragmatic nature of the
way disorder specific models are developed and validated, rather than a genuine
lack of interest in these factors amongst therapists.

Particularist

This way of thinking about individuals and their family systems is based on the
idea that people are more different than they are alike. Therapists who hold this
view might go as far as to say that each individual or family is 'a culture unto
itself' (Henry 1963). In taking this position a therapist would be interested in

and respectful of the thoughts and beliefs of the individual service user and their family members, but would not take into account wider issues of inequality, migration histories or social change. The therapist would to some extent be blind to the ethnicity of the service user but intensely interested in their experiences as a unique individual. They would not draw on generalisations about particular ethnic groups based on their past experiences. A therapist who takes this position would start with the assumption that every presenting problem calls for a unique way of understanding or formulating the difficulties of the service user and a unique treatment plan. Although this model was developed for thinking about culture, it can be used as a way of thinking about the provision of CBT. Someone working as a cognitive behaviour therapist with this view would be likely to be aware of disorder specific models but approach each presenting problem as unique and not draw on them as a basis for assessment or formulation. They would recognise the relationship between thoughts, feelings and behaviours and make use of the core components of CBT interventions such as behavioural experiments or Socratic questioning on a case-by-case basis.

Ethnic focused

This position is a way of approaching diversity that stresses the idea that there are differences between individuals and families but that these can be largely understood in terms of the ethnicity of the person or family in question. This way of thinking is particularly interested in culturally specific processes in terms of expectations, life stages and presenting problems. This approach makes the assumption that, as a therapist, it is necessary to develop detailed and thorough expertise about the ethnic groups served by your clinic, and as a cognitive behaviour therapist this might mean being familiar with the emerging literature on Culturally Adapted CBT therapies (which are considered in more detail in Chapters 5 and 6). Research and intervention programmes which specifically adapt CBT for particular communities have been successful in expanding the knowledge base around using CBT with BME groups and have contributed to an awareness amongst therapists of the need to consider adaptation of CBT when working with diverse communities.

Falicov notes that there are shortcomings to this approach. The first is that it might encourage therapists to overgeneralise about what individuals or families are like based solely on their ethnicity. It might set the therapist up to have particular expectations about a service user, what they might think and how their family might be organised. These expectations might cause the therapist to miss important details about how the service user might differ from what the therapist believes the norms are in the service user's community. It also does not fully account for the way that ethnic identities are dynamic processes or the way that migration histories, place of birth and acculturation all interact to shape ethnic identities. Another problem with this approach is that it assumes that there can be an objective observer of difference and that the conclusions this observer reaches are reliable. As cognitive therapists we would be very much aware that opinions are not facts, and this applies equally to beliefs about cultural norms or practices described in Culturally Adapted CBT. Therapists taking this position who were working in ethnically diverse settings would also need to get to know, in detail, every ethnic group in their catchment area and to have access to a specific Culturally Adapted CBT protocol for each one. Given the breadth of diversity in some areas, that seems to be an unrealistic position to take.

The Multidimensional Approach

The Multidimensional Approach is used as the basis for thinking about Culturally Sensitive CBT, which forms the basis of much of this book. It is a more flexible approach to working in diverse settings than the three described above and provides a framework for therapists to understand the culture and ethnicity of each service user through a number of dimensions and variables, in recognition of the idea that individuals usually live their lives in relation to several different contexts and cultures. The case studies in Chapter 2 of women of South Asian origin are examples of multidimensional ethnic identities. They would describe themselves and think of themselves in different ways in different settings, depending on the immediate context, their migration histories and those of their family members, their degree of acculturation, and how they have engaged with different communities they have come into contact with. It is worth repeating the definition Falicov uses in full. Multidimensional ethnicity is:

> those sets of shared world views, meanings and adaptive behaviours derived from simultaneous membership and participation in a multiplicity of contexts, such as rural, urban or suburban settings; language, age, gender, cohort, family configuration, race, ethnicity, religion, nationality, socio-economic status, employment, education, occupation, sexual orientation, political ideology; migration and stage of acculturation.
>
> (Falicov 1995: 375)

This way of thinking about ethnicity is much more fluid and can account for the varied ways that individuals relate to and live within their families, communities, workplaces or places of education, and homes.

Though it has clear strengths in its ability to encompass the breadth and diversity of someone's life, one shortcoming of this approach is that it does not give much guidance about when to stop being inquisitive. Often it is not necessary to have a complete understanding of a service user's sense of identity in order to be helpful, and therapists need to think carefully about the degree to which they explore these issues in therapy. Most people go into work in mental health and train as therapists because they are interested in people and their lives. For white therapists the lives of BME service users might be particularly interesting because of their difference, so the temptation to keep asking and keep exploring is strong.

When we look at using this framework in Chapter 3 we will look at how therapists can get some sense of how much information is enough to achieve the goals that the person attending therapy is presenting with.

The Multidimensional framework suggests that there are four key areas that can be used to organise this information, which are summarised below.

1 Ecological context

This aspect of the life of an individual or family is concerned with the way that they interact with and fit into the communities to which they belong. This can include their relationships within the family home and with other important institutions such as schools, workplaces and professional agencies. Thinking about how someone relates to these aspects of the world gives the therapist a chance to think about what is often called marginalisation. This is the process through which people from BME groups are excluded from or have worse access to opportunities compared to the white majority population.

The therapist might begin to expand on initial questions about how the service user would describe their background by asking questions about how they see themselves compared to other members of those communities, to what degree they might see themselves as fitting in with a particular community they are affiliated with, and whether there are areas of difference. These sort of questions are equally helpful when asking, for example, a second generation British Pakistani man about his relationships to the Pakistani community in which he lives and to the community of predominantly white professionals with whom he works. Service users are likely to vary considerably in the degree to which they feel they belong to and fit with particular groups. Therapists should bear in mind that they are not getting an objective account of communities and the service user's fit with them: rather, they are hearing the highly subjective account of the service user. As cognitive therapists, it should be easy to hold onto the notion that an idea is not a fact. Some of the cognitive biases we might expect in particular presenting problems might be shaping the subjective reports of relationships with particular groups or communities. For example, a Pakistani male service user with social anxiety working in a wholly white workplace might believe that he is being negatively evaluated by co-workers because of his background and religion. He might have strong imagery associated with how he believes others see him and what he believes are their negative views of this difference. The therapist should try not to make assumptions about whether these beliefs are true or not. They may be true – many members of minority groups experience pervasive racism in the workplace – but some experience none or very little. As a therapist, it is helpful to adopt the same position that you would expect the service user to take in relation to their own thoughts: that is, one of genuine inquisitiveness about how you might explore the degree to which these ideas might or might not be helpful or correct.

If we think about the case of Iftar, a discussion with his therapist might proceed as below:

Iftar:	One of the problems is that me and my mum see things really differently.
Therapist:	I wonder if I could ask a little bit more about that?
Iftar:	Sure, yeah, if you think it is important.
Therapist:	When we drew up the family tree you said that both your parents were born in Pakistan but that you were born in Manchester. You still live in an area you grew up in and that area is mainly Pakistani families. I was wondering how you saw yourself fitting in?
Iftar:	Well I still hang out with my mates from college, they are mainly the same as me but a few of them are getting married now and moving out of the area.
Therapist:	And how would you describe how much you are like most of your friends in the area?
Iftar:	Yeah well, not totally like them, because of going to Uni and working as a solicitor I mix with a lot more white people and I suppose I'm less traditional than some of my mates.
Therapist:	Could you rate how typical you are out of ten for me? Where ten is totally typical and zero is not typical at all.
Iftar:	I'd say I'm about 4 out of 10 typical.
Therapist:	And how do you find mixing with the people at the solicitors? How would you rate how well you fit in there?
Iftar:	Well I'm the only Pakistani and the only Muslim there, I don't go out after work with them that much and I'm the only one not drinking. Yeah [laughs], I'd say I only fit in about 4 out of 10 there as well.
Therapist:	And how about how you fit with your family and their values?

In this instance the therapist is beginning to get a picture of someone who inhabits a number of niches (community friendship group, family, work colleagues) and is mapping the degree of fit with each. Therapists should be clear, when beginning this conversation, that the service user is comfortable with this line of questioning and that it is clinically relevant. In this instance, the therapist and Iftar have begun to see how family processes and general work stress are part of the presenting problem and so have a clear rationale for gaining a better understanding of what is going on.

2 Migration and acculturation

Migration to the UK, Europe, Australia/New Zealand and North America has been happening for thousands of years but recently the rates of population change have been considerable, and in many cases greater than at any other time in the history of those countries. Many of the people who have a need for mental health services are migrants or the second or third generation descendants of migrants. There can be many reasons for migration. Sometimes it is driven by opportunities for economic advancement on behalf of the migrant and the need for labour on the part of the destination country, such as the migrations to the UK from areas of the Indian Punjab, Pakistan and the Caribbean in the 1950s and 1960s. These migrations were often carefully planned and supported by family networks and saw migrants from particular geographical areas and social or religious groups move to particular areas of the UK to work in specific industries. Other migrations can be thought of as forced migrations, driven more by the need to escape the dangers of war or natural disasters, and are much more traumatic and haphazard moves. Sometimes they have resulted in dispersal of communities in the destination country but sometimes forced migrants have settled into established communities in their destination country, such as people moving to the UK from what was East Pakistan, now known as Bangladesh, in the 1970s. Whatever the cause, migration can be both a cause of stress to individuals and families, with attendant losses and trauma, and an opportunity for personal and economic advancement and growth.

There is an extensive literature on the changes to risk of developing mental health problems as a result of migration and on theories regarding the possible social, psychological and biological underpinnings for these risks. This literature is by no means resolved, and there remains considerable debate regarding whether there are real differences in the rates of mental health problems amongst migrant groups and what the explanation for this might be, but for an even-handed summary of these issues it is worth looking at the review by Bhugra (2004).

From the point of view of the cognitive behaviour therapist, what is important to understand is what Falicov (1995) calls the migration narrative. This is the story the individual and family have about how they came to move to their new home country. It might be helpful to ask about who migrated and when, what family or community resources were available to support the move and whether the move was welcomed by different family members. It might also be helpful to enquire about who did not join the migration and what links there are to the family left behind. Sometimes those links are very close and involve weekly contact by telephone or Skype. Contact might involve regular visits, or none at all, and economic links where money is sent to support family members in the country of origin. How this is organised can be a cause of considerable conflict and stress within families and may not be a straightforward process. There might be very different ideas about links to the 'home country' within and between generations.

Linked to discussions about migration histories are questions about acculturation. This can be thought of as the degree to which someone is involved and engages with the majority culture. This process takes place through day-to-day contact with the majority culture and the way that relationships with members of that culture are developed in workplaces, places of education, neighbourhoods, places of worship and local community facilities. One pertinent factor is language. Where members of the family do not speak or read the majority language the opportunities for acculturation are limited, and they may undertake the majority of their social and vocational contacts within their own ethnic community where English use is not necessary. These family members may have very valid reasons for not stepping outside their community, such as worries about being subject to racism or other forms of hostility based on how they believe they might be seen by the white majority. Where there are different degrees of acculturation within a family there might be different value systems, some of which have more in common with the dominant ones in the white majority community and some of which may be closer to the religious or community values of the country of origin. How families negotiate these differences can be an important part of family functioning. As a therapist, it is important not to make too many assumptions about how these differences might work. It is not always the case that older generations are more conservative and younger generations more permissive, or that intergenerational differences are necessarily a cause of stress.

The therapist might expand their understanding of Iftar's context and background by asking for some information about the migration history of his family, as illustrated below:

Therapist: I wonder if we could look at the family tree again and get a better idea about how your family came to the UK?

Iftar: Sure, yes. Well my dad came first, when he was about 22. He was already married to my mum then but didn't have any kids.

Therapist: And did he come straight to Manchester?

Iftar: Yeah, his older brother had come for a factory job in Ancoats, an agent in Lahore had sorted it out and he saved up to pay for my dad to come over after a year or so.

Therapist: And what was it like for your father?

Iftar: He said it was really hard, he was sleeping on my uncle's couch trying to save the money to get my mum over and they couldn't get anything nice to eat in those days. He said you couldn't even get proper rice.

Therapist: And how does he see it now?

Iftar: He says it was hard work but worth it to give us a good chance to get educated. I think he regrets never having that chance himself.

Therapist: And what about your mother?

Iftar: She came over a few years later, she hated it at first, she didn't speak English, it was too cold, everybody was unfriendly.

Therapist: And how did she get on later?

Iftar: It was alright, when she had kids she started doing a lot more and making friends round where we lived. She learnt English at this job she got in a sewing factory from some of the women there and ended up being a Trade Union representative.

So in this example the therapist gets a more detailed idea about how Iftar's family came to the UK and what their experience as migrants was like. Again this has to be justifiable clinically, although sometimes just asking and being genuinely curious can play an important part in establishing and enhancing the therapeutic relationship.

3 Family organisation

The ways that families organise themselves vary throughout the world. It is tempting to see the Western model of two adults raising their children more or less in isolation from the wider family as the norm, but even within the white majority communities in the UK there are many and varied ways that the practicalities of family life might work. For example, in some white working class communities kinship ties are strong, and intergenerational arrangements for childcare, shared finances and family decision making are the norm and often managed through networks of mothers, aunts and daughters. The way that the family lives of BME families are organised might, to greater or lesser degrees, have some continuity with how family life was arranged in their country of origin. It can be very illuminating to ask about how families were organised before migration occurred and how current arrangements differ. Falicov (1995) proposes that a useful framework for thinking about family organisation is identifying the dominant dyad in the family. This is the most important relationship pairing around which a lot of economic and practical decision making takes place. In Western nuclear families this is typically the husband and wife; however, this is by no means a universal way of organising family life. In various cultures the dominant dyad might be the mother and oldest daughter, the mother and oldest son, the father and his brother, or the grandmother and her daughter. Understanding this preferred central relationship can help the therapist to work with the service user to understand which relationships are key to bringing about change in the maintaining factors which may be underpinning a presenting problem.

For example, in Iftar's case the therapist and Iftar may have come to the conclusion that his father is quite central to the maintenance of Iftar's OCD. His father is not able to attend the therapy appointments because of work commitments. Once this has been jointly formulated, they decide that Iftar has to ask his father to drop his own response to Iftar's distress, which is typically getting very angry about the way that his mental health problems are impacting on the family and 'making everyone sick with worry'. This increases Iftar's levels of emotional arousal and increases his belief that he has a great degree of responsibility for the well-being of his family. Iftar's home practice is to negotiate a change in behaviour with his father, and Iftar and his therapist look at this in their homework review.

Therapist: So how did you get on discussing things with your father this week?
Iftar: Not very well to be honest, I tried to have a discussion with him about it and he just got really fed up and started on at me again.
Therapist: I am sorry to hear that. What do you think made it difficult?

Iftar:	I don't know, I can never seem to talk to him about things that are important to me. He won't listen.
Therapist:	I wonder if you could tell me a bit more about how that sort of thing works in your family. What would it be like for you as the oldest son to ask your dad to do something?
Iftar:	I don't know, it is not really the done thing. It might be seen as disrespectful.
Therapist:	And if your father feels like he is not being treated respectfully, how might he feel?
Iftar:	Yeah, I see, even more angry.
Therapist:	So who in the family might be able to talk to your father on a more equal footing?
Iftar:	His oldest brother, my Uncle Mohammed.
Therapist:	And what would happen if you asked your Uncle Mohammed to talk to him about this?
Iftar:	Yeah, I could see that working, it's what I did when I wanted driving lessons.

In this instance the therapist retains a Socratic stance of curiosity: she does not come to the dialogue with any answers but provides Iftar with a framework to think through how it might work within his own cultural context, which in this instance includes a family dyad of the brothers having a powerful position in terms of organising family life. This allows for a more realistic approach to change that takes into account the way that power and influence are managed within the family.

4 Family life cycle

Falicov (1995) provides a way for therapists to understand and think with service users about the stage of the family life cycle that they are currently in, and how this might relate to presenting problems. Typically the working model a therapist has regarding how a family is organised and changes over time reflects their own experiences. Often these models are used implicitly as a basis for understanding the current situation of the service user, as it is tempting to assume a universality to the stages of family life. This is understandable, as themes such as birth, growing up, choosing a partner and death are common across cultures; however, within this broad arc there are many culturally specific variations.

These variations can include longer or shorter periods of the child being dependent on parents or main caregivers. In some cultures there is no recognised adolescent period between childhood and adulthood, instead there is a direct transition from one role to the next. Other variations might include there being no point at which children fully leave home (or at least children of a particular gender), or where the norm is intergenerational co-living which does not recognise the role transition to the 'empty nest' of old age and isolation from the family.

Clinicians should also be aware that the patterns of a family life cycle are not fixed and can often change as a result of migration. This might mean that some family members have expectations of life cycle changes that are closer to those of their country of origin, whilst other family members have expectations that are closer to those of the majority culture. These differences can be a source of difficulty within families that might contribute to presenting problems; however, a successful synthesis of the benefits of different traditions might be a source of strength to families.

It is important for therapists to maintain a curious and respectful position when considering this with a service user. It is useful for therapists to spend some time, perhaps in supervision or alone as part of reflective practice, thinking about their own internal map of the life cycle. When working with service users it might be useful to think with them about how different members of their family might understand the life cycle of a family, and the degree to which this understanding differs between family members. It is tempting to see the cycle that you were born into as the most adaptive and successful one, but it will not help the service user if this belief is articulated or underpins the way that a problem is understood. It is also tempting sometimes to be influenced by dominant social narratives about, for example, generational conflict within particular BME communities, and to assume that unhelpful old-fashioned views on family organisation held by older family members are conflicting with the more modern views of younger family members. Therapists might believe they have a role in championing or supporting the younger family member in this situation. Instead of therapists being influenced by this sort of narrative, service users should be given the chance to think about their situation and develop their own formulations about the way that family hopes and expectations about how life will progress might be a strength or a challenge in their lives.

Interviewing a non-clinical family

It can be challenging to begin to integrate this level of cultural thinking into initial assessments, given how much other information needs to be collected. It might also be the case that what the service user and their family might want to talk about most is the presenting problem rather than family histories. It is also sometimes the case that because of lack of trust in services, which might be seen as prejudiced or as agents of a generally unhelpful and unsympathetic state, families might be reluctant to talk about culture, values and migration histories in much detail. In order to begin to develop skills in this area Falicov (1995) recommends that therapists start by interviewing a non-clinical family or individual about these topics. This could be a colleague within the wider service who is from a minority group, a friend or someone working in an allied service in the area. The therapist would need to explain the rationale for this interview and perhaps use some of the principles of role play in CBT supervision, such as:

Establishing how long the exercise will last.

Giving each other permission to pause, rewind and reattempt sections that might need to be improved.

Agreeing that the volunteer is able to give clear feedback about their experience of being interviewed and areas for improvement.

The therapist might also want to video the session for use in supervision later, or at least make use of their clinical supervision to reflect on the process, and use the Kolb (1984) learning cycle as a basis for reflective practice in order to think about how they might do things differently next time. This approach provides a very useful opportunity for transcultural skills to be tried out and developed; the process is summarised below.

Using the Kolb learning cycle

One important point about developing skills in the area of transcultural therapy is that it is very much an ongoing process. This will involve keeping up to date with a developing research literature, and a change in the way that the therapist engages with ideas to do with culture. In order to support this it is useful for therapists to use the Kolb (1984) learning cycle as a framework to enhance reflective practice. This cycle is one of the key models in CBT, underpinning many therapeutic change processes and the way that therapists learn as part of supervision. The cycle has four components. To illustrate these, the example used below is of a therapist who is not used to asking service users about their ethnic background, but who decides to do this more systematically as a result of reading Chapter 2 of this book.

1   Action – where a task in therapy is undertaken, for example in asking a service user from a BME background about their migration history and that of their family members.
2   Observation – where the therapist notes what happened when these questions were asked.
3   Reflection – where the therapist, either in supervision or alone, considers the implications of what they observed in the light of their expectations and understanding of this issue.
4   Planning – where the therapist thinks about how they might ask this question differently next time in the light of what they have learnt.

Ideally this cycle would then begin again, with the therapist asking about this topic with the next service user from a BME background whom they work with.

Hopefully readers of this book will try many new approaches to their work with BME service users as a result of what they have read, and this cycle is likely to be very useful in supervision and personal reflection as a way of refining the practice of these skills.

Summary

CBT with BME groups is likely to be enhanced by approaches which take into account the role of family members in the formulation. This might be supported by collaboratively developing a genogram with the service user in the first or second session as part of the assessment. In some cases it will be helpful to develop a better understanding of cultural and community issues as part of this assessment. When this is the case, Falicov's (1995) framework can be used to enhance CBT assessments. Using these new skills may need practice, and doing this with a non-clinical family will support this learning process.

References

Bhugra, D. (2004). Migration and mental health. *Acta Psychiatrica Scandinavica, 109*(4), 243–258.

Dummett, N. (2006). Processes for systemic cognitive-behavioural therapy with children, young people and families. *Behavioural and Cognitive Psychotherapy, 34*(2), 179–189.

Falicov, C. J. (1995). Training to think culturally: A multidimensional comparative framework. *Family process, 34*(4), 373–388.

Henry, J. (1963). *Culture against man.* New York: Random House.

Kolb, D. A. (1984). *Experimental learning: Experience as the source of learning and development.* Englewood Cliffs, NJ: Prentice Hall.

McGoldrick, M., Gerson, R., and Petry, S. S. (1999). *Genograms: Assessment and intervention.* New York: Norton.

Williams, C. (2001). *Depression: A five areas approach.* London: Arnold Publishers.

Chapter 4

Disorder specific models in transcultural CBT

Overview of ways of thinking about cultural difference and mental health

There is a considerable body of work challenging the idea that models of assessing and treating mental health problems developed in the West can be exported to other cultures and countries (Fernando 2010). Summerfield (2012) provides a clear critique of the World Health Organization's project to develop diagnostic assessment tools and frameworks that can be applied across cultures and illustrates the way that even a seemingly universal concept such as depression was exported to Latvia over a 20-year period and replaced the widely understood and treated condition of 'nervi'. The research literature often represents this process as a dichotomous choice between two ways of thinking transculturally about mental health problems. One position is the emic, or culturally specific perspective, which argues that the differences between the white Western culture and other cultures is so great that models of assessment and intervention must be developed for each cultural group and context. In contrast, those who take the etic, or culturally Universalist, position argue that models of assessment and treatment generalise across ethnic groups and contexts as all humans share the same underlying biology, family structures and cognitive architecture. In reality this dichotomy is a false one, and many clinicians and researchers in the field of transcultural mental health would place themselves somewhere along the spectrum between the two but seldom at either extreme. Even approaches which largely see Western derived diagnostic concepts in mental health as being constant across cultures would recognise the need for some adaptation to account for the different ways that these might be expressed in different cultural contexts. Likewise, most models of mental health that take a very critical view of Western derived diagnosis and treatment having transcultural value would be likely to see that the insights into the assessment and treatment of mental health problems that they bring might have something to offer clinicians working in other cultural settings.

The process of looking for common diagnostic categories is based on the idea of looking for common symptom clusters, with the implication that at a point in the future common underlying causes for these will be discovered. It seems fair to say that if these common underlying causes exist at all, researchers are a long way from finding them. It might also be helpful to consider how this relates to CBT. The majority of the evidence base for CBT has been developed in terms of disorder specific models, formulations and treatments. These have been developed based on assumptions about the underlying mechanisms and maintaining factors of those disorders, but the relationship between a diagnosis (description of a symptom cluster) and a formulation (a hypothesis about what current processes are maintaining the problem) is a tenuous one. There is no evidence to support the idea that because someone from different culture meets the diagnostic criteria for a particular disorder (that is, they have the same symptom clusters), the problem can be formulated in the same way as it would be for a white service user in a Western context. This chapter will consider a pragmatic response to this limited evidence base that is likely to be useful for cognitive behaviour therapists working in transcultural settings.

Interestingly, the direction of travel of cross-cultural adaptation and treatment of distress appears to be largely one way, with very little opportunity for approaches to treating mental health problems developed in non-Western settings being adapted for the use of clinicians in the West. The one possible exception to this is the adaptation of mindfulness based therapeutic approaches initially developed by Kabat-Zinn (1982), which have become increasingly influential in mental health services in the UK and USA over the past 30 years. These can be conceptualised as a non-Western intervention which has become secularised and separated from its ethical values in order to fit in with the cultural expectations of Western mental health settings. The subsequent evaluation of this intervention in line with positivist scientific principles can also be seen as something that fits with Western cultural norms and expectations.

CBT for specific disorders in an international context

In terms of the use of CBT in other cultural settings, there have been numerous studies looking at clinical outcomes when disorder specific models and treatment protocols are used outside the cultural settings in which they were developed. For example, Manjula et al. (2014) demonstrated that both cognitive and behavioural approaches were effective in treating Panic Disorder in an Indian clinical population, although cognitive approaches were associated with better outcomes. In Pakistan there is ongoing research into the effectiveness of CBT for depression (Rahman et al. 2008) in clinical populations of non-literate rural women, and Moradveisi et al. (2013) have demonstrated that Behavioural Activation can be helpful in treating depression in Iran. In Japan there has been considerable research demonstrating the efficacy of CBT for OCD and other common mental health problems (Ono et al. 2011). In China CBT has been evaluated in the treatment of a wide range of presenting problems, from erectile dysfunction (Xueqian and Heqin 1990) to internet addiction (Du et al. 2010), and there has been recent thinking regarding the extent to which this approach fits with Chinese values and cultural norms (Hodges and Oei 2007). A recent paper described a CBT training programme developed in Uganda in collaboration with therapists from the UK (Hall et al. 2014). This paper described some of the challenges and successes when CBT was introduced to the Ugandan mental health system and made important points about how Ugandan therapists adapt the language and metaphors of CBT for the local context; however, the paper does not comment on the degree to which disorder specific models might be helpful in the context of Ugandan mental health. There is also some very useful insight into how therapists respond to religious and spiritual beliefs. Although there is a growing body of research into CBT for Latin American service users, particularly those with PTSD (Hinton et al. 2011) and depression (Le et al. 2011) in the USA (see Hays and Iwamasa 2006 for further details), there is not an equivalent body of research being developed in Central and South America itself.

This suggests that some disorder specific models can be applied to work in some cultures and contexts, but it does not follow that all models can be adapted for all cultures and contexts.

Naturalistic transcultural adaptation

Some disorder specific models have been robustly researched and found to be useful in non-Western cultural settings. What is notable about this body of research is that in these studies the therapy is delivered by clinicians from that particular culture to service users from that culture. As all of these models were originally developed in English and in Western cultural settings, at some point the treatment protocol would have been either translated into the new language by a bilingual trainer who then delivered the training in local languages, or delivered in English to bilingual therapists who then translated the therapy terms and concepts into local languages in clinical settings. A recent paper (Beck et al. 2014) summarised the teaching methods used in the first stand-alone CBT training course in India. This course was taught by white clinicians from the UK who worked collaboratively with the participants using the Kolb Learning Cycle (Kolb 1984) as a basis for adapting the models to local contexts. Aspects of assessment and intervention were presented in English and role play and video used to illustrate these skills. Participants then role played the skill in pairs, often in local languages, in order to observe how the skill could be used. Group discussion was used to reflect on the adaptation of this particular skill and the group worked together to plan how it might be used in clinical settings. Participants were encouraged to use supervision to repeat the cycle in order to continue and refine the process of adaptation.

All of the examples above, where CBT is delivered in another cultural setting by staff from that setting, will have gone through a similar process, whether implicitly or explicitly. What this amounts to is naturalistic adaptation of CBT for other cultures and contexts by clinicians who are able to engage with the core concepts of CBT as it was developed in the West and subtly adapt them for their own ethnic group and culture.

This is a very different situation to one where white therapists adapt CBT as they work with BME service users, as the white therapist will lack the linguistic and cultural expertise to do this naturalistic adaptation, and will have to rely on a more structured and purposeful way to change the way they work and to review the efficacy of these approaches.

When disorder specific models are not helping

Although many disorder specific models have been evaluated in non-Western countries and contexts, it might be helpful to take the view that not all disorder specific models and diagnostic categories are the same in terms of their usefulness in other countries. It is certainly the case that most disorder specific models have not been evaluated in the majority of contexts and countries. It might be useful to think of disorder specific models as existing on a spectrum, with some having more transcultural utility in some contexts than others. For example, as far as it has been researched, OCD appears to be very much the same in terms of patterns of cognitive and behavioural maintaining factors across cultures, though the specific thoughts and rituals are very much dependent on the cultural context, with religious and spiritual themes having greater salience where these are more a part of people's everyday lives (de Silva 2006). Other disorders, such as depression, Panic Disorder and Generalised Anxiety Disorder, however, may have much greater variety in the way they present across cultures or may not be present within some cultures at all. What is even less clear is the extent to which these models can be adapted to meet the needs of diverse communities in the UK, Europe and North America.

There is a pragmatic approach which clinicians might want to take when working with a service user from a BME group who is presenting with the core features of a particular disorder specific model. Assessment, formulation and treatment should commence using the likeliest looking model in the first instance. If the formulation makes sense to the service user, and the treatment approaches that this formulation suggests are bringing about symptom reduction, then the clinician and service user should continue with this approach. This does not mean that the particular disorder specific model is therefore a good fit for everyone from that community or that the disorder really exists as described within that community. What it means is that at this time, for this service user, this model provides a helpful way of alleviating distress. The improvement may be as much due to non-specific therapy factors such as the therapeutic relationship or the provision of a structured and helpful way for the service user to understand their difficulties. It may also be due to general improvements in the life of the service user, which in turn may be due to work with the therapist or to other factors such as accessing support, training or education. It also remains important to appreciate that a percentage of people with mental health problems would become symptom free even without treatment (Whiteford et al. 2013).

There is also a body of research evidence that supports the idea that improvement seen in service users who are treated with CBT is due not to disorder specific models and approaches but to trans-diagnostic therapy factors found in all of these approaches (Mansell et al. 2008). This view, which is described in detail in Mansell et al. (2012) proposes that there are thinking styles and behaviours common to all psychological problems and that these problems can be addressed using CBT without the need to draw on a particular diagnostic framework to inform the model used. This approach has considerable appeal when therapists and service users are working to overcome the challenges in applying CBT across cultures which this chapter has highlighted. Therapists who find that the thoughts, feelings and behaviours described by a service user who is experiencing distress do not fit with a particular model might still be able to draw on a broad range of CBT techniques in order to help to reduce distress.

Therapists might use Behavioural Activation where the activities and daily living of the service user have become diminished. Developing an awareness of the relationship between thoughts, feelings and behaviours is likely to be of benefit. Understanding the role of thinking styles, and the worry about and rumination on presenting problems, will also be of benefit. Safety behaviours, thought suppression and avoidance are possible patterns that service users experiencing difficulties with anxiety would recognise, and using general CBT techniques to identify and change these patterns may well be helpful. All of these approaches can be used without the need for a disorder specific model. Simple thoughts–feelings–behaviours formulations can be used as a framework to explore patterns unhelpful to the service user.

It is important to retain a degree of humility about the current limits of our knowledge and treatment outcomes when working across cultures. Even the most effective research studies do not achieve even close to a 100 per cent rate of treatment success. Published research is typically done with participants who have more straightforward problems and fewer life stresses and who have experienced less adversity than many of those seen in the mental health clinics where most practitioners are based. Therapists who participate in trials often have lower caseloads, more supervision and higher levels of training than front line clinicians. If a service user does not improve, therapists should be realistic about the current limits of therapies and their own limits within the resources they have available. Using supervision and peer discussion can help clinicians in this situation think about whether trans-diagnostic rather than disorder specific approaches might be more helpful, or whether other types of treatment such as different types of therapy or medication might be in the best interests of the service user.

Summary

Although this chapter has raised several difficulties in terms of applying disorder specific approaches across cultures, this does not mean that CBT cannot be a helpful way to effectively treat mental health problems in BME service users. The next chapter will look at two specific disorders, depression and PTSD, and will look in detail at both specific Culturally Adapted CBT and a framework for Culturally Sensitive CBT when working with these disorders.

References

Beck, A., Virudhagirinathan, B. S., Santosham, S., and Begum, F. J. (2014). Developing cognitive behaviour therapy training in India: Using the Kolb learning cycle to address challenges in applying transcultural models of mental health and mental health training. *International Review of Psychiatry, 26*(5), 572–578.

de Silva, P. (2006). Culture and obsessive-compulsive disorder. *Psychiatry, 5*(11), 402–404.

Du, Y. S., Jiang, W., and Vance, A. (2010). Longer term effect of randomized, controlled group cognitive behavioural therapy for Internet addiction in adolescent students in Shanghai. *Australian and New Zealand Journal of Psychiatry, 44*(2), 129–134.

Fernando, S. (2010). *Mental health, race and culture.* London: Palgrave Macmillan.

Hall, J., d'Ardenne, P., Nsereko, J., Kasujja, R., Baillie, D., Mpango, R., Birabwa, H., and Hunter, E. (2014). Mental health practitioners' reflections on psychological work in Uganda: Exploring perspectives from different professions. *British Journal of Guidance & Counselling, 42*(4), 423–435.

Hays, P. A., and Iwamasa, G. Y. (2006). *Culturally responsive cognitive-behavioral therapy: Assessment, practice, and supervision.* Washington, DC: American Psychological Association.

Hinton, D. E., Hofmann, S. G., Rivera, E., Otto, M. W., and Pollack, M. H. (2011). Culturally Adapted CBT (CA-CBT) for Latino women with treatment-resistant PTSD: A pilot study comparing CA-CBT to applied muscle relaxation. *Behaviour Research and Therapy, 49*(4), 275–280.

Hodges, J., and Oei, T. P. (2007). Would Confucius benefit from psychotherapy? The compatibility of cognitive behaviour therapy and Chinese values. *Behaviour Research and Therapy, 45*(5), 901–914.

Kabat-Zinn, J. (1982). An outpatient program in behavioral medicine for chronic pain patients based on the practice of mindfulness meditation: Theoretical considerations and preliminary results. *General Hospital Psychiatry, 4*(1), 33–47.

Kolb, D.A (1984). *Experiential learning: Experience as the source of learning and development.* Englewood Cliffs, NJ: Prentice Hall.

Le, H. N., Perry, D. F., and Stuart, E. A. (2011). Randomized controlled trial of a preventive intervention for perinatal depression in high-risk Latinas. *Journal of Consulting and Clinical Psychology, 79*(2), 135–141.

Manjula, M., Prasadarao, P. S. D. V., Kumaraiah, V., and Raguram, R. (2014). Temporal patterns of change in Panic Disorder during Cognitive Behaviour Therapy: An Indian study. *Behavioural and Cognitive Psychotherapy, 42*(5), 513–525.

Mansell, W., Carey, T. A., and Tai, S. (2012). *A transdiagnostic approach to CBT using method of levels therapy: Distinctive features.* London: Routledge.

Mansell, W., Harvey, A., Watkins, E. R., and Shafran, R. (2008). Cognitive behavioral processes across psychological disorders: A review of the utility and validity of the transdiagnostic approach. *International Journal of Cognitive Therapy, 1*(3), 181–191.

Moradveisi, L., Huibers, M. J., Renner, F., Arasteh, M., and Arntz, A. (2013). Behavioural activation v. antidepressant medication for treating depression in Iran: Randomised trial. *The British Journal of Psychiatry, 202*(3), 204–211.

Ono, Y., Furukawa, T. A., Shimizu, E., Okamoto, Y., Nakagawa, A., Fujisawa, D., Nakagawa, A., Ishii, T., and Nakajima, S. (2011). Current status of research on cognitive therapy/cognitive behavior therapy in Japan. *Psychiatry and Clinical Neurosciences*, *65*(2), 121–129.

Rahman, A., Malik, A., Sikander, S., Roberts, C., and Creed, F. (2008). Cognitive behaviour therapy-based intervention by community health workers for mothers with depression and their infants in rural Pakistan: A cluster-randomised controlled trial. *The Lancet*, *372*(9642), 902–909.

Summerfield, D. (2012). Afterword: Against global mental health. *Transcultural Psychiatry*, *49*(3), 519–530.

Whiteford, H. A., Harris, M. G., McKeon, G., Baxter, A., Pennell, C., Barendregt, J. J., and Wang, J. (2013). Estimating remission from untreated major depression: A systematic review and meta-analysis. *Psychological Medicine*, *43*(8), 1569–1585.

Xueqian, L., and Heqin, Y. (1990). Cognitive behavioural therapy for erectile disorder: A study from the People's Republic of China. *Sexual and Marital Therapy*, *5*(2), 105–114.

Chapter 5

Post-traumatic stress disorder

Culturally Adapted or Culturally Sensitive CBT?

Overview

In Chapter 1 the distinction was made between Culturally Sensitive and Culturally Adapted CBT. Looking at the literature on the treatment of PTSD allows us to contrast these approaches and consider under what circumstances services might adopt one model or another. This chapter will present two models of therapy delivery in specialist PTSD clinics that are informed by these two approaches. Clinicians will then be able to consider which approach fits best with their own clinical practice and team ethos. Both of these models were developed in clinical teams that work predominantly with refugees and asylum seekers. This chapter will look at CBT for PTSD in BME groups in general and for asylum seekers and refugees in particular; however, the emphasis will be on work with refugees and asylum seekers, as the rate of trauma related mental health problems in this population is particularly high. Many of the broad principles derived from work with refugees and asylum seekers can be applied to work with other BME service users with PTSD.

Different legal definitions are used in different countries to describe the populations which are the focus of this chapter. For example, in the UK the term 'asylum seeker' is used to describe someone who is in the process of applying for the right to remain in the country on the basis that they would face persecution or hardship if they returned to their country of origin, whereas the term 'refugee' is used exclusively to describe someone whose application for asylum has been successful. The chapter will use the term 'refugee' in a broad sense, to describe people who have left their country of origin as a result of political persecution, political violence and torture, or community-wide events such as war or natural disasters.

The prevalence of PTSD across cultures

There is no specific prevalence literature on rates of PTSD amongst BME populations in the UK, Europe or North America. The increased risk factors associated with poverty and living within disrupted communities may make some BME groups more vulnerable to experiencing traumatic events and subsequently developing trauma related mental health problems. The potential for high degrees of variance in rates of PTSD between different ethnic groups is supported by the evidence for considerable variance in the rates of PTSD between countries even when they have broadly similar cultures and histories. Rates of PTSD in European countries range from 0.56 per cent to 6.67 per cent of the population (Wittchen et al. 2010). Some of this variance may be explained by recent history. The highest rates (Netherlands, UK, France and Germany) and lowest rates (Spain, Switzerland) are in countries with very different histories in terms of major wars in the twentieth century; however, as these major wars occurred two or more generations ago there are likely to be other explanations than just differences in the degree of traumatic experiences amongst the population. These factors might include variations in cultural values, responses to trauma and how distress is understood within communities, and these factors might go some way to explaining the differences in prevalence even between superficially similar European countries (Burri and Maercker 2014). This suggests that cultural factors may have a marked impact on the likelihood of someone developing PTSD and adds weight to the arguments summarised below regarding problems with the cross-cultural application of models of PTSD assessment and treatment, but it also supports the idea that where PTSD is identified, interventions need to be adapted to take into account cultural variations.

Estimates for the rates of PTSD amongst refugees and asylum seekers in Europe and North America vary considerably depending on the population surveyed and research methodology employed. Hollifield et al. (2002) report rates of between 4 per cent and 86 per cent depending on the community in question, with between 5 per cent and 31 per cent of refugees also suffering from depression. In addition refugees and asylum seekers appear to have markedly lower subjectively reported quality of life compared to patient groups with similar levels of mental health difficulties (d'Ardenne et al. 2005). It is likely that the mental health and quality of life of refugees is compromised by the impact of sudden and unplanned migration, the challenge of acculturation, years of uncertainty about their legal status and the consequences of forced detention in many countries where they have sought asylum. It is also likely that there may be ongoing worries about family members with whom they have lost contact, about the safety of others and, until their application for asylum is accepted, about the consequences of a possible return to their country of origin. A large proportion of asylum seekers live in relative poverty in the country where they are seeking asylum, as a result of not being able to work legally whilst their claim is being processed and having restricted or no access to welfare benefits. These factors will contribute considerably to the emotional distress and poor mental health of asylum seekers.

Criticisms of the cross-cultural application of CBT for PTSD

Before looking at approaches to therapy in detail it is important to acknowledge that the applicability and usefulness of the diagnosis of PTSD across cultures is vigorously contested by many researchers. Tribe (2013) argues that services must be cautious when considering the point at which normal responses to trauma become a mental health problem, and notes that even in white majority populations, where the majority of research into mental health and trauma has occurred, this distinction is not clear. Given the considerable variance in the way that mental health problems are expressed in different cultures, it becomes even more difficult when working with BME service users to differentiate between what is a normal and understandable response and what might be identified as a mental health problem in need of treatment within a mental health service.

Refugees have typically experienced considerable direct trauma such as violence and victimisation, as well as the indirect traumas of displacement, migration and multiple losses. In this situation, overwhelming feelings of anger, sadness or anxiety are understandable. It might also be a normal response to ruminate about or have intense memories of particular trauma episodes. Applying a diagnostic category like PTSD across cultures in these circumstances is clearly problematic. The service users on whom this diagnostic model was based, and who typically enter research studies, are unlikely to have experienced the level of trauma, loss and displacement that refugee service users have. There are also likely to be major differences between cultures regarding how distress following large-scale trauma is expressed and what might be seen as a healthy, culturally sanctioned or understandable responses to this. The culturally normative expressions of distress in some cultures might be seen as pathological and indicative of serious mental health problems when seen from a Western perspective. It is also possible that mental health problems arising as a result of trauma might be missed if they are not expressed in a way that fits with the forms of expression anticipated by mental health services. These problems might not fit the criteria often used to organise how services are provided and resources allocated, which are based on severity, chronicity and symptom profiles.

Tribe (2013) also makes some very compelling points about the politicisation of the decision regarding which communities might be considered to have been traumatised. Communities who are seen as victims of aggression might be more easily understood as being traumatised and therefore deserving of asylum and of support services, whereas communities who have been subject to equivalent degrees of violence but who are seen as belonging to aggressor nations might not be thought of as deserving this consideration. An example of this from recent UK history might be Iraqis, including those in the armed forces, who were traumatised as a result of air strikes initiated by the USA and UK and who might not be seen as deserving of post-trauma support or political asylum even when they find themselves at risk in their home country. In contrast, Iraqi Kurds, who were subject to air strikes and ground based bombardment initiated by the Iraqi government, would have been more readily seen as victims of trauma deserving of support, services and asylum.

The work of Somasundaram (2010) suggests that working at the individual level with victims of trauma might be far less effective than engaging at the community level and that this approach allows for the mobilisation of community resources and the use of culturally embedded methods of healing. This approach provides opportunities for the recovery from trauma to take place within the political and social context of the traumatised community and has clearly been a successful model in both Sri Lanka and Cambodia, where Somasundaram has developed services.

This chapter is, however, concerned with which approaches might be helpful within services in the UK, Europe, North America, and Australia and New Zealand. Therapists in these countries may not have the opportunity to work at the level of the community in question, either because the numbers of people from that community who access services is small or because of a lack of service wide commitment towards community engagement. Faced with the distress of an individual referred into mainstream mental health services, therapists will have a clear remit to provide an evidence based individual therapy that meets the needs of the service user and takes into account transcultural aspects of their presentation and experiences. This chapter provides examples from two services which have adapted CBT to meet the needs of BME and asylum seeking service users in order to consider ways that this therapy might be effectively provided.

The importance of context when formulating problems with service users who are refugees

The first challenge in working with service users who have experienced these multiple difficulties is the degree to which the presenting problem has arisen as a reasonable response to the sustained injustice, disruption and hardship experienced by the refugee service user. It does the service user a disservice to formulate and understand the problem as being predominantly due to factors that are linked to their thoughts and behaviours, and to expect improvement to occur, without some attempt to address these external and often ongoing pressures.

In most Western countries the experience of being a refugee or asylum seeker is not an easy one. Typically the wait for a legal resolution to claims for asylum takes many years, during which access to education and jobs is limited. This means that access to a good standard of housing will be restricted and participation in meaningful activities of daily life such as work, community events or leisure will also be limited. Feelings of helplessness, sadness and powerlessness are understandable in this context and it might be challenging to distinguish these from, for example, depression. Some asylum seekers find themselves in a position of facing deportation, detention or movement at short notice around the country in which they are seeking asylum. Sometimes these removals are done in the middle of the night and there are well publicised instances of asylum seekers being physically harmed as a result of them. Hyper-vigilance for threat and anxiety would be understandable responses to this ongoing threat and need not be indicative of a mental health problem, though that does not mean that a cognitive behaviour therapist cannot help to explain and normalise these responses and teach techniques to reduce their severity and impact.

Part of the role of the cognitive behaviour therapist might be to work with others involved in supporting the service user to resolve legal issues, resume contact with family members, access funds and housing and develop educational or vocational opportunities, even if these are on a voluntary basis initially.

Evidence for the efficacy of treatments for PTSD amongst refugees

Given the high rates of PTSD identified amongst refugee communities, it is important that therapists have some confidence in the efficacy of CBT in treating this disorder. There is evidence that Culturally Sensitive CBT (Basoglu 2004, d'Ardenne et al. 2005, 2007) and Culturally Adapted CBT (Hinton et al. 2005, 2011) result in good outcomes for BME and asylum seeking service users with PTSD. A recent systematic review of the evidence base for all therapies used to treat PTSD amongst refugees concluded that although most studies have small sample sizes and lacked high standards in terms of research methodologies, there was a reasonable body of literature supporting both the use of both Narrative Exposure Therapy and CBT (Crumlish and O'Rourke 2010). NICE (2005) guidelines for the treatment of PTSD are clear that there is a good evidence base to support CBT as a therapeutic intervention for PTSD and that patient groups likely to benefit include refugees and asylum seekers. This guidance is clear that linguistic and cultural barriers should not prevent CBT being made available to service users, though it does not give specific guidance as to how to best consider these factors in therapy.

It is worth mentioning that cognitive behaviour therapists will find many of the techniques used in Narrative Exposure Therapy familiar, but what it does bring to therapy that is unique is a recognition that Western models of mental health may not be universally applicable, that in resource-poor countries treatments need to be of shorter duration and readily adaptable to local contexts, and that survivors of war or torture would benefit from an approach that incorporates some element of seeking social justice or testimony to the events that they have experienced (Schauer et al. 2011). These aspects of Narrative Exposure Therapy make it particularly useful as a therapy to be delivered in low and middle income countries, but it may not be the best fit for teams working with traumatised refugees in the UK. There is also evidence to support the use of Eye Movement Desensitisation and Reprocessing with refugee groups and, again, although there are differences in some of the key change methods there is a lot about this therapeutic approach that will be familiar to cognitive behaviour therapists (June et al. 2014).

Treating asylum seeking service users who face deportation or dispersal or when legal proceedings are ongoing

There are no specific guidelines available regarding whether service users who are at risk of imminent deportation following a failed asylum claim, or likely to be moved to a different area at short notice through dispersal arrangements, should begin trauma focused CBT. In the service in East London described below (d'Ardenne et al. 2005) imminent deportation or removal is an exclusion criteria for referral; however, this is not a universally agreed standard. The sudden removal of asylum seekers within the UK may be as a result of them being placed in a detention centre prior to deportation, or may be done as part of a dispersal policy that can see asylum seekers moved to different parts of the country at short notice and with no choice regarding where they are dispersed to or when this might occur. No therapist would support the disruption of therapy in this way, and it may be possible to support the service user in postponing deportation or dispersal on the grounds of them needing to complete a course of psychological treatment. This negotiation can be done directly through contact with the Immigration team at the Home Office but is generally more effective when done through the legal team working with an asylum seeker, who will have clear and well-established links with the authorities in question. It might be possible to negotiate an agreed time period in which no forced moves will occur, or a permanent agreement that this will not occur. The policies and procedures regarding deportation, internment or dispersal are subject to frequent and sudden change, but specialist legal representatives or dedicated asylum and immigration support groups are likely to have up-to-date knowledge on how best to address this.

Even when there is an imminent likelihood that a service user may be moved and therapy disrupted, it seems unreasonable to withhold evidence based treatments that are likely to be able to reduce the degree of distress the service user is experiencing in a relatively short period of time. Given that dispersal can often be delayed or cancelled at short notice and that deportation can likewise be cancelled or postponed, it is often worth beginning trauma focused CBT even in uncertain circumstances. Initial work such as helping the service formulate the problem, normalising symptoms and teaching some easily accessible emotional regulation strategies will help manage symptom severity and give the service user a helpful explanation for their distress. If time allows, subsequent trauma focused work can sometimes lead to rapid symptom reduction even if the problem is not completely resolved. The decision as to whether or not to treat in this sort of situation may not be straightforward. Care should be taken that the emotional well-being of the service user is not being excessively compromised by the threat of removal or deportation at these times. Asylum seekers' vulnerability to suicide or self-harm should be carefully assessed and managed, as risk levels can escalate. When necessary, advocating for inpatient care to manage this might be an important part of the therapist's role.

Asylum seekers, refugees and BME service users may be referred for therapy when court cases regarding the trauma are about to begin or are ongoing. Many services have policies that recommend that the therapy is not started until legal proceedings have finished. This is an unacceptable position for services to take. In England and Wales there are clear guidelines from the Crown Prosecution Service (CPS) regarding adult witnesses in court cases available at http://www.cps.gov.uk/publications/prosecution/pretrialadult.html, and regarding child witnesses available at http://www.cps.gov.uk/publications/prosecution/therapychild.html. In Scotland, similar guidance is provided by the Procurator Fiscal Service, whose recommendations for work with adults can be found at http://www.gov. scot/Publications/2008/04/21142140/28, and for working with child witnesses at http://www.gov.scot/Publications/2005/01/20535/50114.

What these documents make clear is that therapy can proceed before or during a trial and that the prosecuting authorities recognise the value of doing so in order to ensure the well-being of trial participants. The benefits of therapy are understood to include helping to reduce anxiety and depression that may arise in anticipation of the trial or during the trial and treating the consequences of trauma. Therapists should familiarise themselves with these documents, and make service managers aware of them, if there is concern about providing treatment to someone prior to or during legal proceedings.

Where legal proceedings are likely, outcome measures should be used as part of the initial assessment. This is because courts may be interested in information regarding the severity of the mental health problems that the service user is experiencing and the use of outcome measures gives additional credibility to the mental health assessment. Therapists should anticipate that their records may be requested by the court at some point and so maintain these with this in mind, although this is a good general principle for all case notes.

The differing needs of refugees and BME service users

Refugees and asylum seekers are a sub-group of BME communities in the UK. Trauma is not an experience unique to those seeking asylum, but the trauma those doing so experience tends to differ from the trauma experienced by UK based members of BME communities. Trauma experienced by refugees can include political violence, politically motivated sexual assault or community-wide disasters on a scale and severity seldom experienced in the UK. It is often accompanied by displacement, considerable losses and the stress of asylum-seeking itself. Trauma experienced by BME communities within the UK is typically less severe in intensity and seldom involves the additional political victimisation associated with many refugees' experiences. Trauma experienced by BME service users in the UK can, however, have other complicating elements. Violence might be racially motivated, and the service user may experience intense changes in their sense of the UK as their home, as a safe place or as somewhere that they belong as a result of this. When this is the case, these experiences might change their beliefs about their relationship to white majority culture in ways that are hard to discuss with a white therapist. The experience of violence within the service user's own community or family might lead to changes in how they relate to their own ethnic group, or they might have feelings of shame about discussing this experience with someone from outside of the community. Service users in this position might believe that a therapist from outside of their community would not understand important aspects of matters relating to the assault. Where the violence is gender based or involves sexual assault it is likeliest that the perpetrator is male, and so aspects of this trauma might be particularly difficult to discuss this with a male therapist, especially if the service user is from a community which places a high value on modesty.

It is vital that therapists are sensitive to these possibilities during the initial assessment and engagement process. There are clearly times when service users might prefer a therapist of a specific gender, and this request should be honoured wherever possible. Therapists can usefully check whether there are barriers to discussing certain aspects of an assault on the basis of the difference in backgrounds between the service user and therapist. Often just acknowledging this difference and being curious about its impact is enough to reassure the service user that the therapist is sufficiently respectful of and interested in their background to be able to discuss cultural sensitive issues with them (see Chapter 2). It might be the case, however, that this is not enough to reassure and engage traumatised BME service users, and where this is the case alternative therapeutic provision might need to be sought in order to reduce the risk of the service user dropping out of contact and receiving no therapeutic help at all.

An example of Culturally Adapted CBT for PTSD

Hinton et al. (2012) describe their work using Culturally Adapted CBT (CA-CBT) with both traumatised refugees and BME service users from a wide variety of ethnic backgrounds in a trauma centre in the United States. The ethnic backgrounds of service users with whom this approach was developed is broad, but service users are generally of Central and Southern American or South East Asian (Cambodia, Laos, Vietnam) origin. Most, but not all, are first generation migrants. Many aspects of the approach to treating trauma will be familiar to cognitive behaviour therapists, but the way that PTSD is conceptualised and the treatment protocol is adapted does differ in some significant ways. This approach also includes some specific cultural components in terms of how aspects of imagery and metaphor are used within the protocol which are markedly different to the way that CBT protocols for PTSD might usually work. This approach has been shown to be an effective treatment for both Latin American and South East Asian service users when compared to waiting list and applied muscle relaxation controls (Hinton et al. 2005, 2011) and is a treatment approach that has been used in individual or group formats. Although the service user population is very different to those seen in the UK this approach is one of the most systematically evaluated and clearly described examples of CA-CBT, and there are many aspects of it that could be incorporated into work in the UK and other countries. This approach will be described in detail and then compared to the Culturally Sensitive CBT provided by d'Ardenne et al. (2005) at the East London Institute of Psycho-trauma.

How this approach differs from CBT as usual

The team which developed this CA-CBT for PTSD report that it differs in several ways from standard trauma focused CBT for PTSD (Hinton et al. 2012). It is easily adapted for service users who have a poor level of English language comprehension and includes an approach which emphasises the treatment of somatic symptoms and anger. There are also treatment components which specifically address comorbid anxiety problems (such as worry or panic attacks). The protocol draws on both the use of applied muscle stretching and mindfulness based approaches in order to help service users manage the intense physiological arousal associated with reliving the index trauma memories. The approach also includes techniques that have been developed from compassion based mindfulness exercises.

In terms of the disorder specific models which underpin the approach, Hinton et al.'s (2012) paper adapts the PTSD formulation to incorporate the idea that trauma symptoms (heightened affect, increased self-scanning and culture bound syndromes) lead to an increase in somatisation and panic symptoms. In most Western contexts these might be thought of as comorbid presenting problems; however, in this model they are very much integrated into the core PTSD formulation. Hinton et al. (2012) propose that a number of triggers might lead to trauma recall and the associated catastrophic cognitions. These might include some very culturally specific appraisals such as, 'If I dream about the trauma incident it is a sign of spiritual depletion'. This model also incorporates ideas about the need to train service users in emotional regulation techniques from Dialectic Behaviour Therapy approaches (Linehan 2013) which are not emphasised as part of standard PTSD approaches (Ehlers et al. 2005).

Their full protocol is described in sufficient detail (in Hinton et al. 2012) to be used as a treatment plan by therapists trained in CBT; however, for therapists looking to incorporate aspects of this approach into their own work, key ideas and techniques are summarised below.

Why the usual approach to trauma is not suitable for asylum seekers

Hinton et al. (2012) propose that the state of hyper-vigilance to threat experienced by many survivors of trauma is driven by the activation of trauma memories and key to much of the impairment and distress associated with PTSD. The prolonged exposure approach for PTSD developed by Foa and Rothbaum (1998) involves the repeated exposure of the service user to the trauma memories in a way that invokes high levels of distress, resulting ultimately in habituation to the anxiety provoking memory stimulus. This exposure work can be done verbally, using written or drawn material, and through audio recordings of the session which are listened to by the service user as part of between-therapy assignments. This approach, though effective, has high drop-out rates even amongst white majority service users. There is evidence that as many as 55 per cent of BME service users drop out of this form of therapy, compared to 27 per cent of white service users (Lester et al. 2010). The current emphasis in trauma focused CBT has changed from the habituation model to one more in line with helping people with PTSD learn that trauma memories can be tolerated and experienced without distress and modifying appraisals associated with the trauma memory. Most current CBT approaches place less emphasis on the repeated exposure to very difficult material and more emphasis on modifying cognitions about the tolerability of such material. This protocol also uses this approach and places much less emphasis on direct exposure to trauma memories; however, the protocol does recognise the value of in-session exposure to somatic symptoms in order to modify catastrophic cognitions about their consequences. This approach has much in common with Clark's (1986) treatment approach to Panic Disorder.

The main components of this approach

Hinton et al. (2012) describe their work with traumatised services users as having three main components:

1   Emotional regulation and tolerance of affect.
    Sessions 1–3 include the use of techniques such as emotional regulation skills, applied muscle relaxation, applied stretching and mindfulness based meditation. These skills provide service users with the means to manage and tolerate difficult affect before direct work on trauma memories begins in Session 4.
2   Using the trauma protocol.
    In sessions 4–10 the service user recounts trauma memories towards the start of the session and if this elicits strong emotional responses they are supported to use a trauma protocol. This involves the use of targeted approaches such as mindfulness, stretching and visualisation in order to manage the emotions and thoughts triggered by the trauma memories. This approach is used in order to enhance the service user's belief that trauma memories can be tolerated and managed.
3   Interoceptive exposure and re-association.
    Towards the end of the treatment, in-session exposure to symptoms such as physiological arousal or dizziness is undertaken in order to develop positive re-associations with these stimuli and reduce catastrophic cognitions about the likely consequences of these symptoms.

Within this treatment plan there are a number of processes that will now be described so that therapists can look at which ones can be incorporated into their own practice.

Pairing emotional exposure with emotional regulation

Many refugees who have experienced severe trauma present with considerable emotional regulation difficulties. The most common aversive emotion experienced on a day-to-day basis is anxiety, but strong feelings of shame and anger can also be present following trauma. These emotions can in themselves trigger cognitions such as catastrophic misinterpretation of symptoms and intense worry plus behavioural or cognitive avoidance. Where this is the case, teaching emotional regulation techniques early on in the therapeutic process can play an important part in recovery. Emotional regulation skills are developed by first teaching and practising the technique when the service user is in a neutral emotional state. Then the difficult emotions are elicited in the session through focusing on trauma memories. The service user then actively uses self-regulation techniques in session to respond to these. Emotions can also be triggered in sessions by asking about recent incidents of feeling angry or ashamed. By practising techniques in session such as mindfulness, stretching or acceptance of emotion, the service user develops the ability to use these any time they are feeling overwhelmed. By developing skills in this area the service users begin to pair positive associations of self-control, compassion or mastery with the emotional state, rather than negative associations such as beliefs that they are out of control or are being overwhelmed and cannot cope.

Culturally adapted emotional regulation techniques

The trauma protocol includes core techniques such as noticing areas which have become tense in response to trauma memories and purposefully stretching and relaxing that area. These stretches can be paired with imagery or metaphors which are culturally specific. For example, when working with South East Asian service users the technique of straightening the spine, tensing the stomach muscles and rolling the head is associated with an image of a lotus flower circling on its stem in the wind whilst repeating the saying, 'May I flexibly adjust to each situation just as the lotus flower is able to adjust to each new breeze'. Loving-kindness meditations are also incorporated into this work. Hinton et al. (2012) report that South East Asian service users might be asked to imagine love spreading outwards like water, an image with roots in Buddhist teaching and practice. Latin American service users, generally from Roman Catholic backgrounds, will be given the image of the Sacred Heart of Jesus to associate with this technique. This popular and iconic Catholic image is generally linked to ideas of the love of Jesus being given unconditionally to all people. In the UK the religious background of service users is generally different to that of those seen in the USA. Many BME service users could be of Hindu, Sikh or Buddhist origin if they are from Sri Lanka or India. Pakistani and Middle Eastern service users are likely to be from Muslim religious backgrounds. African service users could be from Catholic, Protestant or Muslim backgrounds. It might be useful when teaching approaches such as loving-kindness meditation to ask if there are images from the service user's own faith or cultural background that resonate with this idea. Hindu service users have used examples like the devotion and love shown to Ram and Sita by Hanuman in the Hindu epic *The Ramayana*. Muslim service users may bring to mind the way that the Mercy of Allah is extended to all humanity.

Hinton et al. (2012) discuss the ways that it might be possible to incorporate existing techniques within the service user's faith backgrounds that might be utilised to support better emotional regulation. These can include reciting the name of Allah (the *dhikr*), visualising the flexibility of the flames of votive candles with Catholic service users, or using the image of speaking in tongues with Pentecostal service users to remind them that there are many ways of acting and responding to situations just as there are many ways of expressing the voice of God.

These religiously inspired images and approaches may sit uneasily with secular health services staff in the UK, where there is a tradition of keeping religious beliefs and practices out of therapy. Atheist or agnostic therapists might feel particularly uncomfortable with the idea of incorporating elements of religious practice into therapy and religious therapists might be uncomfortable with the idea of incorporating the beliefs of another religion into therapy. Service users from BME backgrounds might be agnostic or atheist and may be unhappy with therapist assumptions about their religious faith based on their perceived ethnicity, so it is important to ask about this using the techniques discussed in Chapters 2 and 3 in order to establish how important faith is in someone's life. Therapists should use supervision to think about their own responses to incorporating religious elements into their work, and should work within a framework that is acceptable for them, their workplace and the needs of the service user. As there have been no dismantling studies comparing the impact of this approach with and without the religious elements, from an evidence based perspective the degree to which they contribute to positive outcomes is not known. A more detailed consideration of the integration of spiritual practice in CBT is provided by Hodge (2006).

Increasing emotional and cognitive flexibility

The approach of Hinton et al. (2012) takes into account ideas which underpin a lot of CBT regarding the need to increase individuals' cognitive and emotional flexibility. These approaches are based on the idea that cognitive inflexibility is seen as a maintenance factor across many disorders. This model also suggests that adapting to new cultures and ways of living will be easier for refugees if they are able to approach these challenges in a flexible manner. There are a number of ways that this skill is fostered in CA-CBT. The mindfulness technique of emotional distancing, which teaches service users to notice and label strong affective states in order to reduce the extent to which they are caught up with them, can be a useful way to develop this skill. Another approach which enhances emotional flexibility is emotion switching. Service users are taught to notice an emotion (typically anxiety) and move to another emotional state through grounding their experience in current sensations or associating the trauma state with current and more adaptive thoughts and affect. Applied muscle relaxation coupled with adaptive self-statements about flexibility is also used to enhance this skill.

Understanding and managing worry and Generalised Anxiety Disorder

This model recognises that many refugees experience intense and seemingly uncontrollable worry. These worries are often grounded in the reality of their lives. Service users might be facing uncertainty either about their own right to asylum or the safety of friends and family in their country of origin, or be living in economically and socially marginalised neighbourhoods where the threat of violence is a day-to-day consideration. Hinton et al. (2012) report that in their service it is often the case that service users are caught in cycles of worry and heightened anxiety or panic. These heightened states of affect are then interpreted catastrophically, further perpetuating the cycle of distress. These cycles are addressed using cognitive techniques that might include eliciting worry themes, addressing catastrophic cognitions and understanding the links between worry, trauma recall and panic attacks. Where typically these cycles might be understood as comorbid problems, to be treated once the main PTSD symptoms are resolved, this model helpfully sees them as part of a wider picture of trauma response and integrates their formulation and treatment into the 12-session programme.

Modifying catastrophic cognitions about anxiety and PTSD symptoms

This model incorporates techniques to address the way service users might misinterpret their anxiety symptoms as indicating that something catastrophic may be about to happen to them. This can include beliefs that intrusions and arousal are indicators that they are 'going mad' and will end up with severe and enduring mental health problems.

Hinton et al. (2012) address these concerns by eliciting the service user's beliefs about the origin of these symptoms and what the implications of these might be. Some of these concerns are very similar to the misinterpretation of bodily sensations seen in Panic Disorder as described by Clark (1986). Hinton and colleagues note that many of the symptoms of PTSD, including nightmares, hyper-vigilance to threat and intense affect, are misinterpreted in this way. There may also be culturally specific misinterpretations of these that might link with culture bound syndromes or beliefs such as nightmares being evidence of persecution by the spirits of the dead or magical attacks. Some anxiety symptoms might also be understood within the service user's culture as evidence of heart weakness, in ways that again would fit with the Clark model of Panic Disorder. The therapy team have developed a good understanding of culturally specific syndromes that they might see in their clinic population, but these may not be applicable for service users in the UK, who on the whole are from very different cultural groups. For example, British South Asian men might have concerns about weakness and loss of physical energy linked to the loss of semen through nocturnal emissions or in their urine. This phenomenon, known as Dhat syndrome (Udina et al. 2013), is likely to manifest at times of stress and difficulty such as post-trauma. Feelings of tiredness, confusion and poor sleep may be attributed to *naja*, or bad magic, by South Asians, while Muslim service users may attribute such symptoms to the impact of *djin* (devils).

Sleep related problems

The treatment approach recognises the impact that trauma may have on sleep patterns and, as well as advising on good sleep hygiene, also specifically asks about and addresses sleep paralysis, which is thought to have a high prevalence amongst refugees with PTSD. This paralysis, typically occurring just prior to falling asleep or on waking, is often misinterpreted catastrophically and may have specific culturally informed negative interpretations, such as visitation by ancestors or other spirits. Stretching and relaxation are used to improve sleep, and psycho-education is used to normalise the sleep paralysis phenomenon.

Transitional rituals

Lastly, at the end of therapy the team encourages service users to use ending rituals from their own culture to mark the move on from a difficult time and the start of a new and more positive period of their life. They describe how some cultures might use a ritual steam bath as a way of purifying the self and beginning a new enterprise. They make the very interesting point that this ritual is likely to elicit strong somatic symptoms like increased heart beat and sweating. The service user then has the opportunity to experience these as neutral or positive rather than aversive. Again the reservations outlined previously about integrating spiritual practices into the UK health care context should be considered if this approach is likely to be used by UK based practitioners, but service users may generate their own ideas about a culturally meaningful act or ritual that can be used to mark the end of the work.

Opportunities and challenges when using this approach

There are some important features to this approach that are worth noting. Firstly it is supported by research evidence developed within a clinic setting, and the research and therapy team have clearly worked to develop a rigorous model of cultural adaptation. There may be aspects of this approach which do not translate well from the USA to the UK, in particular the use of spiritual practices, imagery and approaches within therapy. These might be practices that fit better with the more openly religious culture in the USA than the more publicly secular culture of the UK, although as the next chapter illustrates there are good examples of integrating faith based approaches to adapting CBT in the UK as well.

Another strength of this treatment protocol is that it has been developed to be readily explained and applied when the service user has had limited educational opportunities and has little or no English language ability. The treatment seems to be on the whole provided by therapists from within the service user's own community. This is likely to make the cultural adaptations discussed above easier to integrate into therapy

The authors themselves raise the question as to whether the treatment protocol would be as effective with non-ethnically matched therapists providing the intervention. Non-matched therapists would necessitate greater use of interpreters and longer session times. It might be more difficult for non-matched therapists to suggest the use of specific cultural practices. Integrating these might be feasible for a therapist who is very familiar with a particular culture or who can draw on the expertise of colleagues from that culture for advice or supervision; it might not be feasible otherwise. Given that some parts of the UK include areas with just one or two major BME population groups, it might be possible to develop CA-CBT for PTSD for those communities. In these circumstances it could be possible for a white or other non-ethnically matched therapist to develop the levels of familiarity with those cultures necessary to integrate specific cultural adaptations into their work. In such areas it is more likely that the workforce will to some degree reflect the ethnic composition of the population served, so there are also likely to be local BME staff members who can advise on this adaptation. In areas with a greater degree of ethnic diversity this is likely to be less feasible. Where the ethnic composition is very fluid or very diverse, it becomes difficult for teams to hold this breadth of community practices in mind. Developing links and becoming familiar with many different communities becomes a challenge in busy teams, and in these circumstances a culturally sensitive approach might make more sense.

Culturally Sensitive CBT for PTSD

In contrast to the Culturally Adapted work described above, d'Ardenne et al. (2005) describe the work of the Institute of Psycho-trauma in East London. This is a specialist PTSD service which provides Culturally Sensitive rather than Culturally Adapted CBT. The core elements of this service will be described and then contrasted with CA-CBT. This service for adults covers three London boroughs (Tower Hamlets, Newham and Hackney) which have some of the most diverse and economically disadvantaged populations in the UK. These include long established communities such as the Bangladeshi population in Tower Hamlets and the African-Carribean community in Hackney, and large and rapidly changing communities throughout the boroughs. The service is for all adults who have experienced mental health problems as a result of trauma. To give an example of the diversity of the service users referred to the clinic, the 2005 paper describes that almost half of the people referred to the service were identified as refugees and 45 per cent did not speak English. In terms of the ethnicity of those refugees, the largest group was Black African (25 per cent) and 22 per cent were

Albanian/Kosovan. The term 'Black African' is an ethnic category that encompasses many different linguistic, cultural and religious groups. The main source of trauma in those referred to the service was political torture (44.2 per cent) and trauma related to war (41.3 per cent).

Since this paper was published in 2005, the ethnic composition of the refugee referrals will have changed to reflect the current international refugee patterns, and at different times the service will be responding to different humanitarian crises. East London is often the first port of call for new refugees in the UK because of its long history of hosting diverse communities, existing links to established communities and a history of hosting services specialising in work with refugees. This service has published outcome data which demonstrates significant clinical gains for interpreter mediated CBT for trauma, as well as for CBT delivered in English and to non-refugees (d'Ardenne et al. 2007).

A shared team ethos

The service is organised around several core principles and values. The diversity of the population served by the clinic and the changing nature of the population of refugees means that clinicians in a relatively small team would be unlikely to be able to develop a body of specific cultural knowledge and expertise about every ethnic group which might be referred to the service. In these circumstances, a Culturally Sensitive and flexibly applied CBT enables clinicians to work on a case-by-case basis to ensure that the therapy meets the specific cultural and circumstantial needs of the service user. The therapist team are all first or second generation immigrants themselves and each speaks two or more languages, so there are team perspectives, and approaches benefit from not necessarily being based on white majority cultural assumptions and ways of seeing things. The team has also worked to develop and maintain knowledge of the local communities and populations in East London and has a team philosophy which values 'an ethos of cultural relativity in all its work, and places a high value on respect for and curiosity about all new cultures' (d'Ardenne et al. 2005: 31).

This is an important point in terms of supporting this culturally sensitive work. This flexible and adaptive use of CBT is embedded in a team that is in itself diverse, and which values that diversity. By prioritising these issues in team discussions, policies and practices, the team is able to value and support each other in this work and develop high standards of reflective practice in case discussion and supervision. As the team was set up by Dr Patricia d'Ardenne, the team has clearly benefited from the leadership of one of the pioneers of cross-cultural individual therapy in the UK (see d'Ardenne and Mahtani 1999). Cultural competence and reflexivity is therefore not something that is simply added to CBT-as-usual in this service, it is a part of the core values and practice.

As well as this fundamental team ethos there are a number of practical initiatives that support culturally sensitive working, which are outlined below.

Language

Once a referral is received, the team liaises with referrers to understand the language needs of service users prior to the first appointment. This might include ensuring that service users are able to access someone who can help translate the first appointment letters or documentation that will be sent with this, or sending documents in the first language of the service user where possible. Having a team composed of people who speak several languages also sensitises the team to the limits of 'linguistic equivalence'. This is the degree to which ideas that can be readily expressed in one language may have direct equivalents in another language. This may be limited because the language in question arises from a culture that does not use a particular concept as a means of understanding or explaining the world, or because it does not have words that directly map onto ones in English.

The service also understands and values the role of interpreters and has been able to train a group who they work with regularly. The service also gives users a choice about which language they would prefer to use for therapy, as this can be helpful in returning a sense of empowerment and agency.

Assessment

At assessment, the service ensures that the gender match of therapist and service user is acceptable and provides a therapist of the preferred gender where possible. There are many reasons why service users might have a preference for a therapist of a particular gender. For example, this may be because a female service user has been sexually assaulted by a male and would find it difficult to discuss this with a male therapist, or because a male service user is from a culture where discussing intimate details about his life with a younger female might be difficult or shaming.

A range of mental health measures are sent to all service users with their initial appointment letter. If the service user has been unable to complete these they are supported to do so at the first appointment by the therapist, and an interpreter where necessary. The assessment may also include extensive discussion about the migration history, country of origin and background of the service user. This initial discussion will begin to outline the circumstances relating to trauma experiences, as well as the service user's understanding of trauma and its consequences. The therapist might use this assessment to learn about what is happening in the service user's country of origin from their perspective, which may be different from the narratives available in the UK media. The position of the therapist during this assessment process is one of collaborating with the service user to develop a shared understanding of their world and difficulties. The therapist works to maintain an awareness of their own subjective take on cultural factors, and how distress might be expressed and world events understood during this process. Supervision and team discussions encourage this reflexivity.

The treatment process

Service users receive between 2 and 30 sessions, with a mean of 5 sessions. These can be weekly, fortnightly or monthly depending on the competing demands of other responsibilities in the life of the service user. The service uses a three stage model to frame this therapy process:

1   Establishing safety.
    This can include increasing social support, teaching self-care and emotional regulation skills, and linking the service user with a range of appropriate support agencies. This phase might also include addressing sleep hygiene and physical well-being in collaboration with their general practitioner. This approach specifies that no trauma focused interventions occur until the service user has a firm foundation of trust with the therapist and is considered to be low risk in terms of self-harm and suicidal thoughts.

2   Direct psychological interventions.
    The service uses a model of treatment which is based on Ehlers et al.'s (2005) model, in that it involves reliving the traumatic memory with an emphasis on identifying and targeting the 'hot spots', or most emotionally arousing moments, and identifying and modifying the appraisals associated with these using cognitive techniques. For example, the belief that 'I am going to die', which someone may have held at the time of being assaulted, may be associated with high emotional arousal when reliving an incident. This cognition can be replaced with a more adaptive one, such as 'I survived and now I am safe here', through the therapy process. Service users are also taught how to manage the high levels of distress that intrusive memories might trigger.

3   Reintegration with the community.
    Lastly, the service user is supported in developing stronger links to provide ongoing support for their emotional well-being and reduce the chance of relapse. The service makes specific and detailed recommendations to the service user and the referrers in terms of what might be usefully done to facilitate this process. It might involve increasing the support within existing family or community networks, and helping to trace missing family members or strengthening links to family overseas. Support might also include increasing access to language or vocational classes in order to prepare people for life in the UK, or linking service users to sport and leisure opportunities. Service users might be referred on to agencies who can offer support around housing and immigration issues, or supported to contact groups campaigning for social or political justice within their communities.

The following case example illustrates the way that Culturally Sensitive CBT for PTSD can be adapted to successfully treat traumatised BME service users.

Case example: Wendy

Wendy is a 20-year-old woman from Nigeria. She and her family were violently assaulted in their home in Nigeria as a result of her father's political affiliations. They had to leave Nigeria to ensure the safety of family members and at the time of referral were seeking asylum in the UK. Wendy spoke excellent English, was completing a college course and planned to apply to study nursing in the UK. She had been in the UK for three years when she was referred to mental health services by her GP because of intense anxious arousal. This had been triggered by the failure of the family's application for asylum and the threat of deportation. Although an appeal had been made, the immigration authorities had come to their home at 10pm one evening three months prior to the referral. The family were forcibly taken to a secure detention facility. She had heard about an African asylum seeker who had died from a heart attack whilst being detained by UK immigration authorities and at the time she was being removed she had become anxious and had to be restrained. She reports that at the time she was aware of worries about this escalating, and about having a heart attack whilst she was being transported with her family.

Their legal representative had appealed this detention and the family had been returned to their home after three days. Since then, Wendy had experienced intense intrusive memories of being forcibly removed from her home by immigration authorities. At these times she experienced her increased heart rate as evidence of an impending heart attack.

The initial assessment involved establishing the migration history of the family and gave Wendy an opportunity to reflect on how this process had been experienced by different family members. Wendy was able to reflect that migration had provided her with educational opportunities that had been highly valued, but that her parents were much more ambivalent about life in the UK. Wendy had concerns for her safety if she returned to Nigeria, but thought that the threat was mainly towards her father. Her main concerns were around being able to continue her education and to continue with the life she had made for herself in the UK.

Therapy work began with psycho-education about the nature of anxious arousal, and Wendy undertook a homework assignment to research the fight-flight mechanism and how anxious arousal could be mistaken for evidence of heart problems. Developing a more helpful understanding of her symptoms did not reduce her anxiety levels, but did eliminate one element of her worry cycle. She was taught a simple mindfulness based exercise to practise at times when she did not feel anxious, in order to help her develop the ability to shift the focus of her attention to her breath at times when it

(continued)

(continued)

might become focused on worries about the future or trying to avoid triggers for her intrusive memories about her forced removal. She remained hyper-vigilant for the threat of being removed by immigration authorities.

Her therapist contacted the immigration authorities via her legal team and explained the impact that her forced removal had had on her mental health in the context of prior trauma in Nigeria, and an agreement was reached that the family would not be subject to any further unplanned removal. Her hyper-vigilance reduced considerably in frequency and intensity as a result of this agreement, although she continued to have an exaggerated startle response.

After six sessions Wendy continued to experience unwanted intrusive memories about her removal to a detention centre in the UK. There were no intrusive memories about her traumatic experiences in Nigeria, but her shared formulation with her therapist was that she was vulnerable to developing an anxiety response due to these and her worries about the risk of dying whilst being removed. Wendy discontinued sessions at this point, as she reported that she was functioning better and did not want to directly address the trauma memory. Her therapist gave her the option of directly referring herself back to them if she changed her mind. Three months later, Wendy contacted her therapist to say that she was likely to be given refugee status in the UK and wanted to recommence therapy. There had been a marked improvement in her measures on general anxiety and Panic Disorder, but her scores on the PTSD scale used in the service remained high. The Ehlers et al. (2005) model was used as a basis for the trauma focused work. Wendy's appraisal that she might die at the time of her removal was the focus of the cognitive work. After three sessions of therapy focusing on her memories of the removal and developing more adaptive beliefs about the risks she was in, her scores on the PTSD measure were in the normal range and therapy was brought to an end. At one month follow-up she remained symptom free.

Summary: common themes in CA-CBT and CS-CBT

What both of these service models have in common is an acknowledgement that Western models of PTSD might not be universally applicable, but in clinics providing services to traumatised BME populations in Europe and the USA these models may still provide a useful starting point in helping to alleviate the distress of both BME and refugee service users who have experienced trauma. Both of these approaches include developing a whole team ethos where working with diversity is valued and reflexivity becomes part of the day-to-day team processes. It is striking that both teams described above are diverse in terms of the ethnic, cultural and linguistic backgrounds of therapists and it seems highly likely that this has been an important factor in terms of developing successful cultural adaptations.

The models of PTSD assessment and treatment used by both teams may not perfectly fit the way that distress is experienced in all communities, but at a pragmatic level these models are a starting point for adaptations that work. Both of these approaches incorporate elements of emotional regulation work in response to the high levels of distress that service users might experience on referral, and both models acknowledge the need to manage this before trauma focused work can begin. They also acknowledge the need to modify the way that re-experiencing trauma is integrated into the work, although the CA-CBT approach places less emphasis on reliving and modifying appraisals.

What these models have to offer individual clinicians working in general mental health services, with no opportunity to specialise and only infrequent referrals of traumatised BME or refugee service users, is an interesting question. It seems that, first of all, being part of a group of clinicians interested in work with this user group is likely to be helpful. This might be achieved in-service or between neighbouring services and might involve only cognitive behaviour therapists or therapists from different backgrounds. Supporting one another with this work and working together to encourage reflective and safe practice is likely to be very helpful. Arranging appropriate supervision is also likely to help support this work, in terms of helping the therapist both to manage vicarious trauma and to adapt therapies in a way that is transparent and fits with the ethos of the team and service.

Both models include interpreter mediated therapy, although the East London service appears to make much more use of outside interpreters and these appear to be well supported within the service. Chapter 7 considers interpreter mediated CBT in greater detail and provides further information about how to support this work. Given the diversity of the service users likely to be seen in UK clinical settings, it might be useful to develop idiosyncratic formulations and treatment plans for service users which incorporate key elements from both approaches on a case-by-case basis. This treatment plan would follow on from the problem list and goals set with the service user at the assessment. Treatment approaches should be negotiated collaboratively in the spirit of CBT. It is also worth considering that for some BME service users, particularly those who are second or third generation and who speak English as a first language, there may need no need for the cultural adaptation of the preferred models of treatment at all beyond the discussion of ethnicity and background outlined in Chapter 2.

Vicarious trauma in therapists

The impact of exposure to the traumatic accounts of others is considered in Chapter 7. It is an important factor to consider in supporting therapists and interpreters working with traumatised service users. It is likely that working with refugees will expose therapists to trauma histories that are more difficult to hear than those they might ordinarily experience, and supervision should be used by therapists to reflect on how best to manage this.

References

Basoglu, M. (2004). Cognitive Behaviour Therapy with refugees: Proceedings of the XXXIVth Annual Congress of the European Association for Behavioural and Cognitive Therapies. 9–11 September 2004, University of Manchester.

Burri, A. and Maercker, A. (2014). Differences in prevalence rates of PTSD in various European countries explained by war exposure, other trauma and cultural value orientation. *BMC Research Notes*, 7(1), 407.

Clark, D. M. (1986). A cognitive approach to panic. *Behaviour Research and Therapy*, 24(4), 461–470.

Crumlish, N., and O'Rourke, K. (2010). A systematic review of treatments for post-traumatic stress disorder among refugees and asylum-seekers. *The Journal of Nervous and Mental Disease*, 198(4), 237–251.

d'Ardenne, P., and Mahtani, A. (1999). *Transcultural counselling in action*. London: Sage.

d'Ardenne, P., Capuzzo, N., Ruaro, L., and Priebe, S. (2005). One size fits all? Cultural sensitivity in a psychological service for traumatised refugees. *Diversity in Health and Social Care*, 2(1), 29–36.

d'Ardenne, P., Ruaro, L., Cestari, L., Fakhoury, W., and Priebe, S. (2007). Does interpreter-mediated CBT with traumatized refugee people work? A comparison of patient outcomes in East London. *Behavioural and Cognitive Psychotherapy*, 35(3), 293–301.

Ehlers, A., Clark, D. M., Hackmann, A., McManus, F., and Fennell, M. (2005). Cognitive therapy for post-traumatic stress disorder: Development and evaluation. *Behaviour Research and Therapy*, 43(4), 413–431.

Foa, E.B., and Rothbaum, B.O. (1998). Treating the trauma of rape: Cognitive Behavioural Therapy for PTSD. New York: Guilford.

Hinton, D. E., Chhean, D., Pich, V., Safren, S. A., Hofmann, S. G., and Pollack, M. H. (2005). A randomized controlled trial of cognitive-behavior therapy for Cambodian refugees with treatment-resistant PTSD and panic attacks: A cross-over design. *Journal of Traumatic Stress*, 18(6), 617–629.

Hinton, D. E., Hofmann, S. G., Rivera, E., Otto, M. W., and Pollack, M. H. (2011). Culturally adapted CBT (CA-CBT) for Latino women with treatment-resistant PTSD: A pilot study comparing CA-CBT to applied muscle relaxation. *Behaviour Research and Therapy*, 49(4), 275–280.

Hinton, D. E., Rivera, E. I., Hofmann, S. G., Barlow, D. H., and Otto, M. W. (2012). Adapting CBT for traumatized refugees and ethnic minority patients: Examples from culturally adapted CBT (CA-CBT). *Transcultural Psychiatry*, 49(2), 340–365.

Hodge, D. R. (2006). Spiritually modified cognitive therapy: A review of the literature. *Social Work*, 51(2), 157–166.

Hollifield, M., Warner, T. D., Lian, N., Krakow, B., Jenkins, J. H., Kesler, J., Stevenson, J., and Westermeyer, J. (2002). Measuring trauma and health status in refugees: A critical review. *JAMA: The Journal of the American Medical Association*, 288(5), 611–621.

June, T. H., Jackie, F., Mooren, T., Knipscheer, J. W., and Kleber, R. J. (2014). EMDR with traumatized refugees: From experience-based to evidence-based practice. *Journal of EMDR Practice and Research*, *8*(3), 147–156.

Lester, K., Artz, C., Resick, P. A., and Young-Xu, Y. (2010). Impact of race on early treatment termination and outcomes in posttraumatic stress disorder treatment. *Journal of Consulting and Clinical Psychology*, *78*(4), 480.

Linehan, M. M. (2013). *Dialectical Behavior Therapy*. Phoenix, AZ: Milton H. Erickson Foundation.

NICE (2005). *Post-traumatic stress disorder (PTSD): The management of PTSD in adults and children in primary and secondary care*. London: HMSO. www.nice.org.uk/guidance/cg26.

Schauer, M., Schauer, M., Neuner, F., and Elbert, T. (2011). *Narrative exposure therapy: A short-term treatment for traumatic stress disorders*. Cambridge, MA: Hogrefe Publishing.

Somasundaram, D. (2010). Collective trauma in the Vanni – A qualitative inquiry into the mental health of the internally displaced due to the civil war in Sri Lanka. *International Journal of Mental Health Systems*, *4*(22), 1–31.

Tribe, R. (2013). Culture, politics and global mental health. *Disability and the Global South*, *1*, 251–265.

Udina, M., Foulon, H., Valdés, M., Bhattacharyya, S., and Martín-Santos, R. (2013). Dhat syndrome: A systematic review. *Psychosomatics*, *54*(3), 212–218.

Wittchen, H. U., Jacobi, F., Rehm, J., Gustavsson, A., Svensson, M., Jönsson, B., Oleson, J., Allqulander, C., Alonso, J., Faravelli, C., Fratiglioni, L., Jennum, P., Lieb, R., Maercker, A., van Os, J., Preisig, M., Salvador-Carulla, L., Simon, R., and Steinhausen, H. C. (2011). The size and burden of mental disorders and other disorders of the brain in Europe 2010. *European Neuropsychopharmacology*, *21*(9), 655–679.

Chapter 6

Integrating religious or spiritual beliefs and practices with CBT

Overview

So far this book has made the argument that a culturally sensitive rather than a culturally adapted approach is likely to be the most helpful one for the majority of clinicians working with BME service users. This is partly because CA-CBT may make too many assumptions about the degree to which specific service users fit with the ethnic group they are seen as belonging to, and partly because the diversity of communities served by most teams means that it would not be feasible to be trained in or develop and evaluate a culturally adapted approach for each of these. It is also likely to be the case that CA-CBT is more likely to be useful in a team that reflects the ethnic diversity of the population served, as such a team will have the skills to translate the language, concepts and practices of CBT for the local population.

In Chapters 2 and 3 a framework was provided that will enable clinicians to develop a culturally sensitive approach to CBT which engages BME service users by discussing and understanding their cultural background and developing a shared understanding of family-wide factors using Systemic and Multidimensional Approaches. This way of thinking is quite different to the Particularist approach (see Chapter 3) which is implied by CA-CBT. In other words, CA-CBT can be seen as assuming that people within a particular group are more similar than different, and that presenting problems and interventions should focus on the extent to which the cultural factors associated with that group shape the presenting problem and the subsequent intervention. Culturally Adapted CBT can also be problematic in the way that it assumes individuals from BME backgrounds can be thought of as belonging to just one particular culture. Increasingly, people from BME backgrounds describe themselves as belonging to two or more cultural groups and might describe themselves as being of mixed ethnicity, mixed race or dual heritage (Aspinall and Song 2013). Culturally Adapted CBT may not be flexible enough to capture these complex ethnic identities.

That is not to say that CA-CBT will not be useful for some populations and in some service settings, and the treatment of PTSD described by Hinton et al. (2005) in Chapter 5 clearly demonstrates that it is.

Part of what we would describe as the culture of a service user might often be linked to values, beliefs and practices that have developed as part of their religious faith or spirituality. The degree to which culture and religious identity interact and take primacy in identity formation is a topic of considerable dispute, but it seems reasonable to say that they are not mutually exclusive or separate value systems. It is likely that religious beliefs and practices are shaped by the culture of the society in which that religion is practised, and that religion in turn shapes the values and beliefs of that culture. In many ways it can be argued that it is difficult to say where one ends and the other begins. In order to begin to look at how spiritual and religious beliefs might be incorporated into CBT, this chapter will consider the research literature on the cultural adaptation of CBT for depression and then look in detail at the degree to which CBT might be adapted when working with Muslim service users who are depressed. This chapter recognises that what might be considered Muslim values vary considerably, both within specific ethnic groups and between ethnic groups which are predominantly Muslim in their religious faith. The chapter does not assume that religious affiliations are more important than ethnicity in thinking about how to adapt CBT, although they might be for some service users, but it does propose that this aspect of identity can be an important one and that the values and practices of any religion can be incorporated into thinking about adapting therapy practice.

The cultural adaptation of CBT for depression

It would be useful at this stage to briefly consider the research literature regarding the cultural adaptation of psychological therapies for the treatment of depression. A recent review of this has been undertaken by Chowdhary et al. (2014). This review paper looks at all psychological therapies provided both in Western countries for BME populations and in non-Western settings. The paper summarises evidence for the efficacy of the interventions, the process by which cultural adaptation was undertaken and what the adaptations looked like. The adaptations processes in the 19 studies identified were compared to the Medical Research Council four-stage model for adapting and developing complex interventions (Craig et al. 2008). These four stages are:

1   modelling and theoretical development of the approach to be used
2   formative work to operationalise the process
3   piloting of the intervention
4   evaluation of the intervention.

Ideally this evaluation would then lead to further refinements of the intervention based on what was learnt about the efficacy and acceptability of the approach. Of the studies of culturally adapted psychological therapies identified, ten were of CBT, four were of Interpersonal Therapy, three were for psycho-education only, two were for Problem Solving Therapy and one was for Psycho-Dynamically Informed Therapy. A broad range of ethnicities were represented in the studies.

This meta-analysis concluded that culturally adapted psychological therapies led to significantly better outcomes than various control conditions used for comparison. There was no evidence to support the idea that CA-CBT for depression led to better outcomes than other culturally adapted therapies, although none of the studies directly compared different modalities in their research designs. The study search terms specifically excluded research which looked at treating depression in children or adolescents; however, one recent study has indicated that psychological treatments for depression would be as acceptable for BME adolescents as for white adolescents (Caporino et al. 2014). So far, no research has specifically addressed the clinical outcomes of depressed BME adolescents following CBT or other psychological therapies. There is some evidence that psychological interventions which are based on or incorporate faith based approaches may lead to more rapid improvement in symptoms compared to otherwise similar treatments which do not incorporate religious or spiritual elements, though these early gains are not necessarily sustained in the long term (Hook et al. 2010).

A different systematic review of the research literature regarding culturally adapted interventions for anxiety and depression has been published by van Loon et al. (2013). Of the nine research papers identified for review, four were for CA-CBT for depressive disorders. All of these randomised control trials were done with BME groups in the USA. These studies looked at Chinese care givers of adults with dementia (Gallagher-Thompson et al. 2010), African Americans (Kohn et al. 2002), Latino-Americans at risk of Perinatal Depression (Le et al. 2011) and Latino-Americans with likely depression (Miranda et al. 2003). The pooled effects size for the depression interventions was small ($d = 0.35$) compared to those for anxiety ($d = 1.73$), which is similar to the outcomes found in CBT for depression in white majority populations (Linde et al. 2015).

How cultural adaptations were made by the researchers and clinicians varied considerably. Gallagher-Thompson et al. developed Chinese language and culturally specific educational materials for Chinese carers of older adults with dementia. Kohn et al. adapted the language used for materials for African Americans with depression. Le at al. used Spanish speaking trainers for Latino-Americans at risk of Perinatal depression, and Miranda et al. used materials translated into Spanish and Hispanic actors in the video material used in the intervention.

There are a number of considerations to bear in mind when looking at this meta-analysis. All the studies were of interventions delivered with BME groups in the USA. The patterns of migration and countries of origin of BME groups in the USA country are very different to those in the UK, Europe and Australia/ New Zealand, and so it might be going beyond the evidence to say that CA-CBT will be as effective for BME populations in these countries. Although all of the studies were of CA-CBT, the number of sessions varied from 8 to 12 weeks, and the degree to which they were culturally adapted appears to be limited and based mainly on language and the use of ethnically matched actors and therapists.

There do not seem to have been the same kind of extensive changes to CBT in both the CA-CBT and the CS-CBT for PTSD examples described in Chapter 5 of this book.

There is clearly a need for research in the UK to address the gap in knowledge regarding outcomes; however, in the absence of research to inform evidence based practice clinicians have to draw on practice based evidence – that is, the clinical insights developed by therapists which draw on the existing evidence base for CBT for depression – and adapt this for specific communities. This chapter will look in general at the extensive literature on adapting psychological therapies for Muslim service users, and then look in detail at an adaptation of Behavioural Activation for Muslim service users developed in the UK. This approach is based on broad principles about integrating religious and spiritual practices with CBT that will be useful to therapists working with service users from any faith background.

The rationale for CA-CBT with depressed Muslim service users

This chapter will concern itself with the adaptation of CBT when working with Muslim service users. There are a number of reasons why this particular adaptation may be of interest to cognitive behaviour therapists. The first is that in the UK, Islam is the fastest growing religion and followers of this faith comprise the second largest faith group in the country, with the largest being those who identify themselves as Christian (ONS 2011). There are almost 3 million people in the UK who identify as Muslim, the majority of whom live in England, with smaller communities in urban areas in Scotland, Wales and Northern Ireland. Within England, communities tend to be clustered around specific urban areas with histories of migration from a particular region. The majority of Muslims in the UK trace their family origin to Bangladesh or Pakistan, with smaller communities from a number of African countries, Turkey, India, the Middle East and the Balkan regions. Identifying as Muslim is not an ethnic identity, though people of this faith group may often identify their faith as being of equal or greater importance than their ethnicity in terms of self-identity. Muslims in the UK, Europe and other Western countries have considerable diversity in terms of cultural background, traditions, migration histories, economic opportunities and degrees of acculturation. The values, customs and attitudes of people who identify as Muslim will be shaped by a mixture of the culture of their country of origin, their interpretation and understanding of Islam, and how their practices have changed as a result of life in a country that is not predominantly Muslim.

Typically therapists in the UK will find themselves working with service users of Pakistani or Bangladeshi origin. These could be third or fourth generation migrants in CAMHS or when working with younger adults. Older adults may be first generation migrants, and this may also be the case for the husbands and wives of second or third generation migrants who have come to the UK for marriage.

Amongst these very varied groups, rates of acculturation, English speaking and religious observance will vary considerably. New immigration rules in the UK mean that service users who have moved to the UK to marry a British citizen are more likely to speak English, but perhaps not to a degree that would enable therapy to be provided without an interpreter.

This chapter will summarise the evidence base for CBT adapted for work with Muslim communities, consider key points from the research literature about how this work might be facilitated and then look in detail at two treatment approaches developed in the UK for work with British South Asian Muslims.

Key points about the treatment of depression amongst Muslim service users

This section summarises the literature review conducted by Walpole et al. (2013). This is an extensive literature review of both qualitative and quantitative research regarding depression amongst Muslim communities, and includes a consideration of therapy factors and community narratives regarding the causes of depression and suggestions as to how therapy might be successfully adapted for this group. The paper does helpfully acknowledge that it is sometimes very difficult to separate beliefs that are linked to Muslim faith from ones that arise as a result of national or regional cultural practices. It takes the pragmatic view that religion can be an important organising principle in the lives of many BME service users, and that beliefs and values linked to religious faith can cut across ethnic and cultural boundaries. Islam is not the only religion for which this is likely to be the case, but as this is likely to be the faith background of many BME service users in the UK and Europe it is a useful one to consider in more detail.

Beliefs about the causes of depression amongst Muslim groups

Walpole et al. (2013) summarise a number of largely qualitative studies into beliefs about the cause of depression amongst Muslim communities. Traditionally many forms of mental health problems have been attributed to *djin* (supernatural forces akin to demons or spirits in European culture), the influence of Sheittham (Satan), curses or black magic (sometimes called *naja* in North Indian or Pakistani communities), spirit possession, or poison administered by an enemy. As these causes are largely supernatural in origin many people will initially seek supernatural solutions. What is not clear from the research as it stands currently is the extent to which Muslims from various communities living in the UK hold these beliefs, and the extent to which they are held simultaneously with causal explanations that fit with the dominant psychological and biological models found within Western health services. It is certainly the case that people can hold simultaneous views that might appear to be incompatible, as the case examples below illustrate.

Case example: Safina

Safina is a 29-year-old women born in the UK whose parents migrated to the north of England from Bangladesh for work before she was born. Safina is trained as a mental health nurse and has completed an introductory course of training in CBT. In supervision one day she explains that she has taken two days off as sick leave that week as she has been struggling with low mood and confused thoughts for the past several weeks, but that this has got worse. Her supervisor asks her if there is anything they might need to know about what might be causing this. Safina explains that someone in a neighbouring village to their family home in Bangladesh is in a dispute with their father over the sale of some land. She explains that the person in Bangladesh has written her name on a piece of paper and tied this to a fish in a pond near her home village and that each time the fish changes direction it causes her mind to 'flip' into confusion or sadness. She is confident that the intercession of a holy man in her community will help to resolve this problem.

In her role in a mental health team, Safina works using a bio-psycho-social model of depression and is a thoughtful CBT practitioner. Holding this point of view is not seen as incompatible with a magical explanation for her own depression.

Some Muslims can also hold the belief that depression, like other physical or emotional health problems, is caused by God's will or by fate. For some people this might imply that their suffering must be endured passively but with good grace and patience. However, many Muslims believe that for every illness, God has created a cure, and that it is part of their personal responsibility to make use of that treatment. Some people may also believe that depression is caused by a lack of religious observance or by not following the correct religious path. When this is the case, service users might struggle with strong feelings of guilt and shame in addition to depression and the content of their cognitions might include self-critical beliefs about themselves as a bad Muslim. These thoughts might be difficult to express to a non-Muslim therapist unless they have established a good working relationship that includes the therapist communicating their respect for and interest in the religious values and beliefs of the service user.

There is also evidence that social explanations of the cause of depression are common in Muslim communities. These explanations include the individual struggling to reconcile the conflict between secular and religious values, the impact of marital and family problems particularly in terms of the duty to stay in an unhappy marriage, worries about shame being brought upon the family and the impact of migration.

The review by Walpole et al. (2013) did not find literature that considered the extent to which Muslim communities reconcile and synthesise cultural, social, biological and psychological explanations of depression. The extent to which individuals manage these differing systems of belief will vary considerably as a result of their education, exposure to other ideas about mental health, level of acculturation and personal belief systems, but it is important to note that these four explanatory systems are by no means mutually exclusive. The case example of Safina above illustrates that someone trained in biological and psychological models of mental health might still prefer cultural explanations in some instances. The illustration below provides a different perspective on this.

Case example: Zahida

Zahida is a 74-year-old woman originally from a rural district in the Punjab in Pakistan. She came to the UK to join her son and his family when she was 56 years old. She has not been educated, is illiterate and does not speak English. She is, however, seen as a key figure in her family in terms of offering advice and guidance, and when in Pakistan had a role as a traditional healer for people who were suffering from problems relating to magic. She is interviewed in an inpatient setting when she attends with her son to visit his wife, Rashma, who has been admitted with severe depression following a suicide attempt.

Whilst on the ward Rashma does not speak and takes no role in her own self-care. With a bilingual co-worker the therapist begins to ask about the understanding of the current problems held by different family members. Zahida explains that she has seen people with this sort of problem in Pakistan and that sometimes it can be brought about by *djin* (demons) or through poisons being administered by others who hold a grudge. Zahida is asked what she thinks the cause of her daughter-in-law's current distress is, and she says that in this case her daughter-in-law is not behaving in the way that people whose problems are caused by magic or poison act. She can see that her daughter-in-law has a lot of worries and responsibilities and thinks that this worry has made her unwell. Zahida reports that she would like the doctors to treat her daughter-in-law with the correct medicine and return her to her own home when she is beginning to get better. When a psychological therapist explains that as well as anti-depressant medication they will be using Behavioural Activation to help her daughter-in-law, Zahida says that she can understand why it is important to get active again and to spend some time each day doing pleasant and worthwhile tasks.

This example demonstrates that explanations are not derived from mutually exclusive belief systems and that service users might use one type of explanation or another depending on the circumstances. It might be necessary for therapists and service users to integrate explanations and work within two explanatory models in order to bring about improvement in functioning. This case example also illustrates the link between beliefs about causes, and the ideas about healing and treatment that follow from these. As previously mentioned, there is a clear idea within many Islamic traditions that God has provided a cure for all illnesses and that it is the duty of Muslims to find and use these cures in an active way. There are, however, other competing narratives such as the idea that illnesses are tests or punishments from God that must be endured rather than treated, although this would not stop most Muslims seeking help to alleviate symptoms or treat the underlying causes.

Where there are competing explanations it is interesting to consider the impact of depressive thinking styles on which explanation is preferred. Negative beliefs about the self, the world and the future might lead to those who are struggling with depression being more likely to adopt an explanation that reflects their lack of belief about their own agency in bringing about change. A passive response to depression is likely to make it more difficult to engage people in the active collaboration which underpins CBT, so this is an area that therapists could benefit from exploring with Muslim service users.

Some service users might believe that the route to treatment is wholly through religious practice, particularly if their view of the cause of their depression is linked to poor religious observance. They might see increased observance as the only route to being free from depression, or may increase their use of rituals and practices linked to religious cleanliness. When this is the case there is the possibility of comorbid OCD developing, and therapists should take time to consider the degree to which these rituals are linked to appraisals of specific cognitions and anxiety associated with concerns about the consequences of not undertaking specific rituals. Therapists should also assess whether acting out rituals alleviates the anxiety and leads to the establishment of an OCD cycle.

It may often be the case that the first line of treatment chosen by many depressed Muslims is that provided by traditional healers or religious figures. There is a large difference in the degree to which these healers are sanctioned by mainstream Islamic thought. Some Imams (religious leaders) are clear that the use of these healers is haram (forbidden) under Islamic teaching and may issue a fatwa (religious edict) against their use in the community where they have authority. Other mosques and communities tolerate or support the use of these cultural healers. Once a good rapport has been established with the service user, it can be useful to ask about whether they have used this approach. The advice of these healers may be compatible with CBT, and both models can be combined to help to bring about successful treatment outcomes.

The importance of establishing a good therapeutic relationship

Chapter 2 includes detailed thinking about the importance of discussing ethnicity as part of establishing a good therapeutic relationship. However, Walpole et al. (2013)

suggest a number of other helpful approaches to support this process. The gender of the therapist may play a role in determining whether or not Muslim clients engage initially. Some Islamic cultures place a high degree of value on modesty and this may make the discussion of personal aspects of the service user's life difficult with a therapist of the opposite sex. It is not helpful to assume that the gender of the therapist will be an issue for all Muslim service users, although it is more likely to be an issue where the service user has experienced sexual assaults, domestic violence or marital difficulties. The degree to which this is an issue will depend to some extent on acculturation, religious orthodoxy and the nature of the problems being discussed. In CAMHS services it is less likely that a family will have a strong preference for the gender of the therapist. This issue might be compounded by the age of the service user and the therapist. For example, an older, first generation, Muslim service user from Pakistan might find it difficult to work with a younger, white, female therapist in a way that they might not with an older, white, female therapist. Where possible all service users should be given a choice in this matter, regardless of their religious or ethnic background. Realistically speaking, services are likely to be constrained by the availability of therapists.

Therapists developing expertise in Islamic values and practice

There is an interesting question about the extent to which therapists need to understand and work within the world view of service users in order to be effective. Given that the largest ethnic minority community in many areas in the UK and Europe is of a Muslim faith background, it is likely to be helpful for therapists to develop an understanding of the religious and cultural practices of those communities. It might be helpful if therapists demonstrate some knowledge of Islamic practice as part of the initial assessment. For example, during a CAMHS assessment families are generally asked about how well a child is doing in school. To demonstrate an interest in family values and practices the therapist could also ask if the child is taking any additional classes outside of school and how these are progressing. Many Muslim families send their children to a Qur'an or Hafiz class. These studies, which can take place in the local mosque or the family home, are a highly valued practice in many Muslim families, where children are taught to recite the whole of the Qur'an. Demonstrating knowledge that this is part of many people's everyday family life communicates an interest in and respect for Islamic culture that may be welcomed by many families. This rote learning of the Qur'an is not as common in some Islamic communities as it is in others; therapists who get to know the Muslim cultures in their locality will develop knowledge about whether this practice is expected in the families they work with. Therapists should remain sensitive to the idea that the degree of religious observance of a particular service user may be anywhere on a wide spectrum, from being atheist or agnostic to being highly observant.

Some of the suggestions reported in the review paper by Walpole et al. (2013) may not fit well with secular services. These include having a copy of the Qur'an or

Islamic posters and prints visible in waiting areas or female therapists wearing a veil when treating orthodox Muslim service users. These decisions should not be taken lightly in teams, and the possibility that this might alienate non-Muslims or people from Muslim communities who are not observant should be kept in mind. Also, it seems to be a helpful principle that Muslim staff should not feel that they have to conform to a particular interpretation of Islam to facilitate service user engagement.

The huge variance in cultural practices within the Muslim world means that generalisations about interpersonal styles are impossible. There would be as much difference in the interpersonal styles when comparing an Indonesian Muslim from Jakarta and an Afghani Muslim as there would be between an Ethiopian Christian and an Icelandic one. Therapists may well become aware of specific patterns and preferences within communities served by their teams, particularly if they have the benefit of working with colleagues from these communities; however, adaptation of interpersonal styles is best done on a case-by-case basis and where there is uncertainty, for example with the meanings regarding how a service user might be using eye contact, cultural advice should be sought with professionals from that community.

Confidentiality

One factor that is likely to be common across Muslim communities is a concern about confidentiality. Service users may not understand the way that this works in health services, and it is likely to be important that this is explained in more detail at initial assessments than therapists might usually do with white service users. Muslim and other BME service users may be particularly worried about confidentiality if the therapist, co-worker or reception staff are from their own community. Given the stigma around mental health in some Muslim groups, breaches of confidentiality can be realistically appraised as having potentially catastrophic consequences in terms of the impact on family honour, social standing and the marriage prospects of members of the extended family.

Topics that might be difficult to discuss in therapy

Therapists might need to be considerate in the discussion of topics that are thought to be sensitive for cultural reasons. This might include family conflict or difficulties, sex and sexuality, religious faith and observance, and marital difficulties. That is not to say that these topics should be considered off limits: just that a good working relationship might need to be established before they can be raised, and that the service user may need to feel confident that their therapist can respect and understand their culture and will maintain confidentiality before this discussion takes place. The review paper points out that suicide is considered to be a grave sin within Islamic cultures, but that this should not stop therapists assessing suicide risk in depressed service users in the same way that they would do for service users from other faith groups or ethnic communities.

Directive and Socratic approaches in therapy

The review paper makes a salient point about therapy styles and modalities and suggests that more directive therapy approaches, including CBT, might be more appropriate, as many Muslim service users would expect their therapists to make suggestions which they can then follow. This does not quite fit with the collaborative stance that is usually advocated in CBT; however, it might be necessary for the therapist to shift a little further along the spectrum from being collaborative and Socratic to being more directive if this seems to be preferred by the service user. It would not be helpful to make too broad a generalisation about this, but therapists might want to hold it in mind and adapt their style accordingly on a case-by-case basis. Whatever the particular therapy approach used, it should be supported by reflective practice and the use of the Kolb learning cycle to observe what happened, reflect on this in supervision, plan according to the new knowledge and act differently next time if this is indicated.

Including the wider system in the therapy process

Walpole et al. (2013) discuss the importance of drawing on community resources in the treatment of depression. This might include accessing faith or community based projects or initiatives as part of Behavioural Activation, drawing on the guidance of faith leaders when depression is linked to thoughts about religious observance or practice or accessing practical support around vocational training, education, language skills or leisure activities. These initiatives might be seen as more acceptable and accessible if they are located within community and faith organisations rather than being provided through secular institutions. Using faith based resources may also increase the likelihood of good engagement.

Chapter 3 has already considered the degree to which the families of BME service users might be brought into the therapeutic process in order to increase engagement with treatment. There appears to be clear consensus that this is likely to be useful when working with Muslim service users, and that the typical arrangement of parents having a clear role as head of the family, even for service users accessing therapy as adults, should be kept in mind. This should, however, be balanced by an understanding that for second or third generation Muslims in the UK this way of organising family life may be in a state of flux, and that it might not be either desirable or possible to involve the wider family in the assessment and treatment process. It is also possible that involving family members might make it difficult for the service user to discuss issues that are important but which they would not feel able to raise with family members present. This could include issues such as sexuality, domestic violence, or struggles with role identity and their place in the family system. It is also important to understand the power structures in many Muslim families if they are to be brought into the therapy process. Typically fathers and parents have a more powerful role than children and wives. It is not the place of therapists to challenge these practices and beliefs, but it might be the role of the therapist to help people within the family system articulate how these beliefs might be impacting on the mental health of individuals within that system and to consider how tensions around this might be resolved. Sometimes therapists and service users might agree that there are aspects of these family processes that cannot be changed but that the service user can develop skills in emotional regulation or negotiation to reduce their impact. Sometimes therapy might be an opportunity for family members to explore the degree to which these factors relating to gender and power contribute to emotional difficulties within the family, and how much flexibility there is around these.

Incorporating Islamic teachings into therapy

The review paper makes a very important point about the degree to which Islamic teachings could and should be integrated into therapy. The view taken is that given the spectrum of religious observance within the Muslim community, they should only be integrated to the extent to which they match the service user's level of religious conviction. It is also important that this integration of faith based approaches is only done by therapists who have a degree of confidence in their own ability to negotiate issues within the faith community they are working with.

Suggestions made in the paper include drawing on Qur'anic teaching and scripture as a way of challenging pervasively negative or unhelpful beliefs. Azhar and Varma (1995) recommend that these Qur'anic texts can be used to help service users see when they have adopted what they identify as 'wrong values or goals' which can be modified through asking for forgiveness and guidance from God. There is also a very thought provoking point made by Nielsen (2004), which is that within Islam God is the only judge of the worth of someone. Individuals who are caught up in rumination about their own failings and inadequacy are therefore involved in self-judgements which go against Qur'anic teaching. This ruminative process, which can underpin low self-esteem and subsequent depression, would be incompatible with the idea that only God can judge someone. In the spirit of CBT it would be preferable for service users to make these links themselves rather than being presented with them didactically by the therapist. Using a Socratic approach to support service users to think through the implications of these ideas is more likely to be effective in bringing about lasting change to their beliefs and emotions.

It may also be possible to use the idea that illnesses are a test from God in a way that promotes healthy and active responses to them rather than a fatalistic acceptance of these problems. The implication of this is that having developed depression, the service user now has an opportunity to be free from it by actively engaging in ways of acting and thinking that help them overcome this problem and resume their responsibilities within the family and community. This could be framed within the idea of 'positive religious coping' with depression and a therapy approach developed with the service user that uses a faith framework to encourage active responses to the challenges of having mental health problems.

The expertise of local faith leaders can be sought when a service user's understanding of mental health problems is bound up in cultural or religious beliefs and practices. Where there are large faith communities in an area served by a mental health service it is very helpful to build relationships with key members of these communities. Local religious leaders can contribute to steering groups, provide training on religious issues for staff, and provide consultations to staff on particular issues relating to interpretation of teachings where colleagues are not available or not able to do this. It is also sometimes possible for faith leaders to join the therapy process in order to support the understanding of the therapist and service user around particular faith based dilemmas.

Working specifically with Muslim women

In the UK, Muslim women are considered particularly difficult to reach because of both linguistic and cultural barriers. There is evidence, for example, that British Pakistani women with depression lack social support and experience marked difficulties, particularly in marital and close relationships (Gater et al. 2008, Chaudhry et al. 2009, Husain et al. 1997, 2012), and may lack the fluency in English and the resources necessary to obtain help (Chaudhry et al. 2009). Recent studies evaluating a Culturally Sensitive CBT based psycho-social group intervention for the treatment of depression in British Pakistani women reported a reduction in depression and an increase in participants' self-confidence at the end of the intervention (Gater et al. 2010). Crucial factors in the success of this intervention were thought to be the relationship between the facilitator and the participants, and the provision of childcare and transportation. The group based nature of this approach is also likely to have had a positive impact on reducing participants' sense of social isolation and normalising their experiences.

The group facilitators paid particular attention to the role of *izzat*, or honour, in the lives of women. The burden of preserving and enhancing family honour is thought to fall particularly heavily on women in South Asian Muslim families and research has suggested that the risk of compromising family honour is a likely barrier to accessing treatment (Pilkington et al. 2012). Where family honour is compromised there may be a very real impact on marriage prospects for siblings, a loss of social status within the community and the belief that the subsequent stress from this may cause the ill health of family members. The work by Chew-Graham et al. (2002) suggests that *izzat* is a pervasive and internalised pressure on the lives of Muslim women. It is likely that depressive thinking can exaggerate the threat of losing honour, increase the felt sense of the burden of responsibility and lead to rumination about the possibility of honour being compromised, thus exacerbating an already difficult process in the lives of British Muslim women from South Asian backgrounds.

It is worth paying particular attention to the risk of self-harm and suicide when working with British South Asian women, as there is evidence that these risks are higher in this population than in the white majority community (Husain et al. 2009). Given this, it is particularly important that CBT with this population includes risk assessment and active risk management, and an awareness of the need to work towards reducing isolation in the family or the wider community and to repair and strengthen relationships within the family wherever possible. Enhancing community links might involve referring women into culturally appropriate projects, Sure Start or other early-years schemes that are culturally accessible and adapted, and targeted vocational or educational programmes. Work with husbands and other significant family members might also be useful in reducing isolation and enhancing relationships.

The assessment of depression is likely to be particularly important immediately following births as currently there is evidence that women from all BME groups are not assessed for Postnatal Depression to the same extent that white majority women are (Almond and Lathlean 2011). In some areas the mental health needs of women following childbirth will be met by specialist teams, but practice differs considerably between regions and it might be that local IAPT or primary care mental health services provide this input.

An example of Culturally Adapted Behaviour Therapy for Muslim service users

Mir et al. (2014) have developed an excellent manual for Culturally Adapted Behaviour Therapy to support work with Muslim service users who are depressed. Although the manual focuses on Behavioural Activation for depression many of the principles can be applied to other presenting problems. A link to the manual and other related resources is contained in the References section at the end of this chapter.

The manual was developed as a result of extensive piloting work with the Pakistani and Bangladeshi communities of West Yorkshire in the UK, though it has insights and techniques that would have a lot to offer therapists working with other Muslim communities. One considerable strength of this manualised approach is that it can be used flexibly with service users who are at different points on the spectrum of faith and religious observance and is also likely to be helpful when working with service users who are ambivalent or non-practising in regard to their faith. This flexibility allows therapists to negotiate with clients the degree to which they would feel comfortable in incorporating faith based approaches in a way that is very much in the collaborative spirit of CBT. This approach also recognises that the majority of therapists in the UK are not from a Muslim background, but sees the benefit of therapists in this position familiarising themselves with Islamic ideas that might enhance their therapy and incorporating these into therapy where appropriate.

Mir et al. recommend that therapists who are less familiar with Islamic practices would benefit from supervision from someone who has this expertise. Although this is clearly desirable, in some services it might not be possible to find a supervisor who has skills and knowledge about both CBT and Islamic practices.

Where this is the case it might be pragmatic to approach Muslim colleagues who are not cognitive behaviour therapists for specific cultural consultation and support when using this approach.

Outline of the programme

The 12-week intervention developed by Mir et al. (2014) emphasises the role of Behavioural Activation in the treatment of depression. As with other BA approaches, any cognitive change which might arise from the work is as a result of the BA and is not a target of the intervention in itself. Although the emphasis of the therapy is on behavioural change by the individual there is a clear role for family members where this is indicated, and the model allows the service user and therapist to draw on systemic strengths and resources.

Formulation

The model uses a straightforward vicious-cycle model to illustrate the link between common difficult life events experienced by service users and typical responses to these. One advantage of a formulation as simple as this is that it can be shown as a diagram in a way that service users who are not able to read and write can use. The difficult life events typically experienced by service users include high rates of health problems, increased poverty and unemployment, discrimination and marginalisation, and hostility to Islam in some sections of wider society. In addition, newer migrants may struggle with the process of acculturation, isolation and limited opportunities to develop English language skills. The typical responses to these stressors are depressed mood, anhedonia, anxiety, somatic symptoms and fatigue. In addition, these are likely to lead to a range of unhelpful behavioural responses such as withdrawal, avoidance, not following through with domestic or vocational responsibilities, substance misuse, conflict and suicidal thoughts or acts. One of the tasks in early sessions is to formulate this cycle with the individual and provide a framework for them to understand the particular patterns they might be struggling with. This is very much like BA in white majority populations; however, where it differs is in the use of Islamic teachings or principles to illustrate the vicious cycle and emphasise the need for change. The manual emphasises the need for this initial exploration to be Socratic and exploratory where possible in line with good CBT practice, and then uses this shared formulation as the basis for changing the passivity which is often identified.

Values based behaviour change

This model emphasises the importance of behaviour change as something that needs to be embedded in the core values, goals and aspirations of the service user. In many respects this looks like the Valued Living approach which is so integral to Acceptance and Commitment Therapy (Orsillo et al. 2004). However, where it differs is in the explicit integration of spiritual values into the initial negotiation regarding behaviour change. By aligning the behavioural changes with core values, the therapy increases the likelihood that they will be readily acted upon. In the early sessions the therapist is clear that BA will focus on things the service user has been avoiding doing or things that might be hard for them to begin to do without additional support. There is also a clear message given that in undertaking these tasks the service user is likely to increase their own resilience and change their view of themselves or the world.

Whilst CBT might usually place considerable emphasis on helping service users develop a clear understanding of the link between their thoughts, feelings and behaviours, this model acknowledges that within some Muslim communities describing and discussing emotions is less easy, due either to there being no direct linguistic equivalence between emotional descriptors in English and in their first language or to this kind of discussion not being part of typical cultural practice. The advice given in the manual is that when, for example, a therapist asks, 'How did that situation make you feel?' and the service user replies, 'I just didn't feel like I could do anything about it', the therapist should accept this response. This is different to a typical response in CBT, where the therapist might then say, 'So your beliefs about that situation were that you could not do anything about it, but I'm curious about the emotion that was linked to those thoughts. Perhaps you could describe that to me?'

Acculturation struggles and discrimination as risk factors for depression

The model makes some important points about acculturation and discrimination struggles faced by many Muslims in the UK and explicitly incorporates this into the way that low mood is formulated. This is an important adaptation. Although unmodified CBT would be able to incorporate these experiences, they are phenomena that might easily be missed by therapists who are unused to working across cultures and who are not confident in asking about these experiences, and where service users might believe that the therapist would not be able to understand these issues and might therefore choose not to disclose them.

Acculturation issues for first generation migrants can include getting used to how families from their community are organised in a UK setting, differing expectations in terms of gender roles, learning English, negotiating with statutory and non-statutory agencies, and engaging with the different value systems embedded in white majority culture. Experiences of discrimination are potential drivers for subsequent avoidance of institutions or settings where the discrimination occurred. For example, a Bangladeshi Muslim mother who approaches her child's school regarding concerns about their child's educational development might find the response unsatisfactory and believe she were not taken seriously because of her ethnic background. Given this, she might be reluctant to engage with educational settings in the future. This is likely to create a vicious cycle of avoidance in terms of engaging with schools and colleges, and a vicious cycle of helplessness and passivity in the face of problems her children might face in the future. The manual describes other areas of discrimination, for example at work or when dealing with the white majority community where someone lives, which might also lead to patterns of passive avoidance. Passivity and avoidance do provide a short term solution, as these behavioural responses might reduce immediate negative emotional states, but perpetuate long term patterns of marginalisation and discrimination.

Diagnosis and terms used

Mir et al. (2014) take a very pragmatic view of whether or not therapists need to be explicit about the diagnosis of depression in order for the therapy to be helpful. They note that the bio-psycho-social model does not fully encompass the beliefs of many Muslim service users who also have a spiritual and paranormal set of explanations for their difficulties. Mir et al. also note that the way that depression is manifest in some Muslim communities may also have more somatic components than in the white majority, and that engagement might be compromised by an overemphasis on psychological explanations for difficulties when a physical or supernatural one might be preferred. Given this, it might be helpful for therapists to undertake work without making a specific diagnosis and focus instead on helping the service user 'with the problems you have described' or 'to achieve your goals'. By focusing on what the service user has brought to therapy and by using their terms and frameworks rather than a diagnostic category that may not necessarily be meaningful to them, the therapist is likely to enhance engagement and collaboration in the therapy process.

Avoidance of negative affect

The simple vicious-cycle model which underpins this approach can be expanded to incorporate avoidance of negative affect. The approach makes use of the idea that the desire not to feel bad might be a powerful driver for some service users and that people will tolerate quite significant costs in the short or long term in order to avoid negative emotions. This phenomenon is more often incorporated into formulations for anxiety disorders, but can be very helpful in thinking about depression as well. Where this is the case the manual advises making a clear distinction with the service user between their emotional and behavioural responses (or 'getting stuck', as it is called). This is a useful approach where the formulation calls for an understanding of costs of emotional avoidance. Although not part of the manualised approach, it might be useful to draw up a list of costs and benefits of avoidance with service users at this stage in order to enhance motivation to change.

Emphasis on behavioural rather than cognitive change

Although cognitive change may happen as the result of the intervention, the manual is clear that the emphasis of the intervention is on behavioural change. This seems to be a useful adaptation when working across cultures, as it is one that can fully incorporate ideas about change based on core values whilst avoiding problems about the degree to which particular cognitive styles, or even ways of thinking about thoughts, might be culture bound. This approach has been used in therapy with depressed Latino service users in the USA, a community which faces similar challenges in terms of economic and social marginalisation to Muslim communities in the UK. Santiago-Rivera et al. (2008) summarise this research and note that Latino service users value the practical and problem oriented nature of this approach, as well as it being amenable to adaptation around the cultural values, specific challenges and culturally specific manifestations of depression experienced by this community. Part of this adaptation for Latinos includes activation targets that are culturally specific and take into account the greater degrees of poverty amongst this population. Behavioural Activation might also address specific losses experienced as a result of migration, such as community roles and responsibilities, church attendance and contact with family and friends from the service user's home country. This work with Latino-Americans also explicitly includes looking at goals around acculturation such as learning English and engaging with the white majority culture.

Although there is a consideration of issues regarding acculturation in the manual for working with Muslim communities in the UK, the issue is less straightforward. There are dominant political narratives in the UK relating to the perceived problem of Muslim communities not acculturating sufficiently. Therapists might believe that acculturation would be a useful process for their service users; however. the principle of working towards goals set by service users rather than those set by therapists remains an important one. It could be helpful for therapists to be reflective about their own values regarding acculturation and use supervision as an opportunity to reflect on the degree to which they might emphasise this in therapy to ensure that goals are the service user's rather than their own. One useful exercise that might inform this thinking is the Values Assessment which is provided in full in the appendices of the manual. Again this process looks very similar to approaches used in Acceptance and Commitment Therapy, but is a useful technique to enhance Behavioural Activation by ensuring that goals fit with service user values while also providing a rapid way for the therapist to understand and engage with the values of the service user.

The role of the family

In keeping with recommendations made by Walpole et al. (2013), there is the possibility for involving service users' family members in the Behavioural Activation programme. Even when this is seen as a useful approach, it remains important that the service user has some time in each session on their own with the therapist. There are a number of reasons why this is likely to be helpful. There may be information the service user wishes to discuss or which the therapist is aware of that the service user might not want to be shared with their family members. What information can be shared with whom can be negotiated during this time. The manual authors do caution that it might not be seen as appropriate by the service user or their family for them to be seen alone and that the therapist might need to be flexible about this in order to facilitate engagement. Family sessions provide an opportunity to share the rationale for the intervention with family members, to get their perspectives on why things might be difficult and to think through any barriers or facilitative factors linked to the Behavioural Activation.

At this point the wider family can be involved in ensuring that the service user attends regularly even if they appear to be doing well and have no need for treatment. The manual makes the very helpful point that it might be necessary to emphasise the need for the family to encourage participation in assignments rather than criticise the service user when they struggle to complete them. It might be useful at this point to do some role play with family members to practise how they might do this. It might be also useful to remind family members that the best way to encourage desired behaviours is to praise them when they occur.

Therapists might sometimes find themselves advocating for or raising issues on behalf of the service user with the wider family. Where there are complex family processes in terms of authority and power it might be useful to do this only after the therapist has developed an understanding of these and a good working relationship with the family. This advocacy role might involve negotiating for the service user to have time and resources to undertake specific tasks as part of the Behavioural Activation programme. For example, women in a family might have quite high expectations placed on them in terms of their availability within the household to meet the needs of others. The service user might have identified a particular activity that they would like to do that necessitates some time away from the household, and the therapist can act as a neutral broker with the family to think about how they might adjust expectations to accommodate this. Eldest sons might also find that there are considerable demands placed on their time by younger siblings and parents and that some renegotiation of expectations with the family is necessary as part of the therapy process.

It might also be difficult for some family members to develop friendships or activities outside of the family due to cultural practices. One advantage of a group based treatment for depression in South Asian women described by Gater et al. (2010) is that it is a group format encouraging the development of links outside of the family system. Groups can also be run in settings with links to culturally appropriate vocational, educational or leisure opportunities. When working individually with service users, therapists should make themselves aware of local resources that might meet the need for culturally acceptable activities outside of the home. For example many mosques now run vocational, recreational and educational programmes for Muslim women which have the support of local Imams.

When the service user is a younger unmarried adult living with their parents or a teenager seen in CAMHS, extra consideration needs to be made regarding the role of the family in treatment. In these instances it might be useful to develop enhanced thinking about family processes using the principles outlined in Chapter 3.

This extended assessment of family migration and acculturation allows for greater consideration of any differences in values and perspectives between different members of the family, and some mapping of where the dominant dyads and influential relationships are within the family.

The manual notes that service user may struggle to complete homework assignments or, when they are completed, to record them systematically. This is not something that is unique to Muslim service users. There are a number of options available to address this. It might be enough to use verbal reports in session to get sufficient information to help review and set new homework; however, it is likely that recording tasks between sessions increases the likelihood that they will be carried out and improves outcomes (Thase and Callan 2006). In order to facilitate this, service users could be encouraged to use notebook apps on mobile phones to write down the planned activities and their results. Where there are literacy problems or this is difficult to commit to for other reasons, service users could use alarms on mobile phones as reminders to undertake specific activities, or use the audio recording function to record observations when activities are undertaken. Therapists might also use religious calendars which can be prominently displayed in the service user's home as a means of planning and recording activities. They may have the benefit of communicating a clear message in terms of respect for the faith of the service user and linking Behavioural Activation with religious practice where this is likely to be useful.

Specific faith based metaphors, strategies and approaches

The manual highlights a number of very specific ways that Islamic teaching can be used in the support of CBT and provides an information sheet for service users that summarises these. This resource is available through the link in the References section of this chapter. Some of the Islamic ideas which are brought into therapy to enhance engagement are ideas about stress and challenges in life and the importance of God's mercy at these times. There is an idea in Islam that illness and difficulties are a test from God and that the way to respond to this is with both patience and perseverance. This can help counter the passive response to illness that is underpinned by the idea that it is God's will and therefore something to be tolerated rather than actively addressed. Prayer and reciting passages from the Qur'an are also used as ways to help service users experience some relief from depressive feelings or rumination cycles. There are stories of the Prophet contained in the client information booklet that have been selected to foster hope about the future.

One very interesting idea is used to support service users who are troubled by self-criticism or beliefs about the criticism that others might make of them. The Qur'an teaches that God is forgiving and compassionate and that only God can pass judgement on someone. This idea might allow a service user to break cycles of negative thinking about themselves and begin to see that only God can really judge their actions. This may help improve self-esteem and reduce guilt, although care should be taken to ensure that beliefs such as 'I think I am no good' are not replaced by 'God thinks I am no good'. Service users should be reminded of the compassionate nature of God, with reference to suitable texts to support this.

The manual makes some subtle points about the use of prayer. Service users can use prayer as a way of enhancing their sense of well-being and reconnecting to their spiritual lives if these have been disrupted by depression or life events. Service users should be supported to reflect on whether prayer has become ritualised and so part of a maintenance cycle with qualities similar to those found in OCD. Prayer can also become part of a passive problem solving style and replace active engagement in the changes that are needed to improve the service user's situation. Where this is likely, service users are reminded of the popular Islamic saying that one must 'Tie your camel first and then trust in God'. This saying originates in a story from the life of the Prophet Mohammed (pbuh), who on meeting a desert nomad asked him why he had not tied his camel to something to stop it wandering off. The nomad replied that it was because he trusted in God, and the Prophet told him clearly that he should 'Tie his camel first and then Trust in God'. This is a very helpful distinction to make, as it emphasises the need for active problem solving and change processes in addition to religious faith.

Behavioural scheduling can include agreeing times for religious practice throughout the day. This is thought to be helpful in terms of providing purposeful activities and reducing the service user's sense of hopelessness or isolation. Practice can include prayer, reading the Qur'an and undertaking *dhikr* (remembrance of God). The manual also suggests that some service users will find that talking to God or addressing a diary to God helpful, though only when this fits with the established values and goals of the service user.

There is a possibility that aspects of depression are maintained by unhelpful interpretations of Islamic thought. It might be possible for the therapist to support the service user in understanding these beliefs through Socratic dialogue, but this is not likely to lead to a great deal of change in firmly held religious beliefs. Where this is the case it might be useful to look for more helpful interpretations of Islamic thought through gaining the input of people who will have the religious authority to discuss this with the service user. This might include Muslim hospital chaplains, Imams in local mosques or other community figures who have an understanding of mental health and its relationship to religious thought.

The challenge of faith based approaches for atheist or agnostic therapists or those of different faiths

The manual helpfully acknowledges that not all therapists will be comfortable with integrating religious themes into their therapy practice. Although awareness in terms of cultural sensitivity has become a mainstream part of most mental health training, there is much less consideration of the role of religion and spirituality in mental health. Some therapists might be uncomfortable integrating faith based teaching processes altogether. This may be because their own religious faith puts them in a position of not being comfortable promoting a different set of faith based values, or because their own lack of religious belief and practice makes them uncomfortable discussing faith with others. This might mean that they are unable to make use of therapy developed to incorporate religious values and practice.

It is important that services are able to adapt to best meet the needs of service users, and if this involves incorporating faith based approaches then staff should be supported to do this. However, good therapists know their own limits and it should be seen as reasonable for a therapist to decline to do this work if they feel strongly that they are not able to incorporate these elements into their therapy. Therapists who are using this approach and who are not Muslim themselves might want to explain to service users that although they are not Muslim and are not experts on Islam, they have been trained to incorporate Islamic teachings into therapy. The therapist could add that they that would appreciate the service user working with them collaboratively to support their understanding of how the service user's faith can be used to support and enhance the therapy. Therapists are also advised to keep in mind that the degree to which someone might value incorporating religious practice into therapy might vary across the course of therapy and that this should be an element that is subject to review and re-evaluation.

The role of group based approaches

Social isolation and limited opportunities for making friendships outside of the family system might be part of the maintenance cycle for some Muslim service users, particularly women for whom social expectations are more aligned to spending time around the family home. In order to address this, a short group based social intervention for British Pakistani women has been developed by Gater et al. (2010). This study established the cultural acceptability of such groups, and women in the treatment arm of the study showed clear improvement in their social functioning; however, there was no difference in the depression scores of participants. This is likely to be because there were no specific components in this study addressing the management of depression. A recent study in rural Pakistan (Naeem at al. 2011) has piloted a group based approach to CBT for depressed women which has significantly reduced the depressive symptoms of participants in the treatment arm compared to the control group. This project has led to the development of a CBT based intervention for British Asian women of Muslim and other faith backgrounds which is currently being piloted in the UK.

Safeguarding concerns and spiritual practices

It can sometimes be difficult for therapists to understand the boundary between cultural or religious practices and ones that are potentially physically or emotionally harmful to service users. It can be helpful to seek the advice of colleagues who share the faith or ethnicity of a service user around whom there is a concern if this distinction is not clear. The usual safeguarding procedures should be followed when families are using spiritual approaches to managing mental health problems which seem abusive. Though rare, there are documented instances of abuse done under the guise of spiritually sanctioned approaches in the UK, and this abuse has been seen within many communities and religions. Abusive practices have included beating or starving people with mental health problems in order to drive out the spirits causing the difficulty, forced ingestion of herbal remedies, and involuntary confinement. Child and Adult Safeguarding Teams in Social Services have developed increasingly sophisticated thinking in terms of how to assess and manage this risk. They should be contacted for advice on how to negotiate the sometimes complex boundaries between reasonable and unreasonable cultural or religious practices and may well assess the situation directly if it meets their threshold for risk. If a child or adult is being, or is at risk of being, physically or emotionally harmed by spiritual practices, therapists should see the management of this through referral to Safeguarding Teams as taking priority over the risk of damaging the therapeutic relationship.

Summary

At the moment there is a small but growing evidence base to support group or individual therapy for treating depression in Muslim communities in the UK. There is a clear need to consider the integration of other religious frameworks into therapy. As CBT is considered to be an effective intervention, therapists should be confident in using this approach with Muslim men and women referred to their service. The extent to which therapists will feel able to integrate elements of Islamic teaching into their work will very much depend on their own knowledge and confidence about these modifications and the supervision they have available to support this. In services which serve areas with large Muslim populations, it is worth investing resources in staff developing expertise around discussing and integrating faith based approaches into their work. At the very least, it would be helpful for staff to think about the degree to which faith might be an organising factor in the lives of service users and to see this as a potential resource to draw on to support recovery from mental health problems. The Behavioural Activation manual developed by Mir et al. (2014) provides an excellent framework for enhanced thinking about the role of faith in CBT and a manualised approach for values based Behavioural Activation where transcultural or linguistic barriers might make cognitively focused work less feasible. Values based approaches could be adapted for service users from other faith groups. The next few years are likely to see further trials of CBT for Muslim groups in the UK and other countries which will further inform practice.

Although this chapter has focused on how CBT might be adapted in response to Islamic religious views, the broad principles highlighted seem to be relevant to work with any faith community. Adapting CBT for service users in Uganda, for example (Hall et al. 2014), highlighted the importance of understanding spirituality and the way it interacts with mental health in order to provide more effective therapy. It seems to me that these principles could be summarised as:

Ask about faith and spirituality with the same respect and care that you would when discussing ethnicity and use the principles highlighted in Chapter 2 to do this.

Appreciate that within all faith groups observance occurs on a spectrum from highly religious to agnostic or atheist.

Understand that mainstream religious beliefs and magical beliefs that are more cultural in origin can co-exist even when they might not appear compatible.

Draw on the expertise of colleagues from particular faith groups or religious figures when you are unsure about particular beliefs or practices.

The therapeutic relationship can be enhanced by demonstrating respect for or knowledge about religious or spiritual practices.

Religious or cultural practices might impact on the service user's preference in terms of the gender or age of the therapist.

Spirituality and religion can be a strength to draw on in order to support recovery.

Awareness of your own faith and beliefs about the faith of others will enhance reflective practice and improve therapy.

Asking about and working with a service user's faith and spirituality can be anxiety provoking at first, but is likely to lead to better engagement and a better understanding of the life of the service user, and be a valued part of therapy for many.

References

Almond, P., and Lathlean, J. (2011). Inequity in provision of and access to health visiting postnatal depression services. *Journal of Advanced Nursing*, *67*(11), 2350–2362.

Aspinall, P., and Song, M. (2013). *Mixed Race Identities*. London: Palgrave Macmillan.

Azhar, M. Z., and Varma, S. L. (1995). Religious psychotherapy in depressive patients. *Psychotherapy and Psychosomatics*, *63*(3–4), 165–168.

Caporino, N. E., Chen, J. I., and Karver, M. S. (2014). Preliminary examination of ethnic group differences in adolescent girls' attitudes toward depression treatments. *Cultural Diversity and Ethnic Minority Psychology*, *20*(1), 37–42.

Chaudhry, N., Waheed, W., Husain, N., Bhatti, S., and Creed, F. (2009). Development and pilot testing of a social intervention for depressed women of Pakistani family origin in the UK. *Journal of Mental Health*, *18*(6), 504–509.

Chew-Graham, C., Bashir, C., Chantler, K., Burman, E., and Batsleer, J. (2002). South Asian women, psychological distress and self-harm: Lessons for primary care trusts. *Health & Social Care in the Community*, *10*(5), 339–347.

Chowdhary, N., Jotheeswaran, A. T., Nadkarni, A., Hollon, S. D., King, M., Jordans, M. J. D., Rahman, A., Verdeli, H., Araya, R., and Patel, V. (2014). The methods and outcomes of cultural adaptations of psychological treatments for depressive disorders: A systematic review. *Psychological Medicine*, *44*(06), 1131–1146.

Craig, P., Dieppe, P., Macintyre, S., Michie, S., Nazareth, I., and Petticrew, M. (2008). Developing and evaluating complex interventions: The new Medical Research Council guidance. *BMJ*, *337*.

Gallagher-Thompson, D., Wang, P. C., Liu, W., Cheung, V., Peng, R., China, D., and Thompson, L. W. (2010). Effectiveness of a psychoeducational skill training DVD program to reduce stress in Chinese American dementia caregivers: Results of a preliminary study. *Aging & Mental Health*, *14*(3), 263–273.

Gater, R., Tomenson, B., Percival, C., Chaudhry, N., Waheed, W., Dunn, G., Macfarlane, G., and Creed, F. (2009). Persistent depressive disorders and social stress in people of Pakistani origin and white Europeans in UK. *Social Psychiatry and Psychiatric Epidemiology*, *44*(3), 198–207.

Gater, R., Waheed, W., Husain, N., Tomenson, B., Aseem, S., and Creed, F. (2010). Social intervention for British Pakistani women with depression: Randomised controlled trial. *The British Journal of Psychiatry*, *197*(3), 227–233.

Hall, J., d'Ardenne, P., Nsereko, J., Kasujja, R., Baillie, D., Mpango, R., Birabwa, H., and Hunter, E. (2014). Mental health practitioners' reflections on psychological work in Uganda: Exploring perspectives from different professions. *British Journal of Guidance & Counselling*, *42*(4), 423–435.

Hinton, D. E., Chhean, D., Pich, V., Safren, S. A., Hofmann, S. G., and Pollack, M. H. (2005). A randomized controlled trial of cognitive-behavior therapy for Cambodian refugees with treatment-resistant PTSD and panic attacks: A cross-over design. *Journal of Traumatic Stress*, *18*(6), 617–629.

Hook, J. N., Worthington, E. L., Davis, D. E., Jennings, D. J., Gartner, A. L., and Hook, J. P. (2010). Empirically supported religious and spiritual therapies. *Journal of Clinical Psychology*, *66*(1), 46–72.

Husain, N., Creed, F., and Tomenson, B. (1997). Adverse social circumstances and depression in people of Pakistani origin in the UK. *The British Journal of Psychiatry*, *171*(5), 434–438.

Husain, N., Chaudhry, N., Husain, M., and Waheed, W. (2009). Prevention of suicide in ethnic minorities in the UK. *Ethnicity and Inequalities in Health and Social Care*, *2*(1), 10–17.

Husain, N., Cruickshank, K., Husain, M., Khan, S., Tomenson, B., and Rahman, A. (2012). Social stress and depression during pregnancy and in the postnatal period in British Pakistani mothers: A cohort study. *Journal of Affective Disorders*, *140*(3), 268–276.

Kohn, L. P., Oden, T., Muñoz, R. F., Robinson, A., and Leavitt, D. (2002). Brief report: Adapted cognitive behavioral group therapy for depressed low-income African American women. *Community Mental Health Journal*, *38*(6), 497–504.

Le, H. N., Perry, D. F., and Stuart, E. A. (2011). Randomized controlled trial of a preventive intervention for perinatal depression in high-risk Latinas. *Journal of Consulting and Clinical Psychology*, *79*(2), 135–141.

Linde, K., Sigterman, K., Kriston, L., Rücker, G., Jamil, S., Meissner, K., and Schneider, A. (2015). Effectiveness of psychological treatments for depressive disorders in primary care: Systematic review and meta-analysis. *The Annals of Family Medicine*, *13*(1), 56–68.

Mir, G., Kanter, J., and Meer, S. (2014). BA-M treatment manual. Addressing depression in Muslim communities. University of Leeds: Faculty of Medicine and Health. Resources available at: http://medhealth.leeds.ac.uk/info/615/research/327/addressing_depression_in_muslim_communities.

Miranda, J., Duan, N., Sherbourne, C., Schoenbaum, M., Lagomasino, I., Jackson-Triche, M., and Wells, K. B. (2003). Improving care for minorities: Can quality improvement interventions improve care and outcomes for depressed minorities? Results of a randomized, controlled trial. *Health Services Research*, *38*(2), 613–630.

Naeem, F., Waheed, W., Gobbi, M., Ayub, M., and Kingdon, D. (2011). Preliminary evaluation of culturally sensitive CBT for depression in Pakistan: Findings from Developing Culturally-sensitive CBT Project (DCCP). *Behavioural and Cognitive Psychotherapy*, *39*(02), 165–173.

Nielsen, S. L. (2004). A Mormon rational emotive behavior therapist attempts Qur'anic rational emotive behavior therapy. In Richards, P. S., and Bergin, A. E. (eds), *Casebook for a spiritual strategy in counselling and psychotherapy*. Washington, DC: American Psychological Association, 213–230.

ONS (Office of National Statistics) (2011). *Religion in England and Wales*. London: ONS.

Orsillo, S. M., Roemer, L., Block-Lerner, J., LeJeune, C., and Herbert, J. D. (2004). ACT with anxiety disorders. In Hayes, S. C., and Strosahl, K. (eds), *A practical guide to Acceptance and Commitment Therapy*. New York: Springer, 103–132.

Pilkington, A., Msetfi, R. M., and Watson, R. (2012). Factors affecting intention to access psychological services amongst British Muslims of South Asian origin. *Mental Health, Religion & Culture*, *15*(1), 1–22.

Santiago-Rivera, A., Kanter, J., Benson, G., Derose, T., Illes, R., and Reyes, W. (2008). Behavioral activation as an alternative treatment approach for Latinos with depression. *Psychotherapy: Theory, Research, Practice, Training*, *45*(2), 173–185.

Thase, M. E., and Callan, J. A. (2006). The role of homework in cognitive behavior therapy of depression. *Journal of Psychotherapy Integration*, *16*(2), 162–177.

van Loon, A., van Schaik, A., Dekker, J., and Beekman, A. (2013). Bridging the gap for ethnic minority adult outpatients with depression and anxiety disorders by culturally adapted treatments. *Journal of Affective Disorders*, *147*(1), 9–16.

Walpole, S. C., McMillan, D., House, A., Cottrell, D., and Mir, G. (2013). Interventions for treating depression in Muslim patients: A systematic review. *Journal of Affective Disorders*, *145*(1), 11–20.

Chapter 7

Interpreter mediated CBT

The limits of language might not be the limits of cognition

Overview

In the United Kingdom approximately 785,000 people speak little or no English (ONS 2011). Around 60 per cent of this group are women, and people who speak little or no English are more likely to be unemployed or in low paid jobs. The actual number of people with limited English abilities is likely to be higher than the ONS estimate due to the under-representation of BME groups in census data. Recent migrants, particularly those seeking asylum following political persecution, are also more likely to have little or no English language ability, and this group has greater needs for mental health services than the general population (Hollifield et al. 2002). Within some established communities in the UK, such as those with origins in Pakistan and Bangladesh, there is a history of marriage to community members from outside the UK who may not speak English and who have historically had limited opportunities to learn English following their arrival. This is likely to change within a generation as immigration rules now include an expectation of some level of language proficiency before permission to settle in the UK is granted.

Non-English speakers will have at least the same needs for mental health services and support as English speakers, and in some communities, as a result of increased trauma, poverty and exclusion, the need for services is likely to be higher. The guidelines on PTSD issued by the National Institute for Clinical Excellence (NICE 2005) are clear that interpreters should be used in the provision of CBT with non-English speaking populations and that 'differences of culture or language should not be an obstacle to the provision of effective trauma focused psychological interventions', although, as d'Ardenne et al. (2007) point out, there are no specific recommendations as to how this might be provided.

This chapter outlines different models of interpreting that cognitive behaviour therapists might use and provides a summary of different guidelines on the use of interpreters that are likely to be useful in clinical settings.

Who might need an interpreter

Interpreter mediated CBT is likely to be provided to three groups of people: refugees and asylum seekers suffering from mental health problems linked to trauma and displacement; more established migrant groups who may speak some

English, but not to a degree that would enable them to make use of therapy; and very recently arrived migrants, typically from within the European Union, who have migrated for work opportunities.

It is worth thinking about the second of these groups, as some therapists might find it hard to imagine how someone could live in the UK for any length of time and not develop a reasonable level of English language skills. Migrants who come to the UK for marriage purposes, typically from India, Pakistan and Bangladesh though increasingly also from some African countries, tend to move into areas with well-established migrant communities. Although many community members will speak English, their first language is also likely to be widely spoken even by second and third generation members of that community. Social and religious events will largely be held in their first language and there will be a local network of shops where staff speak this language, meaning that day-to-day activities can take place without the use of English. Where it is necessary to negotiate with official bodies in English this can be done by English speaking family members or through interpreters. There may be a reluctance to attend English classes where these are available, due to expectations that the English speaking world outside of their community is hostile and unwelcoming, the community member having had little or no experience of accessing education in their country of origin, or community values regarding the expectation that women in particular would not need to develop English language skills. More recent migrant groups from within the European Union may come to the UK for work purposes either as competent English speakers undertaking professional or white collar work or as non-English speakers working in manual jobs, where there is little need to develop English language skills for professional purposes and where long working hours and community isolation mean that opportunities to learn English are limited (for further reading on this topic see Duff 2012). Whatever the reason for not speaking English, it is important to bear in mind that it is likely to be a disempowering experience that limits the life choices of service users in many ways.

Tribe and Thompson (2008) make the important point that all service users for whom English is not a first language should be given the option of an interpreter even if they appear to the therapist to have sufficient language skills.

It is important to acknowledge that CBT delivered via an interpreter has additional costs to services. This will include the cost of the time of the interpreter, plus therapy sessions being approximately 50 per cent longer, the time taken to prepare and debrief interpreters, and additional organisational costs (d'Ardenne et al. 2005). Where services provide a considerable amount of interpreter mediated CBT, it is likely to be useful to log this and make commissioners aware of the service level implications of this.

Models of interpretation

The most useful way of thinking about different ways that translation may be used in mental health settings was outlined by Westermeyer (1991). This framework looks at the three way relationship between the therapist, the service user and the interpreter and notes that this is a very different way of organising the process of therapy to the typical two person dyad. The three models Westermeyer outlines and how they might fit with CBT are outlined below.

The black box or linguistic mode

This model sees the interpreter having a minimal role in the relationships during the therapy process. Their role in the session is simply to translate, word for word, what is said by the therapist into the language of the service user and what is said by the service user into the language of the therapist. In this model there is no role for the interpreter to offer opinions regarding the cultural meaning of what is said or the behaviours described, and in this role an interpreter is not expected to develop any degree of ongoing working relationship with the service user or the therapist. Interpreters in this role are effectively interchangeable from one session to the next.

This model has considerable shortcomings. In particular it fails to appreciate the degree to which relationships underpin therapy processes across all mental health interventions. It is likely that the service user will look to the interpreter to build an alliance in a health services environment they are unfamiliar with and that they may value the cultural common ground they may share with the interpreter. Failing to account for this and use it as a positive process in therapy may have a negative impact on outcomes. This model of interpreting also ignores the degree to which cultural practices impact on how distress is expressed and how treatment can be delivered, and the useful role that interpreters can play in helping the therapist understand these factors. Although there may be times when this approach is the most appropriate, it should be used with an understanding of the limitations that it brings.

The triangle

This model sees the therapist and interpreter playing equal but different roles in the therapy session. It acknowledges that there will be an important relational element to the session between the interpreter and the service user, the interpreter and the therapist and the therapist and the service user. The therapist–service user relationship will be mediated by the interpreter in terms of the linguistic component, although the therapist will still communicate directly with the service user in terms of their tone of voice, gesture, use of eye contact, and other non-verbal cues such as time-keeping and demeanour. These non-verbal aspects of communication between the therapist and service user are not universal. For example, in Western cultures eye contact is seen as an important part of the engagement process, but it may have very different functions in different cultures and contexts. In this model, consistency of interpreter is important from session to session wherever possible.

Bilingual co-workers

This last function involves the interpreter having a more active and involved role than either of the models above. A bilingual co-worker is likely to be employed within a mental health team to work with specific communities, will have developed a degree of specialist mental health knowledge through core training or on-the-job training and supervision, and will be able to advise on the cultural adaptation of specific therapies. In this role they will interpret directly but also be able to advise more on meaning, cultural norms and practices, and think with the therapist about which specific therapy techniques might or might not fit with the lives of service users. Bilingual co-workers can also be used where a BME family is English speaking and there is no need for language translation, but where there is still a need for enhanced thinking about culture and context.

Selecting an interpreter to work with

It is useful to think about what is being interpreted as part of thinking about what you might be looking for when delivering CBT through an interpreter. At its most basic level, interpretation involves the word-for-word translation of what is said in one language into another. This is what happens where the translator is in the 'black box' role outlined above. A more involved form of translation entails the interpretation of meanings as well as just words. The translator might convey the gist of what is said and then add their own understanding of what is meant within the cultural context of the service user. They might also tell the service user what the therapist has said but then add further information in order to help the service user make sense of the information being conveyed. It may also include information about non-verbal cues, tone of voice and the degree to which expressed views reflect cultural norms and practices. This approach has more in common with what happens with bilingual co-workers. This way of working needs interpreters to have a more sophisticated knowledge of mental health and of CBT than interpreters who only work with teams on an irregular basis and who have received no formal training might have, but is likely to be more effective in enhancing the quality of the therapy provided.

   Given that the task in CBT is likely to involve more than just black box interpreting, selecting the right interpreter to work with becomes important. This is not as easy as it may seem and needs more consideration than simply identifying the language of the service user and booking someone who speaks that language. Some languages have several local variations or dialects and it may be important to ensure that the service knows which one of these is spoken by the service user before a booking is made. For example, a service user whose country of origin is Bangladesh might speak Bangladeshi, as spoken in the capital Dhaka, as a first language; however, in the UK they are more likely to speak Sylheti, a regional dialect, as a first language and have only a limited ability to understand and communicate in the style of Bangladeshi as spoken in Dhaka.

Care should be taken in choosing an interpreter for a service user from a country where there has been ethnic conflict and civil war. Members of different communities from this country might speak the same language and be identified as being from the same ethnic group as recorded by services, but an interpreter and service user may be from ethnic, religious or political groups that have been in conflict. Where the service user has experienced trauma as a result of this conflict, their ability to work constructively with an interpreter from the community they see themselves as having been in conflict with might be severely compromised. There might, however, be an opportunity for post-traumatic growth and reconciliation through this work; but realistically speaking it is better to assume that an interpreter from what the service user identifies as their own community or affiliate group will be more appropriate.

Lastly the issue of what is expected of the interpreter needs to be considered. If the therapist wants a black box interpretation then the emphasis will be on the shared languages of the interpreter and service user. However, it would seem to be more helpful in the majority of cases to be able to benefit from a cultural consultation and advice as well as direct linguistic interpretation. In this case the ethnicity of the interpreter should also be matched with the service user's as much as possible. This might be an issue when working with a French speaking African service user. Many African countries use French as the first or widely spoken second language, yet these countries differ considerably in cultural practices. An interpreter of European origin or from a different French speaking African country might be able to offer only limited cultural consultation and advice, may not be able to translate subtle aspects of what is being communicated, and may be of limited help in understanding cultural aspects of the lives of service users. This may also be a factor with service users from Spanish speaking Latin America or Arabic speaking North Africa and the Middle East. It is therefore helpful to be as specific as possible when booking interpreters and to be prepared to check their suitability with the service user and the interpreter themselves early on in the session as part of introducing the interpreter or as part of the session review.

It would generally be inappropriate for family members to interpret in a session. Interpreting is a highly skilled process with specific demands in a health care setting. Where family members are brought to an appointment by service users specifically to translate it might be necessary to explain that it is the usual practice of the department to use professional interpreters. Historically, some migrant groups have relied on their UK born or educated children to translate on their behalf. This should never be acceptable in a mental health setting. Using family and friends as translators raises considerable problems in terms of confidentiality and disclosure, as well as increasing the chance that key information which the service user or therapist wishes to communicate will not be communicated if the family member or friend chooses not to do so.

There is also a question as to whether the interpreter might preferably be of the same gender and generation as the service user. It is difficult to make general rules about this, but where the therapy might involve discussions that are related to sexual assault, sexuality or relationships this might be helpful. Once a suitable interpreter has been found, it is best practice to work consistently with that interpreter for the duration of the therapy unless specific problems are identified. Interpreters should be recruited via organisations which adhere to a code of good practice, which includes staff understanding and adhering to the rules of confidentiality, and which offer staff ongoing training and support.

Does CBT delivered via interpreters work?

Although there is a clear evidence base for CBT being an effective treatment for a wide range of presenting problems, there is less of an evidence base for its efficacy when delivered through an interpreter. One particularly impressive study is described by d'Ardenne et al. (2007). Their study compared CBT for three groups of service users attending a specialist trauma clinic in London, all of whom met criteria for PTSD. The groups who were studied were refugees and asylum seekers who did not need interpreters, refugees and asylum seekers who needed an interpreter and English speaking BME service users who were not refugees. This research demonstrated that all three groups benefited from CBT, although gains were sometimes modest. The group that showed the greatest degree of improvement were the service users who received CBT delivered through an interpreter, suggesting that this is a viable way to treat presenting problems even with a service user group experiencing high levels of symptoms and impairment in the context of considerable psycho-social adversity.

There is a disappointing lack of any further research in this area, although there is a body of evidence to support the efficacy of CBT delivered in non-Western cultures in languages other than English. The evidence base for other therapy modalities delivered through interpreters is also very small. This lack of research evidence leaves therapists and service leads with a dilemma: either do not provide any therapy to non-English speakers for lack of evidence regarding the efficacy of this approach, a clearly discriminatory practice, or provide interpreter mediated CBT and use best practice guidelines regarding the use of interpreters, ideally whilst keeping good outcome records to contribute to the evidence base.

Preparing the interpreter

Often interpreters are booked in an ad hoc fashion and there is little consistency between sessions and little or no opportunity to work with the interpreter to prepare them for the particular challenges of work in a mental health setting. A small investment of time in preparation can lead to a considerable improvement in how this interpreting process works.

Training

In some services, particularly where only one or two language groups are represented in the population of service users, a small group of regular interpreters will be used by mental health staff. The interpreters may have full time roles in teams as bilingual co-workers or be regularly employed by the service to such an extent that good working relationships are established. In these instances interpreters may attend team-wide training events or be given bespoke training on mental health issues, particularly regarding the assessment and treatment of trauma where this is a large part of the work undertaken by the team. This training would ideally involve consideration of the effects of vicarious trauma on therapists and interpreters and acknowledge that interpreters may be particularly exposed to this as a result of hearing the accounts of trauma first hand, in the mother tongue of a service user with whom they might closely identify because of similarities in background and migration histories. These regular interpreters might also provide training to the team on the topic of how to best use interpreters or around particular cultural issues and practices.

The emotional well-being of the interpreter

Where this bespoke training and supervision is not provided by services or therapists, there remains some responsibility for the emotional well-being of the interpreter. The majority of interpreters will have had no specialist training in mental health and will not have a clear understanding of the importance of the role of boundaries and self-care when working with people struggling with mental health problems. As part of the work they do with you, the therapist, they are likely to be exposed to a considerable amount of detail about highly emotive events in the lives of service users. This information may have resonance in terms of their own lives or the lives of family members and friends. Even highly trained mental health workers can suffer from vicarious trauma (Sabin-Farrell and Turpin 2003) and interpreters, lacking the years of training and ongoing supervision that makes trauma exposure more manageable, are likely to be more vulnerable to the negative consequences of this. The potential impact of vicarious trauma on interpreters has been recognised for many years (Sande 1998); however, recent work has begun to explore the idea that this exposure to trauma may also lead to post-traumatic growth and personal development (Splevins et al. 2010).

Interpreters might also be asked to give information to service users, such as a diagnosis of learning difficulties or autism in their child, or a diagnosis of psychosis in the service user, that may have profound consequences and lead to strong feelings of sadness or anxiety. Therapists can help reduce the negative impact of this work on interpreter colleagues by carefully working with them before and after the session as detailed below.

Pre-session preparation and post-session debriefs

Ideally, interpreters working in mental health services will have been provided with the training and supervision they need to work in as helpful a manner as possible with the therapist. However, in the majority of cases this will not be the case. The interpreter will probably work over many domains, including legal, physical health and housing, as well as mental health. They are unlikely to have developed much, if any, knowledge of mental health services and models of mental health. They may have some broad knowledge about boundary keeping in their job, but not to the extent that this issue is generally understood in mental health services.

Tribe and Thompson (2008) recommend spending 10 to 15 minutes before the first clinical appointment preparing the interpreter for the work you will be undertaking together. This time can be spent setting out the working relationship you will have together and negotiating how issues such as timekeeping, confidentiality and the debrief will be managed. This will also be a useful time to give an overview of how the sessions are likely to progress and, where the content of the session is likely to include consideration of potentially traumatising material, to prepare the interpreter and check that they are comfortable with this. Technical terms that may be used can be clarified at this time, and it might be supportive and helpful to acknowledge how difficult this kind of work can be when the service user has had experiences that have resonance with those of the interpreter. Tribe and Thompson also discuss that this is the best time to negotiate what kind of interpreting is required and summarise the four main positions that an interpreter might be asked to adopt. These are:

Word for word interpreting – where, as much as possible, the exact meaning of each word and sentence is conveyed in both directions.

Constructionist interpreting – where the meaning or feeling of the words is more important than the literal translation.

The advocate position – where the role of the interpreter involves representing the interests of the service user as well as providing linguistic assistance.

Bilingual co-worker role – where the interpreter also helps the therapist understand aspects of cultural practice that might be important in understanding what is said or the context within the presenting problem occurs.

All of these approaches might be useful at different times, but within CBT it is likely that the bilingual co-worker position is the one that will prove most helpful most of the time. When the interpreter is asked to take this role it might still be important to let them know whether you would like the linguistic aspects of their role to focus on word-for-word translation, or something that is closer to conveying the meaning rather than the exact words.

Following every session it would be helpful to have at least ten minutes scheduled for a debrief. This time could be spent checking with the interpreter about how they thought the session had gone and asking for any feedback and advice they can give you as a therapist in terms of making your work together more effective. This feedback might include practical aspects, such as length of sentences, type of language used and intonation, as well as advice regarding building the therapeutic relationship, such as community specific information about how to convey warmth and positive regard. This time can also be used by the therapist to feed back to the interpreter about what they did well and what you would like to do differently in future. Clarification of any points that could not be fully explored in the session can be sought, and the interpreter might be given the chance to reflect on how the service user presented or on things they said that there might not have been a chance to consider in the session. This is also a chance for the therapist to check in about the emotional impact of the work and to support and advise the interpreter as appropriate if this has been problematic.

The impact on the therapeutic relationship of working with an interpreter

Cognitive Behaviour Therapy usually takes place through a one-to-one relationship between the therapist and service user. Couples based CBT and systemic/ family CBT in Child and Adolescent Mental Health Services are the exception to this. The introduction of a third person to this process can raise some challenges for everyone involved. For the therapist, there is the question as to whether the main relationship is between the service user and themselves, the service user and the interpreter, or the interpreter and the therapist. The relationship between the therapist and service user is necessarily mediated by the interpreter, and the usual ways of establishing and developing the relationship by expressing warmth and positive regard through tone of voice and non-verbal cues are likely to be markedly reduced by this three way arrangement. Some of the barriers might include the service user looking primarily towards the interpreter during exchanges and the closeness that shared language and culture automatically gives the interpreter– service user dyad. Some therapists report feeling excluded from the easy warmth and regard shown between the interpreter and service user during interpreter mediated therapy sessions. As the person with the greatest power and responsibility in the sessions, the therapist should ideally be able to pay attention to all the combinations of alliances and relationships and manage these in the best interests of the service user. In the spirit of active collaboration that underpins CBT, this might involve reflecting on these relationships in the session and asking for feedback from both the interpreter and service user. It might also be helpful to use some of the post-session debriefing time to discuss this with the interpreter, and for the therapist to use their own supervision as an opportunity to reflect on this.

A study by Kline et al. (1980) compared Spanish speaking patients in the United States who used interpreters during the initial psychiatric interview and Spanish bilingual patients who did not use interpreters, and also the members of the mental health team who conducted the assessment. The patients who were interviewed with interpreters reported greater satisfaction than those who were interviewed in English. More than twice as many patients who used interpreters thought the doctor helped them during the initial interview. Interestingly, mental health staff reported that they believed the patients who were interviewed in English felt more appreciated and better understood than those interviewed with an interpreter. The staff members also reported themselves as being more comfortable with interviewing patients in English and it being more helpful when an interpreter was not present. This supports the idea that BME service users value the use of interpreters and rate clinicians who work via an interpreter more highly. It also suggests that whenever English is not spoken as a first language the option of an interpreter should be given, but that mental health staff may not be the best judges of whether interpreter mediated work is indicated or the most effective approach.

Mirdal et al.'s (2011) research involved interviews with psychologists, interpreters and clients involved in what had been identified as successful and unsuccessful interpreter mediated therapy cases. There was a consistent finding amongst successful cases that all participants reported the value of the three way relationship between the service user, the therapist and interpreter. Mirdal et al. (2011) reported that the nature of this three way relationship is poorly understood and, given the general importance of the therapeutic relationship in achieving good therapy outcomes is widely accepted, it does seem to be an area that would benefit from further research.

Penn and Watermeyer (2012) shed an interesting light on what might enhance the quality of the relationships when interpreters worked with mental health staff in South Africa. The study differentiated between 'big talk' (interpreted exchanges that were about service use, assessments and interventions) and 'small talk' (which is not a direct interpretation of what the clinician has said, and which is social in nature, to help align the interpreter and service user). The relationships rated as most successful were those where interpreters worked in more fluid roles and where 'small talk' facilitated trust between the interpreter and client. This study lends support to the idea that verbatim black box interpretation is neither possible nor desirable and that working relationships between all three parties are enhanced by allowing a broader definition of the interpreter's role.

Boss-Prieto et al. (2010) looked specifically at the impact that interpreters had on the therapeutic alliance. In this study, interpreters, therapists and service users were asked to evaluate different aspects of the client–therapist, client–interpreter and therapist–interpreter alliance. The research found that the interpreters' ratings of the alliance were always closer to the clients' ratings than to the therapists' ratings. The researchers suggested that therapists' ideas about the alliances were likely to be more intellectualised and distanced but that the interpreters' and service users' understanding of the alliance was more lived and immediate.

Engstrom et al.'s (2010) research question focused on the ways in which interpreters affect the clinical process. The themes that emerged were predominantly to do with the interpreter's effect on communication and clinical practice. The theme of communication included the use of interpreters as cultural brokers, the possibility of interpreters' inaccurate translation of client responses, the occasional discomfort interpreters feel regarding clinical questions, and the inappropriate linguistic and ethnic match between the client and interpreter. The themes that emerged regarding clinical practice included establishing relationships amongst therapists, clients and interpreters, and the interpreters' complex emotional reactions to clinical material.

Communication and clinical practice emerged as themes in another study on therapists' experiences of working with interpreters. Raval and Smith (2003) interviewed nine Child and Adolescent Mental Health practitioners. They explored potential changes in communication, the content of family responses, the effect of interpreters on the therapy process, and the theoretical frameworks from which therapists draw when interpreters are involved. Similar to Engstrom et al. (2010), communication emerged as a main theme in this study, including possible inaccuracies in interpretation; however, in this study the participants discussed language and its impact on the therapeutic alliance. The therapist participants also described a change in the style of their questioning to simplify their interventions and adapt to both the interpreter's presence and the cultural needs of the client. Raval and Smith (2003) also identified the role ambiguities and power differentials felt by the therapists within the therapist–interpreter relationship. The role confusion created concerns about disempowerment for both therapists and interpreters. These concerns were seen in sessions where the therapists wanted more input from interpreters, but at the same time felt uncomfortable with the interpreters' unsolicited interjections.

How to introduce the interpreter to the service user

It is worth considering the pressure that interpreters might feel under during the session. Some service users may not have a clear understanding of the role of the interpreter and might ask them to provide advice and advocacy that are beyond their remit and expertise. This pressure can be reduced by including a statement about the role of the interpreter at the start of the session.

Preparing the service user for interpreter mediated CBT by including a short introduction during the first session can be a very effective way of setting up how the session will work. It also helps to clarify the roles of each member of the collaborative relationship and to establish appropriate boundaries.

It may also be the case in busy clinics that there is no opportunity to complete a pre-session meeting with the interpreter in order to establish how the working relationship will function. Where this is the case the introduction of the interpreter to the service user can be used to frame this working relationship. This introduction by the therapist might work along the lines described below:

> Hello, my name is Andrew, I am the therapist you will be working with in the service. This is Millie. She is an interpreter who works with our service. Both of us will respect your confidentiality whilst you are working with us here. What this means is that anything you say to us remains private and will not be

discussed with others without your permission. Although I will keep a record of our appointments and will write to your GP to let them know we have met, I will check that you are happy with me sharing any other information I might want to let other people know about and will not share information that you want to keep confidential or private. The exception to this is if I am worried about your safety or the safety of others. Then I might need to talk to other people to make sure that you and other people are kept safe. I will let you know if I am going to do this. The interpreter is not here to give you advice or to help with your problem. Their job is to translate what I say so that you can understand it, and then to translate what you say so that I can understand you. I might ask both of you to help me out if there are things about the way that you and your community do things that I am not sure about. Do you have any questions about that? Are you happy with this way of working together?

This would be far too long a monologue for the interpreter to translate in one go, so it would be helpful to pause after each sentence. You could also ask the interpreter if they have any questions about that, but this runs the risk of the service user feeling excluded from an aspect of the session and it may be a question best left for after the session has finished.

Practical considerations

Tribe and Thompson (2008) provide an excellent summary of the practical aspects of setting up interpreter mediated therapy. These guidelines are summarised below with reference to how this might relate to CBT in particular.

Allow additional time

Both for the session itself and the pre- and post-session meeting with the interpreter.

Avoid complicated technical language

Psychological therapies have many technical phrases and ways of expressing ideas that may not be familiar to the interpreter and which may not be directly translated into another language or cultural context.

Words and ideas may not have direct equivalents

Some ideas which can be expressed in a short sentence in English may take several sentences to properly convey in another language. Tribe and Thompson (2008) caution about the need to be patient if something takes a longer time to translate than expected. After an unexpectedly long translation, the therapist can legitimately check if this was the case. It may be that at times the interpreter is providing the service user with their own opinions or advice, and if this is the case it might be helpful to discuss this briefly during the session or in the debrief. Tribe and Thompson also suggest that a suitable English language medical dictionary should be available to support the interpreter, although they may well attend appointments with their own.

Using proverbs and sayings

Although Tribe and Thompson caution against the use of these in interpreter mediated therapy, other writers on this topic have commented that a discussion of them can enrich the process of therapy as therapist, interpreter and service user collaborate to discuss the meaning and usefulness of particular ways of understanding what has been said in the context of the presenting problem.

Be aware of the risk of losing concentration

Tribe and Thompson warn against the increased likelihood of therapists losing the thread of discussions as sessions take longer and there is a time lag between asking something and receiving an answer via the interpreter. It can help to focus on the tone of voice and non-verbal aspects of the interpreter–service user communication as a means of remaining engaged with the therapy process and looking for additional information that might enhance the formulation.

Checking on the suitability of the interpreter

A service user request to change interpreter should be honoured, but Tribe and Thompson note that it might also be useful to give the service user a form to take away at the end of the first session for them to fill in regarding this, as this would be a difficult question to ask via the interpreter. They note that most service users would be able to find someone in their social circle who could translate the form for them and help them send it back to the service.

Set the room up to enhance the desired relationship between all participants

Some therapists prefer to set the chairs up as a triangle to reflect the equal importance of the participants and the relationships between them in the session, whilst other therapists prefer to seat the interpreter behind the chair where the service user will be sitting. Whatever the choice, it is important for the rationale for this to be considered in advance.

Create a collaborative environment

By communicating regard and respect for the interpreter, the therapist can support them in feeling at ease during the session. The therapist might explicitly or implicitly communicate the collaborative nature of the work, which will enable the interpreter to ask for clarification regarding important points rather than believe that they have to interpret perfectly every time.

In addition it might be useful to consider the following practical points.

Clarity about roles

Ideally interpreters should limit their contact with a service user to one setting (e.g. only interpreting for them in a mental health setting, not on legal or housing matters). In practice, particularly in small language communities, interpreters might have worked with a service user in several settings and this might be unavoidable. Where this is the case it would be helpful to use the session debrief to ask about what challenges this brings to the interpreter's role and to maintain a Socratic and helpful stance to help them clarify how best to manage this.

The content of therapy

It seems reasonable to suggest that the translation of the cognitive aspects of CBT is a more complex process than translation of the behavioural aspects. Even working across cultures in English, there is a recognition that the ways we understand how thoughts impact on our emotions and behaviour is not necessarily universal and that the models we use to describe this in CBT might need considerable modification to work across cultures. This process is even more challenging when done through an interpreter, as terms and ideas may not have direct equivalents. It seems likely however that therapy regarding the behavioural aspects of CBT might be more straightforward to translate. So for example when working with depression the therapist might more usefully emphasise Behavioural Activation and aspects of the intervention that increase social contacts, purposeful behaviour, and meaningful and satisfying activities. Likewise with anxiety disorders, including PTSD, the emphasis might be better placed on habituation as the main model of intervention rather than cognitive techniques, although Chapter 5 presents examples of interpreter mediated transcultural work that includes a cognitive element.

Case example: Kamal, a 14-year-old Somalian young man with PTSD

Kamal is a 14-year-old Somalian young man who had been in the UK for one year when he was referred to Child and Adolescent Mental Health Services. He had been shot in the stomach just prior to coming to the UK whilst walking with friends in the Somali capital city, Mogadishu. The shooting had been a random act of violence and the injuries had been life threatening. At the time of referral Kamal was settled in the UK but had not learnt English beyond basic words and phrases. Though he was of above average

(continued)

(continued)

intelligence, he had received no formal education in Somalia. At the initial assessment it was clear that Kamal was suffering from moderate PTSD. In particular he became very upset and emotionally aroused whenever there was a loud sound (such as a car exhaust backfiring or fireworks), or at gun related violence on television. At these times he was troubled by heightened states of anxiety which he rated as 8 or 9 out of 10 in intensity. He had become highly avoidant of any possible triggers and was vigilant for any gun related content on television. At times of being triggered he described intense visual and auditory memories of the shooting. The problem was formulated with Kamal using a Somali interpreter and he was able to understand the commonly used PTSD metaphor of his memory of the traumatic event being like a book put away on the wrong shelf of the library. This was despite having only recently begun to use libraries and being new to using the English language.

It became clear that it was difficult to access appraisals relating to the incident, and that not having a consistent interpreter to facilitate work with subtle cognitive processes meant that a more behavioural approach would have to be taken. When a graded hierarchy of traumatic memories was developed as part of exposure and habituation work, Kamal reported no emotional response to trauma memories in session. This may be due to the work being interpreter mediated or the prompts in session not being the right ones to bring this about. The therapist sought a consultation from a specialist refugee trauma service and attempted more creative ways of accessing the trauma memories in session using drawing, making scale models and multi-sensory prompts. After six sessions Kamal rated his symptoms as unchanged. At this point the therapist reformulated the problem with Kamal as one of a simple phobia of sounds or imagery relating to gun shots. This enabled the development of a graded hierarchy of stimuli starting with a recorded sound of a gunshot and moving through images of someone being shot in old cowboy movies (which were not very graphic) right up to very graphic movie excerpts of people bleeding following being shot in the stomach. Over seven sessions Kamal worked through this hierarchy, with further exposure work undertaken as homework assignments, and by the end of this further seven sessions there were no symptoms of PTSD or any anxiety responses to environmental stimuli. There were also no intrusive memories of the trauma. When reviewed in school one year later Kamal remained symptom free.

The relatively simple nature of the intervention was very amenable to interpretation and the focus on simple mechanisms proved effective. Not having access to a regular interpreter because of organisational difficulties meant that the rationale for the intervention had to be explained to several different colleagues from the interpretation service. Post-session debriefs established that although some of the interpreters had relatives who had been shot, this form of exposure work was not distressing in itself. It might have been if the interpreter themselves had been a victim of gun related violence or the work involved intensive first person reliving.

Whether to use telephone interpreting

Some services include telephone based interpreting as an option, particularly for minority languages that might not be readily available in local services. Although this approach has the benefit of being easy to access and generally lower cost to the service, a considerable amount of information is lost when only the basic meaning of the words spoken are conveyed. There is less chance to use the interpreter as a resource for cultural consultations and the therapy will not benefit from the considerable gains to be made from the physical presence of an interpreter in terms of helping the service user feel valued and respected.

Telephone interpreting can also be helpful in translating where the information to be conveyed is quite practical in nature (such as arranging subsequent appointments) or where the service user presents unexpectedly and there is a need to have a ready understanding of why they have attended.

Summary

Interpreter mediated CBT presents challenges to the therapist, the service user and the interpreter. However, it can also bring clear benefits in terms of outcomes. Services have a duty to ensure that the service users have a choice about whether to use an interpreter and which interpreter to use. Services also have a duty to take care of the emotional well-being of interpreters and offer them appropriate preparation time before a session and a post-session debrief. Additional training and support for interpreters are also useful. Although it is resource intensive, there is an evidence base to support interpreter mediated CBT.[1]

Note

1 Additional information can be found in the doctoral thesis by Janet Robertson which is an excellent resource for therapists looking for more in-depth consideration of these issues. Robertson, J. (2014). Therapists' and interpreters' perceptions of the relationships when working with refugee clients. Keene, NH: Antioch University New England, available online at http://aura.antioch.edu/etds/177/.

References

Boss-Prieto, O. L., de Roten, Y., Elghezouani, A., Madera, A., and Despland, J. N. (2010). Differences in therapeutic alliance when working with an interpreter: A preliminary study. *Schweizer Archiv für Neurologie und Psychiatrie, 161*(1), 14–16.

d'Ardenne, P., Capuzzo, N., Ruaro, L., and Priebe, S. (2005). One size fits all? Cultural sensitivity in a psychological service for traumatised refugees. *Diversity in Health and Social Care, 2*(1), 29–36.

d'Ardenne, P., Farmer, E., Ruaro, L., and Priebe, S. (2007). Not lost in translation: Protocols for interpreting trauma-focused CBT. *Behavioural and Cognitive Psychotherapy, 35*(3), 303–316.

Duff, P. (2012). Identity, agency, and second language acquisition. In Gass, S. M., and Mackey, A. (eds), *The Routledge handbook of second language acquisition*. New York: Routledge, 410–426.

Engstrom, D. W., Roth, T., and Hollis, J. (2010). The use of interpreters by torture treatment providers. *Journal of Ethnic & Cultural Diversity in Social Work*, *19*(1), 54–72.

Hollifield, M., Warner, T. D., Lian, N., Krakow, B., Jenkins, J. H., Kesler, J., Stevenson, J., and Westermeyer, J. (2002). Measuring trauma and health status in refugees: A critical review. *JAMA: The Journal of the American Medical Association*, *288*(5), 611–621.

Kline, F., Acosta, F. X., Austin, W., and Johnson, R. G. (1980). The misunderstood Spanish-speaking patient. *The American Journal of Psychiatry*, *137*(12). 1530–1533.

Mirdal, G. M., Ryding, E., and Essendrop Sondej, M. (2012). Traumatized refugees, their therapists, and their interpreters: Three perspectives on psychological treatment. *Psychology and Psychotherapy: Theory, Research and Practice*, *85*(4), 436–455.

NICE (2005). *Post-traumatic stress disorder (PTSD): The management of PTSD in adults and children in primary and secondary care*. London: HMSO. www.nice.org.uk/guidance/cg26.

ONS (Office of National Statistics) (2011). Census data. London: HMSO.

Penn, C., and Watermeyer, J. (2012). When asides become central: Small talk and big talk in interpreted health interactions. *Patient Education and Counseling*, *88*(3), 391–398.

Raval, H., and Smith, J. A. (2003). Therapists' experiences of working with language interpreters. *International Journal of Mental Health*, *32*(2), 6–31.

Sabin-Farrell, R., and Turpin, G. (2003). Vicarious traumatization: Implications for the mental health of health workers? *Clinical Psychology Review*, *23*(3), 449–480.

Sande, H. (1998). Supervision of refugee interpreters: 5 years of experience from Northern Norway. *Nordic Journal of Psychiatry*, *52*(5), 403–409.

Splevins, K. A., Cohen, K., Joseph, S., Murray, C., and Bowley, J. (2010). Vicarious posttraumatic growth among interpreters. *Qualitative Health Research*, *20*(12) 1705–16.

Tribe, R., and Thompson, K. (2008). Working with interpreters in health settings. Guidelines for psychologists. Leicester: BPS. Available at: https://www.ucl.ac.uk/dclinpsy/training-handbook/chapters/handbook-pdf/appendix6.

Westermeyer, J. (1991). Working with an interpreter in psychiatric assessment and treatment. *Journal of Nervous and Mental Disease*, *178*, 745–749.

Chapter 8

Why service-wide change is needed to support transcultural CBT

Changing what therapists do in sessions is important in terms of ensuring good clinical outcomes for BME service users, but in order to really ensure equality of access change must take place in terms of how services are organised and in the way that services interact and engage with the communities they serve.

In order to understand how to meet the needs of BME communities it is important to understand something about the way that BME communities use services. This enables services to identify barriers which might prevent BME communities accessing them and then take steps to reduce these barriers. The ideas about access and outcomes in this chapter can be best understood with reference to Figure 8.1. This pyramid is based on the work of Goldberg and Huxley (1980), which provides a way to describe the pathway that someone with a need for mental health services in the community might need to negotiate to get to the point of successful treatment. At each stage of this model the number of people who might successfully negotiate moving to the next stage will be a proportion of the number at the level below, leading to only a small number of those with a need for mental health services being successfully treated.

This model was further developed in Beck (2005) to illustrate the barriers that were likely to make it more difficult for BME service users to move up through each step of the pyramid in order to be able to access the treatment necessary to improve their mental health. In Figure 8.1, we can see that for any population there is a level of need for mental health services, but that not everyone in that community will have their problem identified by someone who can refer or direct them towards the specialist help that they need. This is true for white majority populations as well as BME populations, but there is research evidence to support the idea that BME populations are less likely to have their problem identified by primary care staff and so are less likely to be referred on for specialist mental health treatment. Once someone has been identified as needing specialist mental health treatment the person has to be referred to the right service, attend their initial assessment appointment and then engage with the assessment and treatment process. Even engaging with treatment is no guarantee of improvement, and unless psychological therapies are provided in a way that takes into account the culture and values of BME service users they are less likely to have a successful outcome than white majority service users.

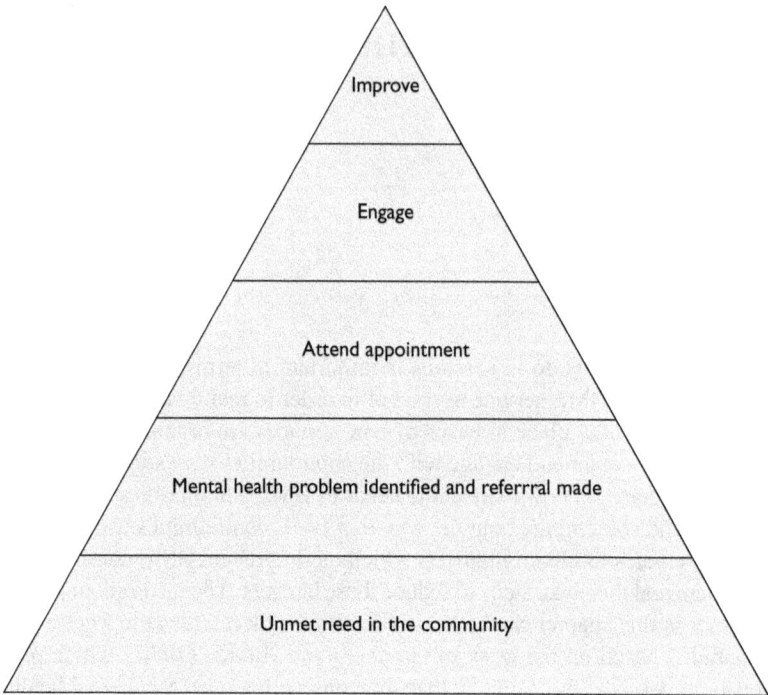

Figure 8.1 The barriers to improvement

In the UK, previous studies have highlighted disparities between the way that white majority service users access services compared to BME communities. Ethnic minority service users are less likely to receive psychological interventions, preventative interventions or aftercare, and are also more likely to be given medication, receive inpatient care or enter the mental health system through criminal justice routes (Nazroo 1998). Black user groups and BME community organisations have also consistently requested better access to psychological interventions (Wilson and Francis 1997).

Each one of these steps up the pyramid towards improvement can be seen as a potential barrier for any service user and it is likely to be the case that people from a culture that is different to the majority are less likely to successfully negotiate these barriers. Some BME community members may be less likely to recognise mental health problems or understand that they can discuss these with their family doctor in order to receive help. They may not know about specialist mental health services or how to access them even when self-referral routes are available. Assessing clinicians in primary care may be less able to identify mental health problems in some BME communities, or may believe that psychology services are not appropriate for BME service users and so may not refer them to specialist treatment teams. The service users themselves may also be less likely to express distress to primary health care professionals. For those who are referred, the way that mental health treatment and services are understood or explained may not fit with their cultural model of distress, leading to non-attendance at first appointments or initial poor engagement. Individual therapists who are less skilled in work with BME service users may struggle to engage the service user through being unable to present a rationale for mental health care that fits with their beliefs about the causes of distress, or may be unable to adapt their approach sufficiently to account for cultural, contextual or family issues that the service user sees as being important. This lack of therapist flexibility will in turn lead to poorer therapeutic outcomes.

The legal and commissioning context for meeting the needs of diverse communities

The Equalities Act (2010) establishes an obligation for UK mental health services to ensure equality of access and outcomes in services irrespective of the ethnicity or religious background of service users. In terms of how this might apply in practice, most of the barriers to successful treatment which service users might need to negotiate will be a result of what the Act terms 'indirect discrimination', that is, a policy, rule or practice that applies to everyone who uses the service but which may disadvantage someone from a minority ethnic or religious group. The Act can be interpreted as meaning that services need to establish whether there are inequalities and then to adapt policies, rules and practices to address any discrepancy that might arise as a result of these. This chapter will provide clinicians and service leads with a broad framework to help them do this.

In the UK, recent commissioning guidelines for mental health services emphasise a number of key points which are likely to have implications for services offering CBT (Joint Commissioning Panel for Mental Health 2015). These guidelines summarise the legal requirements for mental health teams to ensure equality of access. They make a number of recommendations, which are summarised below.

Joint Commissioning Panel for Mental Health key recommendations

There are a number of important points about reducing inequality in terms of access to services and equality of outcomes in mental health services. The ones that are most likely to impact on CBT services are summarised below. The guidelines state:

1   That commissioners have a legal duty to ensure equality of access to mental health services.
2   That commissioners need to understand the mental health needs of their communities and work to understand likely organisational barriers to equality of access.
3   That where necessary specific measures should be used to reduce inequalities and that progress should be monitored.

4   That Clinical Commissioning Groups and Health and Wellbeing Boards have a duty to develop local initiatives and strategies.
5   That there should be targeted investment in specific initiatives regarding BME mental health and that these should recognise the impact of racism and socio-economic inequality.
6   That service users should be involved in any developments aimed at reducing inequality in access to services.
7   That commissioners should ensure that services collect the appropriate data to monitor the service use by BME communities.
8   That care pathways should be better integrated with community and non-statutory agencies to ensure better access.
9   That services should be culturally capable and be able to adapt to the needs of diverse communities.

These initiatives all call for change at an organisational as well as a therapeutic level and are likely to have an impact on the way that services providing CBT work over the next several years. A link to the full guidance can be found in the References to this chapter. The majority of this book is concerned with point 9; however, this chapter looks at service-wide issues that have implications for several other recommendations made in the document. A step-by-step approach to responding to these commissioning demands is outlined below.

Step I – Understanding the population served by your service

In order to begin to understand whether a service is achieving equality of access it is necessary to be clear about the ethnic composition of the population being served. This is not necessarily easy. Census data in the UK is collected every ten years and within a short time period the data is made available by the Office of National Statistics (www.ons.gov.uk). Local authorities and public health departments will have this information readily available, but it is widely believed that census data under-represents BME populations. There are a number of reasons why BME communities might be under-represented. Recently arrived migrants might initially be living in transitory housing and so will not register on any census data. Some people may be wary of participating in official data collection because of uncertainty about their legal status as migrants, tenants or employees, and some might not read English to a sufficient standard to complete the census forms. Because it is only collected every ten years, this data is not responsive to what can be rapidly changing patterns of migration in some areas. Estimates of population data are made available at mid-way points between census reports, but again this is likely to underestimate the size of BME populations.

Given this, it is worth establishing whether local authorities and public health departments have reasonable estimates of the size and ages of BME populations in the area your team serves. These estimates are often made from a range of sources and do not just rely on census data. This will allow your team to make a comparison between the ethnic profile of the population served and the population who are referred to your team. This initial piece of mapping work will enable teams to see how good a fit there is between the population the team serves and the people who are referred.

There are two reasons why this comparison might not be a simple process. The first is that the ethnicity categories used by public health or local authorities might not be the same as the ones used by mental health services. This might make it necessary to collapse or expand categories of ethnicity used to get as good a match as possible between the categories used in service and those used by whoever is supplying the population data. Given that Chapter 2 established how fluid ethnicity is as a concept and how it is best defined by the individual, this is clearly not a straightforward thing to do; but given that the alternative is not to compare the ethnic profile of the population and those referred at all, some flexibility around the use of categories seems like an acceptable compromise. It would be good practice for decisions about how to collapse these categories to be made by a group of interested clinicians so that a consensus can be reached. It might be, for example, that in some areas the number of people of Bangladeshi, Pakistani and Indian origin is so small that it is helpful to collapse this group into the category of British South Asian; however, in other areas these groups might make up substantial numbers of the local population and so these can sensibly remain separate categories in order to discern potential differences in patterns of service use between these communities.

It is likely to be the case that referrers do not routinely report the ethnicity of those being referred, particularly if the referral comes in the form of a GP letter. If services are committed to equality of access it might be important to insist on this information before a referral is accepted, or to ensure that all referrals are via a standard referral form which includes this information. Where local data sharing agreements allow, administrative staff could routinely check this information with the referring agency when it is not given in the initial information.

Where ethnicity is not recorded in the referral and when this information cannot be easily obtained, services have a difficult choice between not looking at whether the ethnicity profile of the area they serve matches the ethnicity of the people referred to them, or making assumptions about the ethnicity of service users based on information available in the referral such as their name and biographical information provided by the referrer. There is also a body of research which supports the idea that reasonably accurate assumptions can be made about the ethnicity of service users based on just their names (Mateos 2014, Morris et al. 2015). This is not ideal, but it is a better option than not recording the ethnicity of people referred at all.

Once someone has attended their initial appointment there is an opportunity to refine the information on their ethnic background. This might be done via ethnicity monitoring forms collected as part of the routine data set collated by the service reception staff in the initial assessment interview. As we have seen in Chapter 2, asking this question is not a simple process and it might be useful for clinicians to make a distinction between asking as part of initial data collection and a more in-depth consideration of this once a therapeutic alliance has been established. It is often the case, even in services with a good degree of cultural awareness and data systems to support the recording of demographic data, that the ethnicity of service users is not recorded consistently.

It is likely that services will have imperfect data about the population served and about who is referred, but this should not be a barrier to at least attempting to map whether or not there is a broad match between these in order to identify if there are any specific communities who are under-represented in the service.

Step 2 – Using audit to support teams to record ethnicity data more consistently

Some clinicians will feel uncomfortable about asking for information regarding service user ethnicity. It is also possible that data systems in teams are not routinely updated with information about the ethnicity of service users or that this information is not consistently collected. In order to see if there are systematic patterns around this, it might be useful to undertake an audit of whether ethnicity is recorded and entered into the relevant database. The audit standard for this could be:

> Ethnicity will be recorded in case notes and on the database for 100 per cent of service users.

This could be done as part of a regular case note audit or as a stand-alone piece of work. As with all successful audits in mental health services, it is important that staff can see the point of and are invested in this audit. When staff believe that an audit is something that is being done to them they are less likely to engage with any changes recommended by the audit. Discussions about how ethnicity is asked about and recorded can still raise the anxiety of staff, so this process needs to be brought up in a sensitive and collaborative way. A cognitive behaviour therapist should find that being collaborative and Socratic is a skill they can use in team meetings as effectively as they do in therapy. Raising the issue using a Socratic approach gives staff an opportunity to discover why this information is important for themselves, rather than being told it is important and something they have to do.

Where the audit finds that some staff are struggling to record ethnicity, this information needs to be fed back to the team in a way that does not specifically identify any one person as being at fault. Good audit does not single out individuals for censure. As part of this feedback it might be useful to do a presentation regarding why this topic might be important. It is worth bearing in mind that some staff will feel a degree of anxiety or sense of threat when this is discussed if they do not ask about or record information about ethnicity. They might communicate this in a way that seems hostile to the idea, or they might struggle to communicate their reasons for not asking service users about ethnic background because of worries that they will be thought of as culturally insensitive. It might be useful to concentrate on bringing about change in the practice of colleagues who are amenable to this in the first instance and not to expend a large amount of energy on trying to change the practice of one or two resistant members of staff.

Once the discussion about the initial audit has taken place, the audit cycle can be completed by re-auditing using the same standards to see if ethnicity recording rates have improved. Once this has been done it is generally useful to revisit step 1, as a more complete picture of the ethnicity of who is referred to the service will now be available for comparison with the ethnicity of the population served.

Step 3 – Looking at patterns of service use

Once services have a good understanding of who is referred, the next piece of work involves looking at what happens next. There are two components to this. The first is about process issues regarding whether people come to their initial appointment, whether they subsequently DNA or drop out of therapy and how therapy ends. In order to do this it can be useful to compare measures such as the number of appointments offered, the number attended, and whether therapy ended as a result of not attending initial appointments, dropping out of therapy following assessment or a planned ending. The second task is to look at clinical outcome measures to ensure that rates of improvement are the same for white majority and BME service users. There are specific challenges regarding outcome measures in transcultural work which are addressed in Chapter 9 of this book.

Analysing symptom severity scores at initial assessment, during therapy and at the end of therapy provides some very useful information. This comparison allows services to understand whether the severity of distress on referral is comparable between different ethnic populations using the service, whether rates of improvement differ and whether outcomes at the end of therapy are comparable. In order for this information to be analysed it is important that clinicians are using outcome measures for all service users. Looking at this data might highlight that measures are less likely to be used for BME service users, which is an important finding in itself.

Case example: A mental health team working with an ethnically diverse area in East London

Beck (2005) describes using this methodology to look at the use of a specialist mental health service in East London. Users of this service were people attending an infection and immunity outpatient clinic which was part of a large hospital trust. Service users who were identified as having mental health problems by medical and nursing staff were referred to the specialist mental health team attached to the clinic. The main therapeutic orientation of all mental health staff was CBT and the team had historically placed a high value on transcultural working, in recognition of the ethnically diverse population served by the team.

(continued)

(continued)

Methods

Therapists prospectively recorded information for each service user during routine clinical contacts. Demographic information including service user defined ethnicity was recorded at the initial session. For data collection purposes ethnicity was initially categorised as one of 19 options. Following discussion in the team at the time of data analysis, these were subsequently collapsed into four broad ethnic categories: White, British South Asian (which included service users of Bangladeshi, Indian and Pakistani backgrounds), Black (which included service users of Caribbean and African backgrounds) and Other ethnicities. Where someone had not attended their initial mental health clinic appointment their ethnicity was recorded using information held on the central clinic database.

The Hospital Anxiety and Depression Scale (HADS, Zigmond and Snaith 1983) was completed for each patient at the first, fourth, eighth and final session. A 5-point visual analogue scale was also used to record the patient's and therapist's ratings of symptom change at the fourth, eighth and final session.

Results

Sample characteristics: A total of 318 patients entered the study. The mean age of the sample was 33.7 years (range 17–69 years). The gender of the sample was 45.4 per cent female, 54.6 per cent male. Using the collapsed ethnicity categories, 71.8 per cent identified themselves as White, 16.4 per cent as Black, 4.9 per cent as British South Asian, and 6.9 per cent identified as Other. A total of 44 per cent of the sample were in paid employment, 6.5 per cent were students and the remainder were on unemployment or sickness benefits.

Referral rates to the clinic: Because the clinic did not serve a geographically defined area it was not possible to compare the ethnic composition of those referred to those in the population served by the clinic. It was, however, possible to compare the ethnic characteristics of those referred for specialist mental health care to the ethnicity to those using the infection and immunity service. It was clear from this analysis that Black and Other ethnicity service users were significantly less likely to be referred for mental health services than White service users, but that British South Asian patients were referred at a rate that was proportional to the number using the infection and immunity clinic.

Level of distress on referral: Chi-square was used to compare HADS scores on referral (collapsed into three categories of case level severity, borderline level of severity and non-case level of severity for both depression and anxiety). BME service users had higher levels of depression on referral than white patients (significant at 0.02, chi-square = 11.25, df = 4) but the same levels of anxiety.

Mean number of appointments offered/attended/missed: The mean number of appointments offered to white patients was 5.7, compared to 2.9 for ethnic minority patients. This difference was significant (at the 0.005 level), and was reflected in the mean number of appointments attended (5.3 for white patients, 2.1 for BME patients, significant at the 0.05 level). However, the mean number of appointments missed (1.3 for white patients, 1.1 for BME patients) was not significantly different.

Therapist and client outcome ratings: Subjective measures of change were recorded at the fourth, eighth and final sessions using a 5-point Likert scale. There was no significant difference in subjectively rated outcomes of therapy by clients or therapists between any of the ethnic groups in the analysis. There was no significant difference in changes to HADS scores over time when analysed by ethnicity. All ethnic groups showed similar rates of improvement over time and the majority of cases went from case to non-case levels of severity.

Therapy ending: Significant differences in therapy endings were found in the analysis (significant at 0.002, chi-square = 34.7, df = 16). Black clients were more likely never to be seen than White service users, or to drop out of therapy before an agreed ending. British South Asian patients were more likely than White patients to DNA their first appointment and so never be seen. Service users from the Other ethnic category were more likely never to be seen than White service users. There was no difference in rates of service users whose ending was agreed or who were referred on to another service.

Conclusion of the study

Malanda et al. (2001) state that a lack of familiarity with ethnic minority cultures means that there is less recognition of distress by professionals and less disclosure of distress by patients, leading to fewer referrals for specialist psychology input. This was partially supported by this case study, as it seemed to be the case that some BME groups were under-represented in the referrals to the clinic and that, for depression at least, the level of distress needed to be significantly higher than for white service users to trigger a referral. As rates of not attending initial appointments and dropping out of therapy were higher amongst BME patients, the overall number of sessions offered and attended was lower for ethnic minority patients. Once engaged, however, both the subjective and objective clinical outcomes for BME service users were as good as those for white service users, despite levels of initial distress being higher. This suggests that accessing the service in the first place was the main barrier but that once BME service users had been referred in and attended their first appointment, the Culturally Sensitive CBT provided by the team led to improvements in service user mental health.

(continued)

(continued)

Subsequent changes to practice in the team

The mental health team worked with referrers to feed back the results of the work and look at ways that they could identify mental health problems in BME patients more effectively.

They worked with referrers to help them explain the rationale for the referral for CBT in order to improve initial engagement with therapy and increase the likelihood of attendance at first appointment.

The mental health team also became more proactive in engaging BME service users who did not attend their initial appointment. This involved changing the service policy of closing a case if the first appointment was missed. Instead, the mental health team called the service user in order to discuss the referral and what the service could offer, and to offer another appointment if this was requested.

Limitations of this case example

This research raised some methodological problems, most notably the validity of ethnicity categories. In order to analyse the data, service user generated ethnicity categories were collapsed into four researcher derived categories. This is difficult to justify from the point of view of promoting a subtle understanding of the interplay between ethnicity and the use of mental health services; however, from a practical point of view it made it possible to identify some important patterns in terms of service use that would not have been apparent otherwise.

Ideally, a follow-up study would have assessed whether the changes brought about as a result of the study had an impact on rates of referral and engagement; however, this was not done.

The findings from this case example are interesting, but may not be applicable to other services. Different populations and different service configurations are likely to have unique challenges in terms of ensuring equality of access and outcomes for BME service users. What is reproducible is the methodology, which would provide a useful framework for specialist CBT services to gain an understanding of whether there is equality of access and outcomes for BME service users. Interestingly, outcomes data from the IAPT pilot sites also indicated that BME service users were as likely to respond positively to treatment as white majority service users (Clark et al. 2009).

Step 4 – Using this approach to analyse data from your team

The most straightforward form of analysis is to compare white majority service users with BME service users on:

- Whether they DNA the first appointment
- How many appointments were offered/attended
- Whether therapy ended by mutual consent or through dropping out of therapy
- How severe the problems were at referral
- Whether the service user improved.

T-tests and chi-square analysis can be used to test whether differences are statistically significant depending on whether the measures are parametric (such as most outcome measures) or non-parametric (such as whether or not there was a DNA). Where there are a large number of ethnicities represented in the study it might be necessary to compress the ethnicity categories into a smaller number of categories. It is more helpful if a decision to do this is made as a team process so that an agreement about the utility and appropriateness of this decision can be shared.

This analysis can be done using a statistical software package such as SPSS. It is usually the case in mental health services that there are trainees from nursing, psychiatry or psychology who are looking for small scale audit or research projects and who will have access to the necessary statistical software. It might be a good idea to collaborate with their supervisor initially and then with the trainee to set this up in a way that meets the needs of the service and the needs of the trainee.

It is much more complex to analyse the population level data, specifically whether the population served by the team is reflected in the population referred and the population who attend. As we have discussed previously, it is difficult to establish the numbers of BME service users in a population and to get information about the ethnicity of those who are referred. Once this has been achieved by services, it might be enough to view the figures and see if the referral rates are broadly the same as the rates you would expect from the population in the area. Again it might be necessary to simplify ethnicity categories at either the population or service level to do this.

Step 5 – Participation as a further way to improve services

The Improving Access to Psychological Therapies (IAPT) programme has placed considerable emphasis on the need to involve service users in participation programmes (Layard 2006). This is in recognition of the fact that services have historically developed without fully taking into account the preferences of service users. Where there is a mismatch between how a service is set up and organised and how it might need to be run to best meet the needs of potential users, barriers to engagement and improvement run the risk of becoming entrenched in the service. A service which listens to the views of users and adapts to meet these is likely to be one that achieves better rates of attendance, better engagement, better clinical outcomes and higher levels of service user satisfaction.

Tambuyzer et al. (2014) suggest that there are a number of factors which have driven the increased recognition of the need for user participation. These include society-wide trends towards greater self-determination and self-advocacy and an increased emphasis on empowerment, civil rights and individual autonomy. These social processes can be understood as having their origins in late twentieth century social and political changes, as well as the mental health service user/survivor movement which became increasingly influential in advocating for the empowerment and involvement of users of mental health services from the 1970s onwards.

The emergence of market perspectives in health care and an idea of service users as customers which began in the 1980s has also contributed to the drive for greater user participation. Having users contribute to the way that services are organised helps to ensure that they are set up in a way that is responsive to their needs. This might involve users being involved in decision making around practical matters such as opening times and how initial contacts from services are arranged. User groups might also contribute to staff training, and to ensuring that the literature and resources developed by services are accessible and user friendly and that the language used to describe services and therapies is respectful and understandable. User voices also give a valuable perspective on how mental health is understood within minority communities and can greatly enhance transcultural working.

Limitations in the way that participation is often organised

The participation process often involves establishing a user group, which meets regularly in a way that looks very much like the kind of formal professional meetings typically held in health settings. These groups are usually chaired by a member of the staff team, and ideas and outcomes from these groups are fed into local management and team meetings. There is no question that these user groups are a valuable part of developing services that place the needs and views of service users at the heart of decision making and service development. But there is a risk that service users who join these groups may not be representative of the majority of users of a service (in that they may be more likely to be from middle class backgrounds, more likely to be white, less likely to be in work or education and so have the time to attend, and may not have presenting problems of the same severity as the majority of users). This may not be a good format in which to hear a breadth of views, as the formal nature of these meetings can be intimidating for some service users. Given this, it is possible that the perspectives of a great number of users will not be heard if this is the only format used to collaborate with users of a service.

The value in specifically seeking out BME service user voices in participation

Although the importance of participation has been recognised for many years (Rose et al. 1998) there has been no clear call for ensuring that user groups are representative of the communities served by mental health teams. Given that stigma may play a considerable role in preventing BME service users accessing mental health care (Knifton et al. 2010) it seems reasonable to assume that many BME service users will not readily identify themselves as having mental health problems and so will be unlikely be able to engage with participation projects to the same degree that white majority users are able to.

It is therefore important that participation projects within teams include a commitment to ensuring that they reflect the ethnicity of the population served. This means that where the team serves a diverse population the project should look at ways of facilitating the involvement of BME groups. One model which may be helpful is described in detail in Beck et al. (2005). This work looked at improving access to sexual health services amongst the Bangladeshi population of Tower Hamlets. It was clear that establishing a participation group made up of Bangladeshi service users to inform service development was unrealistic. Instead the process of adapting services to meet the needs of the local community was started by developing a stakeholder group comprised of professionals who were from and could speak for the local community.

What is the local community?

One problem often faced by statutory services is a lack of clarity as to what constitutes the community and who is able to speak on their behalf. Typically community consultation is done with community leaders who are often older, male, used to dialogue with statutory organisations and more likely to be linked to religious institutions. These views are unlikely to be representative of the wider community, but they are the views that are most typically heard by statutory services. In the participation project described in the next case example, the team set out to establish a diverse steering group in order to understand a wide range of views about the service.

Case example: Working with the Bangladeshi community of Tower Hamlets (Beck et al. 2005)

Everyone on the steering group was of Bangladeshi background, but in establishing the group the project team considered worked to ensure that a diverse range of Bangladeshis were represented. The age of members ranged from youth workers who were in their early 20s and working with adolescents to professionals in their 50s working with adults over 65 years of age. The steering group included first and second generation British Bangladeshis, a member of a project working with LGBT Bangladeshis, an academic who was a member of the community and a senior Imam from a local mosque. Thus, secular and religious, first and second generation, young and old, male and female, and heterosexual and gay voices were included in the process of thinking about service development.

(continued)

(continued)

An iterative process of developing, asking, interpreting and refining questions

This steering group helped the participation team develop appropriate research questions about service configuration, unmet needs and preferences in terms of clinical care. These questions were then taken to local community members through quantitative questionnaires or qualitative interviews in order to develop provisional ideas about how to improve the service. These initial research findings were then taken back to the steering group, which helped to interpret the answers and further refine research questions. This iterative process allowed the participation group to consider the voices of community members who were not accessing the service, and those who were accessing it but who would not have felt able to join a formal participation group.

Outcomes of the participation project

The research findings in themselves are not relevant to CBT services but are reported in Beck et al. (2005); however, the methodology is one that could be used to enhance the way that a CBT service engages with and understands the needs of particular BME communities. The impact of this particular project on the service was both practical and subtle, and similar benefits are likely to be felt by CBT services developing projects using this model. In terms of how the clinic was run, resources were identified to develop bilingual co-worker posts. These posts, one male and one female, were developed in response to a preference for same-gender workers from their own community expressed by older participants in the study. Developing these posts meant that specialist clinicians could work with a bilingual co-worker colleague and, where necessary, benefit from interpretation or cultural information and guidance. A preference for older workers was expressed by older members of the community, whereas younger members of the community expressed a preference for workers closer to their own age. One consistent finding was that members of the Bangladeshi community of all ages did not access the service because of worries about confidentiality, or that they might not disclose specific information to their worker because of worries about this. Many members of the community were particularly worried about confidentiality where the worker or reception staff were from their own community. As a result of this concern, information disseminated about the service was adapted to emphasise its confidential nature and staff were encouraged to take additional time to explain how confidentiality worked at the initial assessment session.

In more subtle terms, there was shift in how key members of the Bangladeshi community in the steering group understood the service, and

> this in turn facilitated better use of the service by community members they were in touch with. As a result of the links developed during the project, the service was also able to publicise itself through Friday sermons in local mosques, Ramadan radio and community newspapers. Bringing members of the community into the service in a more equitable relationship, and subsequent joint training events with local mosques which explored assumptions about community values and ideas, were also invaluable in helping staff, who were on the whole from white majority backgrounds, to better understand the values and cultures of the local community. The qualitative research published from this work led to a wide dissemination of both the methodology and the findings, which were of interest to other services working with South Asian communities.

It seems that an important step in adapting CBT for work with service users from BME backgrounds could be to start a community engagement project in order to bridge the gap between staff and the populations served. As BME communities are likely to have a plurality of voices and perspectives on how services might adapt to meet their mental health needs, this work needs to go beyond listening to the easily heard voices of community leaders and a narrow range of service users who are willing to be involved in a more traditional participation process.

Improving the way that clinicians understand their local communities is likely to positively impact on the way service users progress through all steps of the pyramid (Figure 8.1) in order to achieve successful outcomes. There is likely to be better community recognition of need, more referrals in to the service and better engagement with the service following referral. Service managers are also likely to be supportive of practical and structural changes which might facilitate these processes if the suggestions are backed by research evidence and the support of community steering groups. Furthermore, staff, being better sensitised to community values and cultural practices, are better able to engage users, understand how to adapt therapies and, ultimately, have better treatment outcomes.

Step 6 – Ensuring service managers and staff members support change

It is vital that both service managers and staff, support work which looks to change the way services are run. If projects looking at service use and participation are going to lead to improvements in the way that BME communities access and benefit from CBT then this work needs to be broadly understood and supported by the service leads and service managers who can make these changes happen. If a colleague's first real exposure to a BME participation project is when they are presented with findings which show the service is not doing very well in some areas and suggestions from service users as to how to improve things, they are less likely to get behind the changes that need to take place. One way to ensure staff ownership of the project is to begin to think about these issues with the whole staff group before the project starts. Team meetings or academic presentations can be used to raise this topic and find out what the thoughts of colleagues are about BME access and outcomes within the service. Ideas regarding how to better understand these issues should ideally be developed collaboratively across the whole team.

Typically at this stage it will be clear that some colleagues are very interested in this but that some are not. It is likely to be very difficult to change the minds of people who are not interested, so at this stage developing a working group of interested colleagues might be a good way forward. Ideally this should represent the different disciplines in the team and have some input from or report to a service manager. It might be worth starting a project like this by presenting general information regarding patterns of service use amongst BME communities to the staff group in order to begin to build interest in this area. This might lead to some initial interest in mapping the ethnicity of the local population and the users of the service. It might be helpful to see the work as a staged project, with each stage being fed back into the team to develop and refine ideas for the next stage of the project. Although this is time consuming it does ensure that these issues remain on the agenda of the team and that the project can incorporate the interests of team members as it progresses.

Service managers should be aware of the legislative framework that emphasises the need to ensure equality of access to services, but might need to be convinced that it is worth allocating valuable staff time to a project like this. Generally, IT improvements in departments have made collating and analysing data easier and less resource intensive. Managers might also be more likely to support a project like this if trainees from disciplines working with the team are used to doing the majority of data collection and analysis.

The ethnicity of staff involved with this sort of project or research is also a topic worth considering. Often it is BME staff members who take a lead in raising issues and undertaking audit or research looking at how BME service users make use of services. Staff from minority communities can often bring a great deal of expertise to teams in terms of helping white majority staff develop a better understanding of subtle cultural issues that might take place in therapy or in the use of services. But if the sort of work outlined in this chapter is done wholly by BME staff then this might reduce the likelihood that white majority staff feel invested in understanding how the service is used and perceived by BME communities. There is a risk that thinking about diversity issues then becomes something that only staff from BME backgrounds do, rather than something that is an important part of everyone's practice. Staff who do not see this sort of thinking as important to their own work may be less likely to invest in bringing about the necessary changes to improve the experience of BME communities using the service. Ideally, staff working groups looking at diversity issues should be diverse themselves and include representation from BME and white team members.

Step 7 – Getting to know the area you work in and the community you work with

This chapter has looked at several approaches which will support therapists, service managers and commissioners in understanding the BME communities they work with. However, there are also other more straightforward and enjoyable approaches that staff can take in order to do this. These are to get to know the area they serve and the lives of the people who live there outside of clinical settings. This might involve using lunch breaks, evenings after work and weekends to engage with the cultural life of the locality. Joining the boards of community organisations provides opportunities to get to know community members as colleagues, not just as service users, and cultural knowledge and understanding will be developed as a result.

It is also greatly enriching to get to know the music, films and literature of the communities you work with. Some of the literature from particular BME communities might be about the migrant experience and some about life in the country of origin, but both will illuminate the therapist about aspects of cultures they might otherwise only ever get to know in a health service setting. Music can be another route into new cultures; this might be the music of the country of origin or music created in the destination country following migration which incorporates the music of both countries. Films might be harder to access unless the community is from an English speaking country, as foreign language films are seldom available in subtitled form unless they are made with an international audience in mind. Finally, non-fiction about the history of particular countries can provide the therapist with a richer knowledge regarding the lives of the communities in their area. This information might sensitise them to the struggles that service users or their families might have faced or make staff aware of the richness of cultures and histories that have been left behind by migrant families.

During the time I worked in Tower Hamlets I became aware that I had no real knowledge about the lives of the Somali families I worked with. One evening after work I went to a local Somali café and asked for advice about what to eat. This led me to becoming a regular customer and I was recognised and drawn into conversations with the Somali men who ate there regularly. We would discuss the news, broadcast continually on a television in the corner of the café, the situation in Somalia and local politics. Doing so made me interested in reading about the history of Somalia and enhanced my ability to understand the lives of the families I was working with. I also subsequently took an opportunity to become linked with a project working with Somali families and had the opportunity to develop working relationships with Somali professionals, which again enhanced my understanding of this community.

Summary

Although the majority of this book is concerned with what happens at the therapeutic level, improving access to and outcomes within services needs to happen at the service and community level as well. Improving therapy practice in isolation will have only limited benefits for BME service users if the issues in terms of access to services and service-wide responsiveness to the needs of BME communities remain unchanged. Collecting and analysing data provides services with quantitative information about who uses services and likely local barriers to this. Developing community participation groups helps services gain a better qualitative understanding of the values and practices of their local communities, and can ensure that key members of the local community gain an understanding of how the service works and the values and practices of mental health staff.

This work has resource implications. It takes time to do it, and improving access may well increase demand for the service. At times when services are busy and struggling to meet existing demands this might not be welcome; however, it is likely that commissioners will be interested in this work and will see services proactively thinking about these issues in a positive light. There is also no doubt that team-wide thinking about culture and ethnicity can genuinely enrich the work that therapists do and provide welcome topics to stimulate and inspire staff in their therapeutic work. Community participation events can also contribute to changing attitudes within communities and help reduce stigma associated with mental health problems.

References

Beck, A. (2005). Identifying institutionalised racism in psychology services: A prospective, quantitative study of ethnic minority service use and treatment outcomes in a sexual health/HIV service. *Clinical Psychology, 49*, 36–40.

Beck, A., Majumdar, A., Estcourt, C., and Petrak, J. (2005). 'We don't really have cause to discuss these things, they don't affect us': A collaborative model for developing culturally appropriate sexual health services with the Bangladeshi community of Tower Hamlets. *Sexually Transmitted Infections, 81*(2), 158–162.

Clark, D. M., Layard, R., Smithies, R., Richards, D. A., Suckling, R., and Wright, B. (2009). Improving access to psychological therapy: Initial evaluation of two UK demonstration sites. *Behaviour research and therapy, 47*(11), 910–920.

Equalities Act (2010). London: HMSO.

Goldberg, D. P., and Huxley, P. (1980). *Mental illness in the community: The pathway to psychiatric care.* London: Tavistock Publications.

Joint Commissioning Panel for Mental Health (2015). *Guidance for commissioners of mental health services for black and minority ethnic communities.* London: JCPMH. Available at: www.jcpmh.info/resource/commissioning-mental-health-services-for-bme-communities/.

Knifton, L., Gervais, M., Newbigging, K., Mirza, N., Quinn, N., Wilson, N., and Hunkins-Hutchison, E. (2010). Community conversation: Addressing mental health stigma with ethnic minority communities. *Social Psychiatry and Psychiatric Epidemiology, 45*(4), 497–504.

Layard, R. (2006). *The depression report: A new deal for depression and anxiety disorders* (No. 15). London: Centre for Economic Performance, LSE.

Malanda, S., Meadows, J., and Catalan, J. (2001). Are we meeting the psychological needs of Black African HIV-positive individuals in London? Controlled study of referrals to a psychological medicine unit. *AIDS Care, 13*(4), 413–419.

Mateos, P. (2014). Classifying ethnicity through people's names. In Mateos, P., *Names, Ethnicity and Populations*. Berlin, Heidelberg: Springer-Verlag, 117–144.

Morris, M., Woods, L. M., and Rachet, B. (2015). A novel ecological methodology for constructing ethnic-majority life tables in the absence of individual ethnicity information. *Journal of Epidemiology and Community Health, 69*(4), 361–7.

Nazroo, J. (1998). Genetic, cultural and socio-economic vulnerability? Explaining ethnic inequalities in health. *Sociology Health & Illness, 20*(5), 710–730.

Rose, D., Lindley, P., Ford, R. (1998). *In our experience: User focused monitoring of mental health services in Kensington and Chelsea and Westminster Health Authority*. London: Sainsbury Centre for Mental Health.

Tambuyzer, E., Pieters, G., and Van Audenhove, C. (2014). Patient involvement in mental health care: One size does not fit all. *Health Expectations, 17*(1), 138–150.

Wilson, M., and Francis, J. (1997). *Raised voices: African-Caribbean and African users' views and experiences of mental health services in England and Wales*. London: Granta.

Zigmond, A. S., and Snaith, R. P. (1983). The Hospital Anxiety and Depression Scale. *Acta Psychiatrica Scandinavia, 67*(6), 361–370.

Chapter 9

How confident can clinicians be about using outcome measures across cultures?

Overview

One of several significant developments in mental health practice in recent years has been the widespread introduction of the routine use of clinical outcome measures in services. Although measures have been used by clinicians for many years they have typically been used in an ad hoc fashion rather than systematically across a whole service, and the choice of measure was left to the clinician. The use of measures brings many advantages. For service users and clinicians, it provides an objective measure of the severity of the presenting problem, and both enables them to track changes in severity over time and provides an opportunity for this information to be incorporated into formulations and therapy. The regular use of session-by-session measures has also been found to significantly improve service user outcomes when compared to service users where measures are only used at the beginning and end of therapy (Anker et al. 2009, Reese et al. 2009). Service managers and commissioners also increasingly see the collection and analysis of measures as an important way of understanding effectiveness at a therapist and a team level, and in England and Wales this information is collated centrally by the Department of Health in order to support the planning and funding of mental health services for children and adults.

Most mental health services have clear expectations in terms of which outcome measures will be used with service users, yet these service-wide arrays of measures typically make no allowance for the degree to which they might or might not be appropriate for BME service users. As Goldberg (2010: 225), one of the most eminent psychiatrists of his generation, said:

> It is quite possible that depression manifests itself differently in different cultures, or at different ages, or between men and women. If that is so, a measure which implicitly imposes a universal definition of depression on the whole world might be mistaken.

This problem of cultural variance is likely to be true for all presenting problems seen by cognitive behaviour therapists. If we accept the idea that CBT needs to be adapted to reflect culture and context then it follows that how we measure symptom severity and change over time will also need to be adapted.

Adapting measures of mental health problems across cultures

Flaherty et al. (1988) propose a model for adapting measures across cultures. This framework is a useful one for clinicians interested in whether measures that they might use have been subject to an appropriate level of transcultural adaptation. It also provides a way of thinking about what a service might need to do in order to adapt existing measures where this work has not been done previously. The approach incorporates the direct translation of terms used in measures, and the ideas that the way mental health problems are expressed is mediated by culture and that some disorders may be culturally specific and have no direct equivalent across ethnicities. Although the assumption in these stages of adaptation is that the test is being adapted across languages and across cultures, it is possible that some tests may be adapted from one English speaking culture to another. In this instance these stages would still need to be followed, as the cultural manifestation of distress may still differ between cultures and terms and idioms in one English speaking country may not be the same in another. The five levels of transcultural adaptation that this approach recommends are:

Content equivalence

That is, the extent to which the content of each item on the questionnaire is relevant to the way a particular disorder is expressed in the cultural setting in question. This is important where there is reason to believe that a particular disorder is culturally mediated in some way. This could only really be established through extensive population based research looking in some detail at how distress is manifest in different communities. For a particular disorder in any particular community it is possible that this work has already been carried out, for example by the World Health Organization. This primary research can then be used as a basis for adapting outcome measures.

Syntax equivalence

This is the idea that the meaning of each item on the test should remain the same when it has been changed from the original language to a new one, and that this consistency of meaning might need to include thinking about the direct equivalence of words, sayings and colloquialisms. This is usually established through back translation, where the test is first translated into the new language by a panel of bilingual practitioners with expertise in mental health and then translated back into the original language by a new group of experts. Where a good level of syntax equivalence has been achieved the resulting measure should have much in common with the original one, and where there are significant differences the research team has the opportunity to look in detail as to why this might be the case.

Technical equivalence

This relates to whether the particular assessment method (which is usually pencil and paper) is comparable in the culture the test was designed for and the one it is being adapted for. It is difficult to see how this could be established without research comparing culturally mediated styles of communication, but it is still a factor that needs to be considered.

Criterion equivalence

This relates to whether the interpretation of the measurement of a particular test variable remains the same when it is being compared to the norm for the cultural group in question. For example, the cut-off point above which someone can be thought of as being depressed in one culture might not be the same in another as a result of the different ways that depressive symptoms are expressed. This is a very difficult point to establish without primary research which specifically establishes the norms for this test in the population it is being adapted for. Again it is possible that, for a particular disorder in a particular community, this work has been undertaken by an international body such as the WHO.

Conceptual equivalence

This relates to whether the measure is looking at the same mental health problem (such as OCD or Panic Disorder) in the culture the test was developed for and the one it is being adapted for. This question relates to the question about whether mental health problems are universal processes, perhaps only differing in terms of specific cultural manifestations, or whether they are different and distinct manifestations of distress. It is likely that some diagnoses are more culture bound than others, and that clinicians can be fairly confident that something like OCD has the same processes across many different cultures but that a disorder such as Chronic Fatigue Syndrome might not.

Salvador-Carulla and Gonzalez-Caballero (2010) conclude that the process of establishing the reliability and validity of transcultural tests is extremely difficult, time consuming, and may still often lead to unsatisfactory results. They acknowledge that the resource intensive nature of adapting and translating new tests is seldom undertaken and that it might be better to develop new disorder specific tests from scratch for each cultural group. This process would need a lot of resources and will not be feasible in a service where people from many different ethnic groups are routinely seen.

The need for caution when using measures with BME service users

Tribe and Thompson are clear in their recommendations regarding the use of measures developed in one cultural context for service users from another. They say that clinicians 'need to be extremely cautious in the use and interpretation of psychometric tests' (Tribe and Thompson 2008: 15), and that failing to use extensive test adaptation procedures such as those outlined above is likely to compromise the usefulness of the tests used. There is a risk that tests might not be measuring what the clinician and service user think they are measuring and so will not be helpful in providing measures either of problem severity or of change over time. Service users who are shown a graph of their disorder severity scores remaining unchanged when they feel considerably better, or service users who are shown a graph of their symptoms improving when they are feeling with worse, will find this confusing and may lose confidence in the therapist.

Given the lack of adapted tests available in services, cognitive behaviour therapists working with BME service users are faced with a difficult choice. Do they use mandatory measures within their service, knowing that they may not be valid or reliable for the service user they are working with and may not reflect the lived experience of many BME service users? Should therapists in this situation ask interpreters to support the administration of tests with non-English speaking service users, knowing that the answers given may not reflect the mental health difficulties they are supposed to measure? Faced with service level expectations, clinicians may well find themselves using tests with BME service users when they are not confident about how reliable and valid a particular test actually is.

Measures used in CBT research with BME service users

There is some good quality research into the efficacy of CBT for BME service users, and what research is available does provide some ideas regarding which outcome measures might be helpful. In most of the instances described below the measures were not subject to the process of extensive cultural adaptation described previously in this chapter. The choice of measures by clinicians who are experienced in working within this area can at least be considered as practice based evidence. What is meant by this is that evidence for the usefulness of these tests will have developed through clinical expertise and experience rather than through primary research.

Measures for PTSD

The Impact of Events Scale (Horowitz et al. 1979) is used as the main outcome measure by d'Ardenne et al. (2007) for PTSD symptoms, with the Beck Depression Inventory (Beck et al. 1996) and the Manchester Short Assessment of Quality of

Life questionnaire (Priebe et al. 1999) used as additional measures of mental health and overall functioning. Hinton et al. (2006) evaluated the Clinician Administered PTSD Scale for Cambodian refugees and found it to have adequate psychometric properties. Although this evaluation process has not been undertaken with other ethnic groups, the measure is used extensively in the research studies reported by Hinton. Hollifield et al. (2013) have evaluated a generic mental health screening instrument for refugees (the Refugee Health Screener-15) that may also be helpful in mental health services working with this user group. Only three ethnic groups were included in the development trials; the instrument was found to have good reliability and validity for two of these groups but not the third.

Measures for Panic Disorder

Research into the treatment of Panic Disorder in India (Manjula 2014) has used the Panic Disorder Severity Scale (Shear et al. 1997) and the Agoraphobic Cognitions Questionnaire (Chambless et al. 1984), and both measures appear to have had good face validity and the sensitivity to demonstrate change over time with English and non-English speaking service users.

Measures for depression

In the research trials of CBT for depression with BME groups summarised in the meta-analysis by Chowdhary et al. (2014), the outcome measures used varied considerably.

The Beck Depression Inventory (Beck et al. 1996) was used in four of the studies, and this measure has been subject to research to establish its validity and reliability across cultural and linguistic groups. The Hamilton Rating Scale for Depression (Hamilton 1960) was also used in four studies and has also been subject to extensive research in terms of its cross-cultural utility despite Bagby et al. (2004) describing it as more of a 'lead weight' than a 'gold standard' as a measure of depression. One study used the Global Health Questionnaire-28, an instrument which has benefited from extensive validation by the World Health Organization in different languages and cultural settings (Goldberg et al. 1997). The Patient Health Questionnaire was used in one study, and has also been validated in a transcultural mental health setting (Huang et al. 2006) and found to have a reasonable degree of reliability and validity amongst four major ethnic minority populations in the USA. One study in rural Pakistan used an adapted Hospital Anxiety and Depression Scale (HADS, Zigmond and Snaith 1983), which has also benefited from considerable transcultural validation research but which measures anxiety in general rather than disorder specific symptoms. Beck (2005) also used the HADS in an ethnically mixed study population in the UK, where it appeared sensitive enough to show change over time and across the varied ethnic groups represented in the study.

Measures for OCD

The Yale-Brown Obsessive Compulsive Scale (Y-BOCS, Goodman et al. 1989) is widely used in transcultural settings, as is the child version of this measure. For example it has been used to look at OCD in Turkey (Tek and Ulug 2001), India (Okasha et al. 1994) and Pakistan (Gadit 2003), and in ethnically diverse clinics in the United States (Friedman et al. 2003).

General measures

Within CAMHS, the Strengths and Difficulties Questionnaire (Goodman 1997) is widely used in initial assessments and has been extensively translated and validated across cultural and linguistic groups. It is not useful as a session-by-session outcomes measure tool for cognitive behaviour therapists but could be used for initial assessments and at the end-of-therapy review.

Choosing transcultural measures for your service

Given the difficulties in assuming that measures can be used uncritically across cultures, it might be useful for services to look at which outcome measures are preferred by managers and commissioners. Once this has been established, staff would need to check whether there are versions available in the languages most likely to be used in the service and whether these have been validated for the particular population groups most likely to be referred. Where the majority of BME service users are second and third generation migrants who speak English as a first language, clinicians might be justified in using standard measures; however, this should still be done with some sensitivity to the idea that how mental health problems manifest within different cultures may still have some bearing on whether the measures are a valid reflection of underlying problems. Where appropriate validation has not been undertaken and where clinicians are not confident about the reliability and validity of the measures available, it might still be possible to measure change in functioning over time using Goals Based Outcomes and the Outcome Rating Scale.

Goal Based Outcomes

One outcome measure that is likely to have both reliability and validity across cultures is service user ratings of progress towards their goals. Goal Based Outcomes scales are part of the routine measures in many services, and establishing and measuring progress towards goals will be part of routine practice for most cognitive behaviour therapists. It is likely that in the first or second session the therapist and service user will have agreed a clear set of Specific, Measurable, Attainable, Relevant and Timely (SMART) goals and that as therapy progresses the service user will be regularly asked to rate how close they are to achieving their goals on a ten-point scale. Many services have data collection systems which include Goal Based Outcomes, and it might be that these are the most valid and reliable measures of change over time for some service users. They have the advantage of being trans-diagnostic, which is useful where there are questions regarding whether Western models of diagnosis are a good fit for the difficulties experienced by a particular service user.

The Outcome Rating Scale

In CAMHS and adult mental health teams in the UK, the service-wide data sets include the Outcome Rating Scale (ORS) developed by Miller et al. (2003). This visual analogue scale provides a clear way of tracking change over time, and although it has not been widely validated across cultures it does seem to have a good degree of face validity. The scale asks service users to rate how well they have been doing overall (their general well-being), individually (their personal well-being), interpersonally (their family and personal relationships) and socially (their work, school and friendships). It is not clear whether a visual analogue scale like this is wholly valid across all cultures, and so this scale should still be used with some degree of caution. Therapists should be prepared to check whether it has meaning and validity with interpreters and service users when in doubt. The terms used for each of the four scales that make up the ORS can be easily translated in session and there does not appear to be much cultural loading on the four domains listed above, although the degree to which each of them is important to a particular individual may be related to their cultural background. The measure is likely to be sensitive enough to show change over time, and there can be considerable advantages for therapy in checking on changes in these domains on a weekly basis and using a Cognitive Behaviour framework to formulate the reasons for improvements or set-backs.

The Work and Social Adjustment Scale

This scale (WSAS, Mundt et al. 2002) is widely used in adult IAPT services. It is similar to the ORS in that it asks for self-ratings regarding functioning over five general domains. These are work, home management, social leisure activities, private leisure activities, and personal or family relationships. It has been widely used as an outcome measure, but although there is a body of literature regarding its reliability and validity this has not taken cross-cultural issues into account. This measure serves broadly the same purpose as the ORS and may well be a useful measure to demonstrate change for BME service users where disorder specific measures are not appropriate.

Summary

There is currently a shortage of accessible, valid and reliable outcome measures for clinicians working with BME service users. Where English is spoken as a first language and service users are second or third generation migrants, it might be reasonable to use standard measures adopted by the service. Where service users are first generation migrants, whether English speaking or not, considerable care should be taken when using measures. Reliable and valid measures might be available for specific disorders in specific populations, and these may be available in translated or adapted forms. Where these are not available it might still be possible to use standard measures, but clinicians should be aware of the problems associated with doing this. Services working with large BME populations should try to develop a local agreement about which measures will be used, with which communities, for which disorders, in order to develop some consistency around this. At the very least clinicians should be able to use Goal Based Outcomes and the Outcomes Rating Scale or Work and Social Adjustment Scale to ensure that progress is effectively monitored.

References

Anker, M. G., Duncan, B. L., and Sparks, J. A. (2009). Using client feedback to improve couple therapy outcomes: A randomized clinical trial in a naturalistic setting. *Journal of Consulting and Clinical Psychology, 77*(4), 693–704. For further resources and information see https://www.heartandsoulofchange.com/.

Bagby, R. M., Ryder, A. G., Schuller, D. R., and Marshall, M. B. (2004). The Hamilton Depression Rating Scale: Has the gold standard become a lead weight? *The American Journal of Psychiatry, 161*(12), 2163–2177.

Beck, A. (2005). Identifying institutionalised racism in psychology services: A prospective, quantitative study of ethnic minority service use and treatment outcomes in a sexual health/HIV service. *Clinical Psychology, 49*, 36–40.

Beck, A. T., Steer, R. A., and Brown, G. K. (1996). *Beck Depression Inventory-II (BDI-II)*. Toronto: The Psychological Corporation/Harcourt Brace.

Chambless, D. L., Caputo, G. C., Bright, P., and Gallagher, R. (1984). Assessment of fear of fear in agoraphobics: The body sensations questionnaire and the Agoraphobic Cognitions Questionnaire. *Journal of Consulting and Clinical Psychology, 52*(6), 1090–1087.

Chowdhary, N., Jotheeswaran, A. T., Nadkarni, A., Hollon, S. D., King, M., Jordans, M. J. D., Rahman, A., Verdeli, H., Araya, R., and Patel, V. (2014). The methods and outcomes of cultural adaptations of psychological treatments for depressive disorders: A systematic review. *Psychological Medicine, 44*(06), 1131–1146.

d'Ardenne, P., Ruaro, L., Cestari, L., Fakhoury, W., and Priebe, S. (2007). Does interpreter-mediated CBT with traumatized refugee people work? A comparison of patient outcomes in East London. *Behavioural and Cognitive Psychotherapy, 35*(03), 293–301.

Flaherty, J. A., Gaviria, F. M., Pathak, D., Mitchell, T., Wintrob, R., Richman, J. A., and Birz, S. (1988). Developing instruments for cross-cultural psychiatric research. *The Journal of Nervous and Mental Disease, 176*(5), 260–263.

Friedman, S., Smith, L. C., Halpern, B., Levine, C., Paradis, C., Viswanathan, R., Trappier, B., and Ackerman, R. (2003). Obsessive-compulsive disorder in a multi-ethnic urban outpatient clinic: Initial presentation and treatment outcome with exposure and ritual prevention. *Behavior Therapy, 34*(3), 397–410.

Gadit, A. A. (2003). Obsessive compulsive disorder in a fishermen community. *Journal of the College of Physicians and Surgeons – Pakistan: JCPSP, 13*(10), 581–583.

Goldberg, D. (2010). Top-down versus bottom-up measures of depression. In Thornicroft, G., and Tansella, M. (eds), *Mental health outcome measures*. London: RCPsych Publications, 223–236.

Goldberg, D. P., Gater, R., Sartorius, N., Ustun, T., Piccinelli, M., Gureje, O., and Rutter, C. (1997). The validity of two versions of the GHQ in the WHO study of mental illness in general health care. *Psychological Medicine, 27*(1), 191–197.

Goodman, R. (1997). The Strengths and Difficulties Questionnaire: A Research Note. *Journal of Child Psychology and Psychiatry, 38*(5), 581–586. Translations into many languages are available at: www.sdqinfo.org.

Goodman, W. K., Price, L. H., Rasmussen, S. A., Mazure, C., Fleischmann, R. L., Hill, C. L., Heninger, G. R., and Charney, D. S. (1989). The Yale-Brown Obsessive Compulsive Scale: I. Development, use, and reliability. *Archives of General Psychiatry, 46*(11), 1006–1011.

Hamilton, M. (1960). A rating scale for depression. *Journal of Neurology, Neurosurgery, and Psychiatry, 23*(1), 56–62.

Hinton, D. E., Chhean, D., Pich, V., Pollack, M. H., Orr, S. P., and Pitman, R. K. (2006). Assessment of posttraumatic stress disorder in Cambodian refugees using the Clinician-Administered PTSD Scale: Psychometric properties and symptom severity. *Journal of Traumatic Stress, 19*(3), 405–409.

Hollifield, M., Verbillis-Kolp, S., Farmer, B., Toolson, E. C., Woldehaimanot, T., Yamazaki, J., Holland, A., St Clair, J., and SooHoo, J. (2013). The Refugee Health Screener-15 (RHS-15): development and validation of an instrument for anxiety, depression, and PTSD in refugees. *General Hospital Psychiatry, 35*(2), 202–209.

Horowitz, M., Wilner, N., and Alvarez, W. (1979). Impact of Event Scale: A measure of subjective stress. *Psychosomatic Medicine, 41*(3), 209–218.

Huang, F. Y., Chung, H., Kroenke, K., Delucchi, K. L., and Spitzer, R. L. (2006). Using the Patient Health Questionnaire-9 to measure depression among racially and ethnically diverse primary care patients. *Journal of General Internal Medicine, 21*(6), 547–552.

Manjula, M., Prasadarao, P. S. D. V., Kumaraiah, V., and Raguram, R. (2014). Temporal patterns of change in Panic Disorder during Cognitive Behaviour Therapy: An Indian study. *Behavioural and Cognitive Psychotherapy, 42*(05), 513–525.

Miller, S. D., Duncan, B. L., Brown, J., Sparks, J. A., and Claud, D. A. (2003). The Outcome Rating Scale: A preliminary study of the reliability, validity, and feasibility of a brief visual analogue measure. *Journal of Brief Therapy, 2*(2), 91–100. Resources available at: http://scott-d-miller-ph-d.myshopify.com/collections/performance-metrics/products/performance-metrics-licenses-for-the-ors-and-srs.

Mundt, J. C., Marks, I. M., Shear, M. K., and Greist, J. M. (2002). The Work and Social Adjustment Scale: A simple measure of impairment in functioning. *The British Journal of Psychiatry, 180*(5), 461–464.

Okasha, A., Saad, A., Khalil, A. H., El Dawla, A. S., and Yehia, N. (1994). Phenomenology of obsessive-compulsive disorder: A transcultural study. *Comprehensive Psychiatry, 35*(3), 191–197.

Priebe, S., Huxley, P., Knight, S., and Evans, S. (1999). Application and results of the Manchester Short Assessment of Quality of Life (MANSA). *International Journal of Social Psychiatry, 45*(1), 7–12.

Reese, R. J., Norsworthy, L. A., and Rowlands, S. R. (2009). Does a continuous feedback system improve psychotherapy outcome? *Psychotherapy: Theory, Research, Practice, Training*, *46*(4), 418–31.

Salvador-Carulla, L., and Gonzalez-Caballero, J. L. (2010). Assessment instruments in mental health: Description and metric properties. In Thornicroft, G., and Tansella, M. (eds). (2010). *Mental health outcome measures*. London: RCPsych Publications, 28–62.

Shear, M. K., Brown, T. A., Barlow, D. H., Money, R., Sholomskas, D. E., Woods, S. W., Gorman, J. M., and Papp, L. A. (1997). Multicenter collaborative panic disorder severity scale. *American Journal of Psychiatry*, *154*(11), 1571–1575.

Tek, C., and Ulug, B. (2001). Religiosity and religious obsessions in obsessive-compulsive disorder. *Psychiatry Research*, *104*(2), 99–108.

Tribe, R., and Thompson, K. (2008). *Working with interpreters in health settings: Guidelines for psychologists*. Leicester: British Psychological Society.

Zigmond, A. S., and Snaith, R. P. (1983). The hospital anxiety and depression scale. *Acta Psychiatrica Scandinavica*, *67*(6), 361–370.

Chapter 10

How to use supervision to enhance and support transcultural CBT

Overview

There is no specific literature addressing the way that Cognitive Behaviour Therapy supervision needs to be adapted to enable therapists to consider their practice in terms of transcultural work. Therapists are likely to benefit from the opportunity to reflect on their own practice, to be directed to current ideas and to try out some of the specific techniques that this work might lead to. Supervision is likely to be a very effective forum for this to happen. Given this, it seems helpful to develop some kind of framework to support the supervision of transcultural CBT. It is likely that some of the core processes that underpin current thinking about good practice in CBT supervision could be used to support therapists to think about their work with BME service users. This chapter will highlight and illustrate how this might work. Current thinking in CBT supervision does not seem to be sufficient to address all the challenges of transcultural working and so a wider literature on supervision for transcultural psychological therapies has also been adapted for this chapter.

Ultimately the purpose of supervision is to improve the outcomes of service users. This can be done by improving the use of specific therapeutic techniques and thinking about how they need to be adapted for specific service users. Clinical outcomes can also be improved by helping therapists reflect on their own work and on what their own cultural background leads them to bring to their practice.

Collaboration and hierarchies in transcultural supervision

At its best, supervision in CBT mirrors the therapy process in that it is a collaborative process. It is therefore helpful if both participants have a shared understanding of the principles that underpin it. Supervisory relationships are intrinsically hierarchical in nature, with the supervisor having a position of authority and the responsibility to manage and guide the supervisory process (Milne and Dunkerley 2010). Supervisors generally also have some degree of seniority, either implicitly through their greater clinical experience or explicitly through additional roles and responsibilities linked to line management, assessing the abilities of the supervisee or, in the case of a trainee, potentially failing or passing them on a placement.

The emphasis of this chapter is on clinical supervision rather than line management supervision. This distinction is not always clear in practice and sometimes a supervisor fulfils both roles in a single supervision session. Ideally, how supervisory time is spent is negotiated and clarified through the use of agendas. This ensures that both participants are clear about what supervisory task is being undertaken when, and that there has been a negotiation about this. Some of the principles and themes discussed in this chapter are likely to be useful where the task is primarily line management, although thinking about how these themes relate to line management is not the main aim of the chapter.

The responsibility for providing supervision that allows for the constructive discussion of culture and ethnicity lies primarily with the supervisor as the person with more power and seniority. However, it might also be the case that supervisees identify unmet needs for this topic to be more effectively addressed in supervision. In order to address how they might negotiate this, there is a section at the end of the chapter on how supervisees might bring these issues to their supervisor's attention.

Key factors in CBT supervision which might support transcultural thinking

There are a number of approaches used in CBT supervision that readily lend themselves to facilitating transcultural work. These are discussed below, before principles derived from transcultural supervision in other therapeutic approaches are considered.

The supervisor–supervisee relationship

A good supervisory alliance or relationship is considered to be an essential part of effective CBT supervision (Hatcher and Lassiter 2007). The literature across all therapy modalities emphasises the need to start by developing safe and secure supervisory relationships. A good supervisory relationship will provide the foundation for the constructive discussion of diversity and transcultural work with supervisees. Ladany et al. (1999) reported that a poor supervisory alliance was identified by almost half of trainee mental health staff as the reason they would not bring clinical mistakes or difficulties to supervision. Given that there is often a degree of worry about bringing issues relating to transcultural work to supervision, for example due to worries about being considered racist or culturally insensitive, it is highly likely that a poor alliance will act as a barrier to these issues being discussed.

The process of establishing a good alliance includes developing supervisee trust in the supervisor through gaining a sense of their professional and personal competence. Establishing a sense of professional competence is likely to be achieved through several routes. Observing the supervisor's clinical practice can be a useful way for supervisees to gain a sense of their clinical abilities and professional reliability. It is also an effective way for the supervisor to model specific therapy or assessment skills. It might be helpful to prioritise opportunities for the supervisee to observe work with BME service users and families. Where direct observation is not possible it might be helpful for supervisees to have the chance to look at recordings of work, or to observe sessions through one-way screens used in family therapy clinics if this resource is available. Supervisors who are punctual and keep to professional boundaries, who speak in a respectful and appropriate way and demonstrate a good understanding of the relevant literature and best practices, are also more likely to be seen as competent by supervisees. Using CBT approaches to supervision, such as generating problem lists, goals and agendas, is also likely to foster a sense of clear boundaries and professional working.

Trust in the supervisor is likely to be facilitated if they establish and keep to agreed boundaries around availability and time keeping, if they demonstrate an empathic response to the difficulties faced by supervisees and demonstrate warmth and positive regard. Trust can be enhanced by supervisors having an 'open door' policy, where supervisees feel able to approach them outside of supervision times if they are worried about cases and need advice and support.

Once trust is established the supervisor can begin to support discussions about transcultural working in a way that is less likely to make the supervisee feel defensive or worry about getting the discussion wrong. Strategies such as the supervisor reflecting on some of the challenges they have faced as a therapist when working across cultures, or disclosure about their own ethnicity and how this relates to therapeutic work, are likely to further establish a positive and productive therapeutic relationship.

The Zone of Proximal Development

The Zone of Proximal Development (ZPD) is an idea adapted from educational theory (Vygotsky 1978) which provides a useful framework to help supervisors think about what a supervisee might realistically be able to achieve in terms of new skill development at any given time. This model differentiates between three different types of skills that someone might seek to develop. Phase 1 skills are those which a supervisee could achieve on their own with time and practice. Phase 2 skills are those which a supervisee might be able to achieve with practice, appropriate support, feedback and supervision. Phase 3 skills are those which are beyond the current abilities of a supervisee to develop, even with training, practice and intensive support and supervision. In the development of any therapeutic skill, the supervisor needs to be aware of and periodically review their understanding of where a supervisee is in terms of these phases.

It is not in the best interests of service users to work with a therapist who is attempting to develop skills which are outside of their current range. It is also not in the interests of supervisees to invest time and energy into attempting to develop skills that are beyond their current capabilities, as this is likely to be frustrating and demoralising. As supervisees progress, some previously unattainable (Phase 3) skills will become attainable (Phase 2) skills, or skills that might have only been attainable with support (Phase 2) will become attainable just by practice (Phase 1).

This can be a useful framework in terms of thinking about supervision and skills development in transcultural CBT. A supervisee who is relatively new to CBT but who is from a social work background where they have had considerable training in working with BME families is likely to be able to pick up and incorporate ideas of working across cultures quite readily. In this situation there are likely to be useful skills such as asking about a service user's ethnic background that they can achieve without any supervisory support (Phase 1 skills). They may also be able to develop other skills, such as taking a detailed migration history and developing a genogram, with the right supervision (Phase 2 skills). They might, however, struggle with some of the micro-skills involved in CBT, such as making links between cultural practices and the presenting problem through Socratic questioning (Phase 3 skill), which might call for very different skills to the ones they have developed professionally up to that point.

In contrast, a supervisee who has trained in a profession which does not place much emphasis on transcultural work and whose own life experiences might not have included much contact with diverse communities might initially be unable to incorporate ideas of transcultural thinking into their practice (so these might be Phase 3 skills initially). At this stage it might be that the most they can achieve with the right support in supervision is to be able to ask the service users about their ethnicity in a helpful and supportive way (a Phase 2 skill). Doing this without the right support might be beyond their current capabilities (so it is not a Phase 1 skill). By being given the chance to think about their views on this, being directed to helpful reading about this issue and perhaps role playing the use of this skill with their supervisor, they may well find that this skill can be developed. Once this skill has been achieved, more sophisticated ways of asking and thinking about culture and ethnicity in therapy will be likely to enter their ZPD with appropriate support.

Supervision as a place to think about the automatic thoughts and core beliefs a trainee might have about different cultures

Supervision might also provide an opportunity to consider the therapist's core beliefs and automatic thoughts about work with different communities. It is inevitable that when a therapist finds themselves working with someone from a culture they have little direct experience of, they will draw on both their own beliefs and current social narratives about that community. These beliefs might be positive, neutral or negative and may well impact on their ideas about how therapy is likely to progress. This tendency has much in common with what Falicov (1995) calls an Ethnic Focused approach to understanding presenting problems. What this means is that the therapist might understand the presenting problem as being predominantly to do with the ethnicity of the service user or family they are working with. Likewise a therapist who has worked with a particular community for some time may have also developed general rules about how members of that community are likely to think or behave in certain situations, and again these might shape their expectations of the presenting problem and the outcomes of therapy. These rules might be identified and explored in supervision, as illustrated below when a supervisee is discussing a 22-year-old Bangladeshi female service user struggling with depression.

Case example: Supervisee 1

Supervisor: How did Samina get on with the Behavioural Activation work you set her last week?

Supervisee: It didn't go very well at all, nothing really changed.

Supervisor: What happened when you reviewed this at the next session?

Supervisee: She said that she hadn't felt like doing any of the activities I set her.

Supervisor: I am interested in the idea that the activities were ones that you set, why was that?

Supervisee: She was really struggling to set any herself.

Supervisor: Do you have any ideas why that might be?

Supervisee: I just don't think she is used to doing much outside of family activities, and her parents are both quite ill and don't do much these days. In Bangladeshi families the girls aren't really used to being independent so I've found it helps to be a bit more directive about activities.

Supervisor: That is an interesting observation. What do you know about how she spent her time before her parents became ill?

Supervisee: She used to go to the gym a few times a week and help out on a local youth project.

Supervisor: So how does that fit with the idea that it might be community values that are getting in the way of her doing activities outside of the family home?

Supervisee: It doesn't really fit, I suppose.

Supervisor: Maybe there is another explanation?

Supervisee: Could it be to do with how depressed and hopeless she feels?

Supervisor: Is it possible that the observations you have made over the years might have led to you developing too fixed an idea about how Bangladeshi women might act in certain circumstances?

Supervisee: I suppose I don't expect much in terms of people taking an initiative.

Supervisor: Is there a more helpful way of thinking about that observation?

The last part of this exchange, where the supervisee is invited to reflect on a strongly held belief about a particular community, is a strategy that has to be handled carefully. By remaining Socratic and exploratory the supervisor invites reflection without challenging the supervisee too directly, as this is unlikely to help them to reconsider or reflect on their beliefs and expectations. Where the therapist's beliefs are negative and highly generalised they can be thought of as racist, particularly if they prevent BME service users accessing the right kind of support. The therapist would be likely to be embarrassed and unhappy with the idea of being thought of in this way, and direct discussion of this is unlikely to be productive. For many years the prevailing response to the expression of such beliefs has been to forthrightly challenge them, and this is certainly an approach that has been successful in the political world. However, within mental health teams, while this approach is likely to reduce the expression of such views, it may not have much impact on the strength of the underlying beliefs and the subsequent behaviours of the person who holds them.

Where these seemingly fixed and generalised beliefs are expressed in supervision, a skilful supervisor could use approaches such as Socratic dialogue to give the supervisee the opportunity reflect on their beliefs; to consider how they might have arrived at them, whether there is evidence to support them, and whether there are other points of view; and to explore whether they are helpful in progressing therapy. This kind of discussion would be difficult in a public arena such as a team meeting but might be possible as part of a good supervisory relationship.

How supervision contracts might support this work

There are two main purposes to supervision contracts. The first is largely procedural. They can be used to specify when, where and how often supervision occurs and to clarify responsibilities in terms of line management and caseload management. The second use is as a basis for negotiating something about the content and focus of supervision. When beginning a new supervisory relationship it is useful to check with the supervisee about their goals, unmet needs as therapists and preferred ways of working. This also provides a time for the supervisor to ask about their interests and experiences in terms of transcultural work and whether the supervisee has any preferences in terms of how thinking about these issues might be best managed in supervision. Novice therapists might not have much idea about what this might entail, and experienced therapists who have not thought in these terms before might find the idea anxiety provoking. In both these situations it might be useful to agree to consider cultural issues and to review how this is working on a regular basis. Patel (2004) makes the point that this early stage of the supervisory relationship is also a good time for the supervisor to take the initiative in raising issues of power and difference with the supervisee. These points are considered in more detail later in this chapter.

Prioritising transcultural thinking

Incorporating detailed thinking about cultural issues might be an unmanageable burden on a supervisee who is already, for example, trying to incorporate the use of a new disorder specific model of treatment, practise new skills and manage a busy caseload. As part of taking care of the supervisory relationship, a supervisor might want to consider the current level of stress the supervisee is under and the degree to which they have the capacity to think about what can be complex and challenging issues. Remaining aware of the well-being of the supervisees and their priorities and needs is an ongoing and important task for supervisors. Although consideration of cultural issues is important it remains one of many tasks for the supervisor and supervisee, and the degree to which supervision time is allocated to this is something for negotiation and review.

Patel (2004) notes that either the supervisor or supervisee may be dissatisfied with the discussion of cultural factors in supervision. This topic may place additional demands on a supervisory process that is already likely to have other competing priorities in terms of improving therapy outcomes, considering service needs and ensuring fidelity to therapy models.

The usefulness of thinking about power relationships in supervision

Patel (2004), in a paper which addresses issues regarding ethnicity in supervision in general rather than CBT in particular, points out that, historically, BME groups have had less powerful positions in society. An understanding of power relations in therapy and supervision needs to acknowledge this in order for more effective collaboration between the supervisee and supervisor to take place. There are many possible combinations of ethnicities and power relations in the service user–therapist–supervisor triad. For example the therapist and supervisor might be from a white majority group whilst the service user is from a BME group. However, the service user and the therapist might be from BME groups with a white majority supervisor, or a BME service user might have a white therapist who has a BME supervisor. Whatever the combination, an acknowledgement of this difference and the power structures it implies is seen as beneficial by Patel. This paper notes that gender and social class will also impact on power in supervisory relationships and makes the important point that power and inequality are subtle and shifting processes that need careful consideration. There is currently no literature which considers this issue in terms of CBT supervision. This might be a result of models of CBT therapy and supervision developing in what is essentially a context-free environment, where difference of any kind has, until recently, not been thought about.

Patel considers the way that a white majority supervisor might approach working with a BME supervisee. The supervisor might take a 'colour blind' approach and hold the view that the ethnicity of the supervisee is not important. Supervisors who hold this view will probably believe that all supervisees should be treated the same regardless of their ethnic background, as the therapy and supervisory processes to be discussed are the same. This is similar to what Falicov (1995) identified as the Universalist position that therapists might take, as discussed in Chapter 3. The main problem with this approach is that is does not allow any consideration of the way that the ethnicity of the supervisee might have shaped therapeutic processes. There is also no framework to support the discussion of the way that supervisee experiences of racism and marginalisation might impact on their work. Patel also describes the 'colour conscious' position: that is, where the supervisor understands all the challenges faced by the supervisee through the lens of their ethnicity. This is similar to the Particularist position described by Falicov. This might make it difficult for supervisees to raise difficulties relating to culture or ethnicity in case they are seen as being too preoccupied with these issues. A supervisor adopting this position might be less likely to suggest solutions that are linked to culture or ethnicity in a tentative or exploratory way and may miss out on vital aspects of supervision which involve checking with the supervisee that the ideas generated are useful or plausible.

Supervisors might be reluctant to discuss issues of power and ethnicity at all with supervisees. This might be due to concerns about being seen as culturally insensitive or out of date in their thinking. This might be particularly true where the supervisor is from a white majority background and the supervisee is from a BME background. The supervisor might also take a largely culture-free position in terms of using CBT and might find it puzzling or challenging that a supervisee wants to bring these issues to supervision. Given the inherent power difference between the supervisor and supervisee this leaves the supervisee who wants to discuss these issues in a difficult position. They may find themselves unable to raise with their supervisor issues relating to culture or ethnicity that are important to them.

It might also be the case that the supervisor is comfortable discussing issues of culture and ethnicity but that the supervisee is not. In this case the supervisor needs to be very sensitive to the idea of introducing these factors without raising the anxious arousal levels of the supervisee so far that new learning cannot occur. The supervisee might adopt an avoidant response to the feared situation of discussing ethnicity and culture. Ideally this avoidance should be acknowledged and a shared agreement reached to work towards specific goals, such as being comfortable with discussions about culture and ethnicity. The way to negotiate this in supervision might be similar to that in the case example below, where a white supervisor and white supervisee discuss Frank, a 19-year-old male service user who was born in Nigeria and moved to the UK with his parents when he was 11. He has recurrent depression and is often in conflict with his parents. The supervisee has brought the case to supervision in order to develop an understanding about why the service user is struggling to engage with Behavioural Activation work.

Case example: Supervisee 2

Supervisor: I wonder if you could tell me a bit more about the challenges you are facing in bringing about some sort of change?

Supervisee: He just doesn't seem able to get the link between his lack of activity and his low mood.

Supervisor: That does sound tough. What is your hypothesis about what might be getting in the way?

Supervisee: I don't know really, I think he is just so used to staying at home he doesn't see it could be a problem.

Supervisor: I wonder if you have thought about the role that cultural factors might play in maintaining the problem?

Supervisee: I don't think the problem is anything to do with that.

Supervisor: Okay. Is there any way that his family's expectations about how he might spend his time might be making it harder for him?

Supervisee: I don't think his family has anything to do with it either really.

If at this stage the supervisor said 'It looks as though you are uncomfortable talking about how cultural factors might have something to do with this case', the supervisee might respond in a defensive manner or might find themselves in a state of anxious arousal as a result of worries about this discussion. The potential for a Socratic dialogue to develop a better understanding of cultural factors could then be lost. The supervisor needs to manage their powerful position, in terms of shaping the discussion about the case, with sensitivity. This is to ensure that the supervisee is not put into a position of having a discussion they are not comfortable with or of believing they are being negatively judged by their supervisor. The supervisor might begin by asking:

> I wonder if you could just fill me in on the background of this service user? Can we start by drawing out a genogram?

This is likely to bring about a discussion that may be more comfortable to the supervisee. Whilst completing the genogram the supervisor might ask about what jobs different family members have, where they were born and when they came to the UK. This could be expanded upon to include questions about how family members spend their time, what their expectations might be for Frank and how the family resolve differences of opinion. This could lead to questions about acculturation or hopes and expectations about life in the UK. These initial questions allow for the topic of culture and ethnicity to be introduced in a way that might be built on and expanded in subsequent supervision sessions as both the supervisor and supervisee become comfortable with this.

Patel (2004) has written about the importance of explicitly recognising power relationships in supervision if more constructive discussions regarding transcultural working are to take place. Although Patel's work on supervision is written in a generic way in terms of therapy modality, many of the principles will be useful to supervisors using CBT as their main therapy model. Patel points out that the supervisor has a responsibility to the profession, to their organisation and to the service user when providing supervision. If the considerable power inherent in the supervisory process is not recognised and talked about explicitly then there is an increased likelihood that this power will be misused and that the supervisory process becomes more coercive and less collaborative. This process of explicitly naming the power relationship seems different to the way that cognitive behaviour therapists might manage this in the therapeutic relationship. In CBT the therapist is in the position of relative power in terms of social status, access to resources and expertise. The therapist works with the service user to develop a collaborative position in order to progress towards a shared understanding of the presenting problem and to develop shared solutions. The power difference between the therapist and service user is usually not explicitly raised in CBT, but effective therapists do hold this in mind when working towards developing a collaborative approach.

Patel (2004) makes a number of recommendations in terms of supervisory practice that are likely to facilitate better supervision in terms of considering culture and ethnicity, which are summarised below and put into the context of CBT supervision.

Supervision processes

The development of a trusting and secure supervisory relationship is seen as the most important factor, both in effective supervision and specifically regarding supervision on transcultural issues. Where supervisees are worried about being negatively evaluated by the supervisor they are also less likely to take the risk of discussing cultural issues. The supervisor, as the most powerful person in the partnership, has responsibility for creating a climate in supervision where the supervisee can feel safe enough to take the chance of making mistakes. This might be done by being very explicit about acknowledging this, by saying something like:

> It can be difficult to bring some topics to supervision but what I value in a supervisee is someone who can learn from times that therapy becomes difficult, not a supervisee who never seems to find things challenging.

The supervisor could also model being able to tolerate uncertainty or struggling with an issue and might think aloud with the supervisee around issues relating to culture and ethnicity in a way that allows for not always getting it right. Within CBT the principle that the formulation is a provisional hypothesis, and a therapeutic position that supports a willingness to explore ideas about the role of culture and ethnicity through Socratic dialogue, could support this process. It might also be a useful exercise, as part of initial contract setting and discussions about preferred supervisory styles, to negotiate how issues regarding culture and difference can best be raised as part of supervision. This contract setting stage of arranging supervision might be a good time to acknowledge that uncritically applying psychological models across cultures might not be in the best interests of service users, and that thinking collaboratively about these issues will be likely to be an important part of the supervisory process.

Developing supervisees' knowledge about new developments

Within CBT supervision there is an acknowledgement that, at different times, the supervisor can usefully be in a position to provide didactic teaching about particular issues as well as assigning reading or research tasks to the supervisee. Both supervisor and supervisee have an important role in keeping knowledge up to date and current in terms of thinking about transcultural practice, both in the field of CBT and more broadly in mental health care. It is also helpful for both to be reflective about the limitations of current knowledge in this area and the degree to which the research literature they are drawing on is limited in terms of transcultural application. By modelling a reflective and critical approach, supervisors can encourage supervisees to adopt this way of engaging with the relevant knowledge bases.

Skill development is at the heart of CBT supervision. This can be achieved by rehearsal of new skills in supervision through role play, feedback on skills through review of recorded material, or using supervision to reflect on approaches used. Socratic dialogues are typically the way that reflective practice is encouraged in CBT. These Socratic discussions then form the basis for planning new ways of working. Patel (2004) notes a number of skills that can be facilitated through supervision, which are summarised and adapted specifically for CBT below.

Assessment

Supervision can be used to consider the degree to which issues regarding ethnicity should be incorporated into the initial assessment. Where supervisees are not confident about incorporating thinking about culture and ethnicity, experiential learning approaches such as role play could be used to explore how this might be done. Supervisees can also be encouraged to reflect on their own assumptions about the service user based on their ethnicity, and on ideas that might be associated with this in terms of expectations about presenting problems, willingness to engage in therapy and assumptions about the family life of the service user. Any standardised assessment tools used at this stage could usefully be critically evaluated in supervision in terms of how useful they might be in a transcultural context.

Formulation

In CBT the collaboratively derived formulation is a cornerstone of therapy. As we have seen previously, much CBT is based on disorder specific models and very little is known about their applicability across cultures. In supervision the therapist can be encouraged to take a reflective stance about which models they think might fit the presenting problems of a particular service user. They could be encouraged to think about what the strengths and limitations of using these models might be. As the major disorder specific formulations pay little or no attention to family systems or culturally specific ways of expressing distress, supervision can be used to think about whether these models can be modified to include these factors with a particular service user or whether idiosyncratic or trans-diagnostic formulations might be more useful. The role of marginalisation, exclusion and racism in the formulation can also be considered at this stage. These are, typically, difficult areas for novice therapists to integrate with their work and even experienced therapists who are not used to thinking about these issues might find this challenging. The supervisor could introduce this topic as part of the formulation by adopting a Socratic position. Take for example the case of Frank and his therapist, discussed previously in this chapter. A possible discussion might go as follows:

Case example: Supervisee 2, continued

Supervisor: I am curious about these pervasive thoughts about not being good enough and not being liked that Frank has expressed. Do you have any ideas about life events that might have led to him developing these ideas?

Supervisee: I don't know, to be honest. We have been focusing more on their current impact than their origin.

Supervisor: That sounds like a very helpful thing to do. I was just wondering about what the impact might have been of growing up in a town in the UK where his was the only black family?

Supervisee: He didn't say anything about that being important.

Supervisor: Can you think of any ways that this might have presented challenges? I wonder if he mentioned how he was treated by people when he was growing up?

Supervisee: He didn't say anything and to be honest I would not feel comfortable asking.

Supervisor: It can be very difficult to raise this with a service user when you are a white therapist. I still find myself struggling with this sometimes. But could you see how it might be helpful to know this information?

(continued)

(continued)

Supervisee: Well, if he grew up expecting people to have negative views about him because he is Nigerian and he is the only Nigerian working in his office he might think things are just the same there.

Supervisor: That is a very thoughtful hypothesis. It sounds as though it would be important to check but that you are not sure about how to raise that. Do you have any ideas about how we could see how that discussion might go?

Supervisee: I suppose we could role play it.

Supervisor: To help me understand the service user better, could I play the therapist first and you could give me an idea about how this service user might react?

Once this role play has occurred the supervisor would use the Kolb cycle to review how the supervisee experienced this and encourage some reflection on how, as a white therapist, the supervisee might approach having a discussion about racism.

Interventions

In CBT the intervention should ideally lead on from the formulation, with the service user generating ideas on how things could be done differently as a result of insights gained from collaboratively mapping out the maintaining factors. Where the supervisor is supporting the supervisee to make adjustments to their therapeutic work to include an understanding of cultural factors, it might be helpful to encourage clarity about the rationale for the use or adaptation of particular change methods. The supervisor might also need to encourage the supervisee to take a realistic view about the limits of CBT and the degree to which it can be adapted transculturally. Encouraging the therapist to consider alternative approaches might ultimately be in the best interests of some service users. These might include community support organisations and an emphasis on practical help in addition to or instead of CBT where this model alone has not improved the mental health of the service user.

Patel (2004: 113) suggests a number of very pertinent questions that a supervisor might ask in order to facilitate reflective practice when working with BME service users. The most salient for cognitive behaviour therapists are summarised below. These might be experienced as very challenging questions by supervisees and are probably best used when a solid foundation of trust and mutual regard has been established.

- What are the possible assumptions, values and cultural biases inherent in the psychological models and resulting interventions you have planned?

What might be the implications of using the interventions with the client? How useful is it to locate the presenting problem wholly within the service user?

- Are you adequately acknowledging the importance of social context and the external realities of discrimination? If so, how does this fit with locating responsibility for change solely with the client/family?
- To what extent do your interventions focus on the problems, weaknesses and vulnerability of the client? How does this fit with, for example, their experiences of racist abuse in their workplace? Could you be missing out on acknowledging the lived experience of racism the service user is struggling with?
- How could you assess the impact of racism on a client's life and formulate effective intervention strategies? How could your interventions challenge racism in the client's life, as well as in the therapeutic relationship, in the therapeutic work and in the professional network/team?
- To what extent are your interventions or your therapeutic approach designed, adapted or chosen specifically for the client in question?
- To what extent is the client expected to fit into and respond to your own preferred approach, or into the dominant model within your service? What are the impactions of this for the client?

The last question is likely to be particularly pertinent within IAPT services, which often have quite prescriptive models of how CBT should be delivered. Although these models are helpful for many service users, it is likely that for some BME service users considerable adaptation will be necessary in order to help alleviate distress, or different approaches altogether might be more helpful.

Supervision as a forum for supporting BME therapists

Supervision can also be a useful way to support BME staff whose positions in teams working with diverse populations can be complex. Whether or not there is an ethnic match between supervisor and supervisee, it is important for supervisors to be aware of the additional pressures BME supervisees might face when working in white majority settings. For example, BME staff can find themselves positioned as expert in all matters to do with ethnicity and culture by the team. This is likely to be a difficult role to fulfil, particularly if they are trainees or relatively junior and still developing their own practice as therapists. Locating the majority of expertise for transcultural work with BME members of staff also makes it less likely that white majority staff will believe they need to develop confidence and expertise in this area themselves.

There may also be issues regarding perceived authority for some BME staff. Service users (whether or not they are BME themselves) might see staff from BME communities as less authoritative and so less able to help them. This might also be the case for some outside agencies that workers are interacting with.

BME staff members' experience of prejudice at work is something that can and should be thought about in supervision. It might be difficult for BME therapists to raise their experience of racism in supervision, particularly if they have a white supervisor. They might worry it could be seen as not coping, as being over-sensitive or asking for special treatment. Supervisors might communicate a willingness to think about supervisees' experiences of racism by first of all asking about and being interested in how service users' experiences of racism might have impacted on their emotional health. From this starting point, it could be useful to explore how hearing about this impacted on the supervisee. It would be good practice at this point for the supervisor to reflect on how they react to hearing about experiences of racism. It is important to communicate that the supervisor can hear about this and respond in a genuine way without being overwhelmed. As the supervision begins to consider more personal issues, the supervisor could ask something like, 'How would it be for you to bring your own experiences of prejudice or racism in this job to supervision?' or, 'Would it be helpful for me to ask you about your own experiences of racism or prejudice whilst working here?' These questions give the supervisee a choice about what they would to bring to supervision.

Eklund et al. (2014) summarise current thinking about the extent to which supervisees from BME backgrounds might benefit from supervision from someone from a culturally similar background to themselves, particularly during their time as a trainee. They acknowledge that there is a shortfall in the number of qualified therapists from most BME communities and that it is likely that a cultural match between supervisor and supervisee will be difficult to arrange for most trainees. They also acknowledge that a cultural match is not necessary for BME supervisees to report a good level of satisfaction with their supervisor.

Where the supervisor is from a white majority background, the supervisory relationship may be enhanced by the supervisor acknowledging that the way health services, educational establishments and institutions work tends to take the experience of someone from a white background to be the norm or universal. This may be especially helpful where the supervisee is from a different ethnic group, but also allows white supervisees to see reflectivity in action. This is likely to support a more open discussion of the role of culture and ethnicity in therapy practice. If this facilitates trust and a sense of openness it will make it easier for supervisees to feel able to bring to supervision cases which include a consideration of cultural factors. Supervisors might also take the opportunity of introducing ethnicity to ask about the supervisee's own background. Many of the principles outlined in Chapter 2 regarding having this discussion with patients will be helpful in thinking about when and how this might occur with a supervisee.

Where the supervisee is from a BME background, the supervisor should consider that different cultures might have different communication styles that need to be taken into account in. Eklund et al. (2014) provide useful examples of how this might work in supervision. They note that white majority communication styles used when speaking include a relatively rapid vocal style and the use of non-verbal head and hand gestures to facilitate communication. They contrast this to some Asian and Hispanic cultures where the tone of voice used is softer, the rate of speech slower, and where direct eye contact might be seen as disrespectful. They suggest that supervisors might draw incorrect conclusions from the communication style of BME supervisees if they do not have some awareness that the rules and methods of communication they take for granted are not universal.

What good transcultural supervision should include

A very useful summary of what good practice might look like is provided by Eklund et al. (2014). Their work is based on current thinking about the supervision of school based psychologists working in multicultural settings in the United States, though the ideas can be readily adapted to CBT supervision.

Discuss cultural similarities and differences between the supervisor and supervisee

There is some research evidence that BME supervisees find supervision where difference and culture is discussed to be more helpful, and that the supervisory alliance is strengthened through this (Gatmon et al. 2001). Clearly the timing of this is important, and this discussion can serve a number of purposes. This might include helping both to think about their own background and how this impacts on the work. This discussion also communicates that ethnicity is a topic for thinking about in supervision. It might also open up further discussion about power and experiences of prejudice, and how the supervisee and supervisor might usefully raise and reflect on these issues in supervision.

Creating the right setting

This might involve the supervisor taking a general stance of being open, flexible and respectful in order to ensure that the supervisory environment is one in which the supervisee is comfortable discussing their worries, struggles and emotions as a therapist. Responding to these in a concerned and genuinely helpful way reinforces the message that supervision is the right place to bring these concerns.

Model and teach transcultural competencies

Supervisees may be at a less advanced stage of ability than supervisors in terms of transcultural competencies. Taught competencies might include the ability to think critically about existing ways of working, about using specific models of therapy or about assumptions regarding mental health in different cultures. Taught competencies might also include modelling an ability to think about how the supervisor's own ethnicity, social class, gender and sexuality impacts on their therapeutic work.

Support continuing professional development

There is very little formal training available in adapting CBT for transcultural settings. There is also only a limited research and practice literature on this. In order to foster skills in this area, supervisors need to support supervisees in accessing what training is available and ensure that they themselves keep up to date on the relevant literature as it is published. It might be helpful to support supervisees in setting up or joining special interest groups for therapists interested in this work. Supervisees can also be encouraged to develop their own skills and knowledge through research projects, clinical audit or teaching others. Supervisors often benefit from this vicariously, as the new knowledge is brought back into the department and disseminated.

How therapists can prepare their supervisor for supporting their transcultural practice

Although most CBT supervisors are likely to say that they are committed to helping supervisees adapt therapy across cultures and contexts, not all will be up to date in thinking about how this might be best done. This is understandable. Transcultural thinking in CBT is a relatively new area and there is a reasonable chance that it will not have been part of supervisory training. Unless a supervisor has a particular interest in this area they may not have accessed recent training on the topic or be familiar with current research and practice. Supervisors can often feel a degree of anxiety when supervisees ask about areas they do not believe they are up to date with. This might lead to low levels of physiological arousal and might make it difficult to constructively and collaboratively think about this topic.

Supervisors are also as likely to be as worried about getting it wrong when discussing ethnicity as supervisees are. Where this might be the case, supervisees might raise the topic as something for future consideration, perhaps saying that they would like to prioritise it in a future specified session. It might be helpful to say that you have been looking at some literature which might inform this thinking and that you would value the supervisor's opinion on it. Whether or not the supervisee provides this chapter as an aid to support the shared task of supervision is a matter of judgement, but does seem to be in the spirit of collaboration which underpins CBT.

Summary

Therapists practising transcultural CBT need to be supported by a supervisor who understands the challenges that this work brings. Supervisors need to be sensitive to the needs of supervisees and bring topics relating to culture and ethnicity into thinking about cases at a level that fits with the current learning needs of supervisees. This needs to be done in the context of an effective therapeutic relationship. Good practice for supervisors includes a willingness to think aloud about their own transcultural working and a willingness to not know all the answers. Developing a working relationship where critical thinking about current knowledge is encouraged will also pay an important part in supporting more effective transcultural work.

References

Eklund, K., Aros-O'Malley, M., and Murrieta, I. (2014). Multicultural supervision: What difference does difference make? *Contemporary School Psychology*, *18*(3), 195–204.

Falicov, C. J. (1995). Training to think culturally: A multidimensional comparative framework. *Family Process*, *34*(4), 373–388.

Gatmon, D., Jackson, D., Koshkarian, L., Martos-Perry, N., Molina, A., Patel, N., and Rodolfa, E. (2001). Exploring ethnic, gender, and sexual orientation variables in supervision: Do they really matter? *Journal of Multicultural Counseling and Development*, *29*(2), 102–113.

Hatcher, R. L., and Lassiter, K. D. (2007). Initial training in professional psychology: The practicum competencies outline. *Training and Education in Professional Psychology*, *1*(1), 49.

Ladany, N., Lehrman-Waterman, D., Molingaro, M., and Wolgast, B. (1999). Psychotherapy supervisor ethical practices: Adherence to guidelines, the supervisor working alliance, and supervisee satisfaction. *The Counseling Psychologist*, *27*, 443–475.

Milne, D., and Dunkerley, C. (2010). Towards evidence-based clinical supervision: The development and evaluation of four CBT guidelines. *The Cognitive Behaviour Therapist*, *3*(2), 43–57.

Patel, N. (2004). Difference and power in supervision. In Fleming, I., and Stern, L. (eds), *Supervision and clinical psychology: Theory, practice and perspectives*. London: Brunner-Routledge, 96–117.

Vygotsky, L. (1978). Interaction between learning and development. *Readings on the Development of Children*, *23*(3), 34–41.

Index

safeguarding 111–112
safety, in therapy 84
safety behaviours 64
Salvador-Carulla, L. 154
Santiago-Rivera, A. 107
self-concept 25
self-disclosure 26
self-esteem 109
self-harm 72, 84, 102–103
self-regulation 77; *see also* emotional
  regulation
service users: definition of 9; discussing
  ethnicity and culture with 20–37;
  improving outcomes for 162;
  participation of 143–147; *see also* Black
  and Minority Ethnic service users
service-wide change 133–151
sexual assault 74, 83, 98, 121
sexuality 10, 16, 33, 42–43, 47;
  interpreters 121; Multidimensional
  Approach 50; Muslims 100; self-
  defined identity 30, 31; transcultural
  competencies 177; white people 12
shame 77
siblings 41, 108
Sikhs 29, 77
skills development 164–165, 172, 178
sleep related problems 80
SMART goals 157–158
Smith, J. A. 126
Social Anxiety Disorder 43–44, 51
social class 10, 16, 33; Multidimensional
  Approach 47; power in supervisory
  relationships 168; self-defined identity
  31; transcultural competencies 177;
  white people 12
Socratic approaches 25, 49, 56, 138;
  depressed Muslim service users 100,
  101, 104, 110; family context 45;
  formulation 173; interpreters 129;
  rapport 32; supervision 167, 170, 172
Somalis 129–130, 149
Somasundaram, D. 69–70
South Africa 125
South Asians 7, 11, 29–31, 80; data
  collection 137, 140; Muslims 93,
  94; women 102–103, 108; *see also*
  Bangladeshis; Indians; Pakistanis

South East Asians 11, 74, 77
Sri Lankans 11, 70, 77
staff support for change 147–148
stigma 144–145, 150
Strengths and Difficulties Questionnaire
  157
Sue, D. W. 28
suicide/suicidal thoughts 72, 84, 96, 99,
  102–103, 104
Summerfield, D. 13, 14, 16, 60
supervision 4, 15, 64, 107, 162–179;
  assessment 172; BME therapists
  175–177; contracts 167–168, 172; East
  London Institute of Psycho-trauma
  83; family life cycle 57; formulation
  173–174; good practice 177–178;
  interviewing non-clinical families 58;
  Islamic practices 103; knowledge of
  new developments 172; power relations
  168–171; processes 171–172; PTSD 87,
  88; supervisor-supervisee relationship
  163–164; transcultural thinking 168;
  Zone of Proximal Development
  164–165
syntax equivalence 153–154
systemic issues 39–40, 43, 46
Systemic Therapy 39, 47

Tambuyzer, E. 143–144
technical equivalence 154
telephone interpreting 131
terminology 8–12
therapeutic relationship 3, 7, 55; discussing
  ethnicity with service users 21, 22–27,
  28, 36; ethnic matching/non-matching
  of therapist and service user 32, 34;
  interpreters 124–126; managing
  difficulties 34–35; Muslims 95, 97–98;
  respect for religious practices 113;
  supervision 164, 178
therapists 2, 3; CA-CBT 5; challenge
  of faith based approaches 110–111;
  cultural competence 15; discussing
  ethnicity and culture with service users
  20–37; East London Institute of Psycho-
  trauma 82; ethnic focused approach
  49–50; ethnicity of 31–34, 36–37,
  81; family life cycle 57; interpreters

For Product Safety Concerns and Information please contact our EU
representative GPSR@taylorandfrancis.com
Taylor & Francis Verlag GmbH, Kaufingerstraße 24, 80331 München, Germany

www.ingramcontent.com/pod-product-compliance
Lightning Source LLC
Chambersburg PA
CBHW070426270326
41926CB00014B/2961

9 7 8 1 1 3 8 8 9 0 4 8 0